Shades of Gray

Little, Brown Series on Gerontology

Series Editors

Jon Hendricks
and
Robert Kastenbaum

Published

W. Andrew Achenbaum
Shades of Gray:
Old Age,
American Values,
and Federal Policies
Since 1920

Donald E. Gelfand
Aging: The Ethnic
Factor

Jennie Keith
Old People
As People: Social
and Cultural
Influences on
Aging and Old Age

Theodore H. Koff
Long-Term Care:
An Approach to
Serving the Frail
Elderly

Forthcoming
Titles

Linda M. Breytspraak
The Development
of Self in Later Life

Paul Costa and
Robert R. McCrae
Emerging Lives,
Enduring Dispositions:
The Stability of
Personality in Adulthood

Carroll L. Estes
Political Economy,
Health, and Aging

C. Davis Hendricks
Law and Aging

John L. Horn
Aging and Adult
Development of
Cognitive Functions

Noel D. List
The Alliance
of Health Services
and the Elderly

John F. Myles
Old Age in
the Welfare State:
The Political Economy
of Public Pensions

Jan D. Sinnott,
Charles S. Harris,
Marilyn R. Block,
Stephen Collesano,
and Solomon Jacobson
Applied Research
in Aging: A Guide to
Methods and Resources

Martha Storandt
Counseling and
Therapy with
Older Adults

Albert J.E. Wilson III
Social Services
for Older Persons

Shades of Gray

Old Age, American Values, and Federal Policies Since 1920

W. Andrew Achenbaum
Carnegie-Mellon University

Little, Brown and Company
Boston   Toronto

Library of Congress Cataloging in Publication Data

Achenbaum, W. Andrew.
   Shades of gray.

   (Little, Brown series on gerontology)
   Bibliography: p.
   1. Aged—Government policy—United States—
History—20th century.   2. Old age assistance—
United States—History—20th century.   3. United
States—Social conditions—1918–1932.   4. United
States—Social conditions—1945–   I. Title.
II. Series.
HQ1064.U5A626   1983   305.2′6′0973   82-14912
ISBN 0-316-00652-1
ISBN 0-316-00654-8 (pbk.)

Library of Congress Catalog Card Number 82-14912

ISBN 0-316-00652-1

ISBN 0-316-00654-8 {pbk.}

9 8 7 6 5 4 3 2 1

ALP

Published simultaneously in Canada
by Little, Brown & Company (Canada) Limited

Printed in the United States of America

In Memory of My Father
and
For My Mother

Foreword

Where is aging? In each of the billions of cells in our bodies? Or in our minds? Then, again, perhaps it is something that happens *between* people. Ought we not also take a look at the marketplace as well? And at the values expressed through our cultural institutions? Undoubtedly, the answer lies in all these factors—and more. The phenomenon of aging takes place within our bodies, in our minds, between ourselves and others, and in culturally defined patterns.

The study and analysis of aging—a burgeoning field—is deserving of an integrated spectrum approach. Now, Little, Brown and Company offers such a perspective, one designed to respond to the diversity and complexity of the subject matter and to individualized instructional needs. The Little, Brown Series on Gerontology provides a series of succinct and readable books that encompass a wide variety of topics and concerns. Each volume, written by a highly qualified gerontologist, will provide a degree of precision and specificity not available in a general text whose coverage, expertise, and interest level cannot help but be uneven. While the scope of the gerontology series is indeed broad, individual volumes provide accurate, up-to-date presentations unmatched in the literature of gerontology.

The Little, Brown Series on Gerontology:

—provides a comprehensive overview
—explores emerging challenges and extends the frontiers of knowledge
—is organically interrelated via cross-cutting themes
—consists of individual volumes prepared by the most qualified experts

—offers maximum flexibility as teaching material
—ensures manageable length without sacrificing concepts, facts, methods, or issues

With the Little, Brown Series on Gerontology now becoming available, instructors can select the texts most desirable for their individual courses. Practitioners and other professionals will also find the foundations necessary to remain abreast of their own particular areas. No doubt, students too will respond to the knowledge and enthusiasm of gerontologists writing about only those topics they know and care most about.

Little, Brown and Company and the editors are pleased to provide a series that not only looks at conceptual and theoretical questions but squarely addresses the most critical and applied concerns of the 1980s. Knowledge without action is unacceptable. The reverse is no better.

As the list of volumes makes clear, some books focus primarily on research and theoretical concerns, others on the applied; by this two-sided approach they draw upon the most significant and dependable thinking available. It is hoped that they will serve as a wellspring for developments in years to come.

Acknowledgments

When Jon Hendricks invited me to contribute a volume to the Little, Brown Series on Gerontology, I was delighted to accept his offer. As a teacher and public speaker, I had become increasingly aware that most people held erroneous ideas about the course of recent American history, particularly as it has affected elderly men and women. With few exceptions, they really did not understand why current programs for the aged and aging evolved in the ways that they did. Many could not see "the big picture" into which changes in the meanings of growing older and the experiences of being aged fit. As a professional historian, I had to acknowledge that a comprehensive and definitive overview of twentieth-century developments in U.S. history that have had an impact on older people did not yet exist. This present work is not, and does not pretend to be, a study that will tell gerontologists, historians, or general readers everything they need to know about the "modern" history of old age in America. It is simply too short and selective in focus to cover all of the topics. In length and style, *Shades of Gray* more closely resembles an extended essay than a major monograph; it is more of a synthesis of the literature produced by scholars working in a variety of disciplines than an inquiry based on extensive research into primary sources. Nonetheless, the work tries to say some very important things about the ways Americans have defined and dealt with the challenges and opportunities of an aging and graying society during the twentieth century. I offer it as a work-in-progress, though of course I am prepared to take full responsibility for its contents.

Many kind people and generous institutions helped me in the course of my writing. A first draft of this manuscript was executed between 1977 and 1979, when I was a visiting assistant research scientist at the Institute of Gerontology in Ann Arbor, Michigan. There, I worked on the "American Values and the Elderly" project, funded by U.S. Administration on Aging Grant No. 90-A-1325. My intellectual and personal debts to the other principal investigators on the project—Harold R. Johnson, Jane K. McClure, Terrence N. Tice, and John E. Tropman—are enormous: they encouraged me to challenge their interpretations and gently helped me to wrestle with my own hunches and ideas. Stephen M. Kruk, Gail Lewis, and T. A. Meyer served as able research assistants; John Campbell, Henry Meyer, Eric Rabkin, Andrea Sankar, Judith Shuval, and Sue Stein offered penetrating criticisms based on their own interdisciplinary research and professional experiences.

I have also learned much from the people who have taken the time and shown the interest to react critically and constructively to earlier drafts. I want to thank my students in several summer courses offered at the Institute of Gerontology between 1976 and 1980, the undergraduate and graduate students in classes at Canisius College and Carnegie-Mellon University, and members of seminars sponsored by the Hastings Center, the Employee Relations and Public Affairs departments at E. I. DuPont de Nemours Co., the Brookdale Center on Aging at Hunter College, Kent State University, and Columbia University. I also had a chance to learn something about the politics of aging by participating in two Public Policy Symposia convened to prepare materials for the 1981 White House Conference on Aging.

The final draft of this work, completed during a year of research and thinking underwritten by the National Endowment for the Humanities, was greatly improved by recommendations from several quarters. I especially wish to thank my friend and colleague Peter N. Stearns for his boundless encouragement and support. Members of Carnegie-Mellon's Program in Applied History and Social Science, particularly David W. Miller, Daniel P. Resnick, and Joel Tarr, offered valuable suggestions about the introductory section. George Wm. Bergquist, Edwin Fenton, David H. Fowler, Charles and Sara Hill, Jan Lewis, H. R. Moody, Robert J. Myers, Anne C. Rose, and J. David Valaik critiqued several chapters. Byron Gold, John F. Myles, Mildred M. Seltzer, Ludwig F. Schaefer, and Edmund H. Worthy, Jr. offered sage advice at critical junctures. Preparation of this manuscript was greatly expedited by the word-processing facilities at Carnegie-Mellon: John Stuckey introduced me to the latest state of the art, and Ellen Parkes helped to transfer handwritten chapters into machine-readable files. Jon Hendricks and William W. Kelly edited the penultimate draft with their scholarly concern for precision and clarity. With tact and style, Madelyn Leopold, Julia

Winston, and Sally Lifland presided over the editorial process at Little, Brown. My wife, Mary Schieve, and two daughters, Emily and Laura, helped me keep my perspectives straight and priorities in order. I have dedicated this book to my parents with deep respect and thanks, for it is the chronicle and interpretation of events, people, collective tensions, personal choices, national options, societal victories, and individual disappointments that shaped their lives and those of their generation.

Contents

Shades of Gray

Philip Evergood's painting
"Through the Mill" (1940)
offers a bitter commentary
about the effect of "modern"
economic structures and social
processes on people's attitudes
and behavior. Yet its rich
detail highlights key elements
shaping the development of
early twentieth-century
American life. Note the
peripheral role that the aged
play in this scene. [Philip
Evergood. *Through the Mill.*
(left section) (1940) Oil. 36 ×
52 inches. Collection of
Whitney Museum of American
Art.]

Chapter

1

American Modernization in Historical Perspective

Musing About Clio's Relation to Gerontology

It is impossible to imagine a topic in the field of aging that lacks a temporal dimension. For gerontologists doing research in the natural sciences, describing and explaining the nature and dynamics of change over time is an essential task. Some scientists analyze structural and functional changes in the lives of cells. Others study processes of aging in organisms with life spans ranging from a few hours to more than a century.

This life-cycle perspective is not limited to bio-medical disciplines. Social scientists, health-care deliverers, and social workers have shown that older people's responses to changing circumstances are influenced by previous experiences and current relationships, as well as by their racial, educational, occupational, and economic backgrounds. Similarly, economists, psychologists, political scientists, and sociologists typically assess the assets and liabilities of age in terms of the allocation of resources, influence, power, and roles over the life course. Demographers distinguish between long-term and short-range trends in estimating the future size of the elderly population. Public officials, policy analysts, and those who administer institutions and programs in the private sector also must be sensitive to shifts in the needs of different segments of the aging population over time.

It seems very clear that students of old age confront the same type of issues that engage historians. Like contemporary-minded gerontologists, traditional historians are interested in the relationship between "past" and "present," even though their particular definitions of "time" and specific uses of the past vary considerably.

To be sure, many historians write about times and places that seem to have little in common with our present world. Yet in so doing, they frequently elucidate a range of human experiences that transcends temporal and spatial boundaries. Studying the past enables them to distinguish between the timeless and the distinctive features of contemporary life. Historians, moreover, share gerontologists' preoccupation with change and context. "The big picture" counts in both disciplines. Thus the heirs of Clio, that venerable muse of history, define their task and go about their business in a manner compatible with practices prevailing among experts on aging.

Nevertheless, while there are parallels between the gerontologist's interests and the historian's aims, several points of divergence in orientation, method, and style frustrate efforts to foster interdisciplinary research. Gerontologists typically view history as prologue. Some use snippets from the historical treasure trove as a backdrop for discussing the "real" issues, which tend to be the pressing matters of the moment. Others invoke the past in an effort to underscore the novelty of contemporary circumstances. A few (mis)use legal precedents, philosophical positions, or supposedly analogous situations in former times to justify the status quo or to sanction a proposed amendment (for more on this point, see Mandelbaum, 1977). Historians, on the other hand, tend to view the study of the past as an end in itself. Heeding Voltaire's injunction not to play tricks on the dead, many attempt to interpret history by meticulously reconstructing the social milieu and by using terms and concepts consonant with the period under inquiry. Some quail at "the tyranny of present-mindedness," fearing that too much concern for current events blinds one's critical eye and reduces the likelihood of a dispassionate perspective. More than a few historians probably would prefer to have lived during the period that sustains them intellectually.

Not only do gerontologists and historians view the past differently, but they also have received divergent training to prepare them for their present work. Gerontologists like to claim that their methods of analysis are "scientific." Rigorously refined theories, empirical evidence, and statistical significance count for more than a felicitous phrase.[1] History, too, has its "scientific" branch, whose proponents utilize sophisticated quantitative analyses and incorporate methodologies first developed by econometricians, sociologists, and political scientists. Yet many within the historical profession scoff at such efforts. The world's most eminent practitioners typically de-

[1] The desire to define gerontology as a science perpetuates a legacy from the formative years of the discipline, when physicians and laboratory researchers dominated the field. It also reflects the fact that most gerontologists continue to identify themselves as clinical medical personnel, biological researchers, applied social practitioners, or behavioral or social scientists.

scribe the historian's craft as both art and science, a discipline nurtured by its deep connections in the humanities and social sciences. Characterizing history as an academic *via media* has advantages, of course, but it also ensures that many historians will find the research goals and procedures of gerontologists objectionable.

Because of these differences in orientation and training, gerontologists and historians often find it difficult to talk to one another, much less to see any reason for doing so! Consequently, any fruitful dialogue will depend on identifying a contemporary social issue that attracts attention and stimulates creative work in both camps. Analytic strategies that can survive careful scrutiny in historical and gerontological circles—even among scholars who formulate and operationalize research designs in significantly different ways—will be required. Happily, such a research problem and methodological framework currently exist.

Surveying Common Ground for Collaborative Research

Both gerontologists and historians have a stake in learning more about the history of older people in twentieth-century America. This is an important challenge for gerontologists because they generally have relied on their own casual impressions or recollections in order to understand the recent past. Such a historical perspective is bound to be biased, since few individuals experienced the impact of specific ideas, socioeconomic currents, or political events in precisely the same way as did people born in different years. Nor can gerontologists mention a few cliches from civics textbooks and assume that the subject has been covered. Hackneyed descriptions of "contemporary America" as a monolithic, static entity are woefully inadequate. Professional historians' understanding of the elderly's recent past, moreover, is often as impressionistic and fallacious as that held by nonspecialists. Historians to date have done a far better job in detecting shifts in the aged's images and conditions prior to the passage of Social Security than they have in elucidating the social, cultural, political, and economic history of older Americans during the last half-century.

Reconstructing dominant American values and social patterns since World War I—especially as they have affected the elderly—is a major intellectual priority that ought to command interest in both disciplines. Salient clusters, contradictions, ambiguities, paradoxes, and shifts within American value systems must be identified. Scholars then have to describe and explain their relationship to other

socioeconomic and political developments. Historians and gerontologists who engage in this task will quickly find themselves moving
into other disciplines' territories. As Canadian sociologist John F.
Myles recently noted,

> The development of a "political sociology of aging" requires going
> far beyond the gerontologist's traditional concern with the elderly as
> such and extending the traditional boundaries of the discipline to
> include those social groups and institutions which produce the social
> policies which do shape the experiences of growing old in contempo-
> rary societies. This does not mean, however, that such a political
> sociology of aging must now be created *ex nihilo*. Although the national
> and comparative studies of social policies for the elderly are still re-
> stricted in number . . . the larger body of both theoretical and empirical
> research which subsumes such policies is now vast indeed. . . . It is from
> within this broader tradition in political and social theory that any
> analysis of the "politics of aging" must perforce begin (1981: 1–2).

Making connections among American values, alterations in the
political economy, and the transformations in life-styles occurring at
a national level will be hard. Yet the endeavor should enable gerontologists and historians to place the evolution of current old-age
programs and policies, as well as changes in the meanings and experiences of being old, into a broader socio-historical context than they
are accustomed to using.

Now, having identified a common problem, how can researchers
best proceed? Gerontologists and historians searching for a way to
put all of the disparate information and issues that are indispensable
for understanding old people's place in recent American history
immediately find themselves overwhelmed by a dazzling array of
alternatives (see the Technical Appendix). Faced with such a wide
range of interpretations, one is tempted to pick and choose until one
finds an interpretation that seems to surpass all others. Alas, no
single theory is all that compelling. There is one candidate, however,
that merits special consideration.

Toward a New Conceptual Framework

In my opinion, the concept of "modernization" offers a useful
framework for asking the right questions about the connections
among old age, American values, and federal policies since 1920.
Since "modernization" is an idea familiar to both gerontologists and
historians, it facilitates interdisciplinary efforts to study structure and
process over time. A good modernization model eschews the

monocausal, deterministic notions of social change implicit in most other constructs, because it does not assign, *a priori,* primary causal significance to any economic, demographic, political, social, or cultural agent. A well-designed modernization model increases the likelihood that researchers will identify developing interdependencies in the political economy, recognize patterns of autonomy and exchange among various groups in the social structure, and be sensitive to pivotal dysfunctions in popular attitudes, collective behavior, and public policy.

Accordingly, let me distinguish my views on modernization from other versions by summarizing at the outset some of my ideas about three specific issues. The modernization model that I set forth here is meant to be a road map for all that follows. My conceptual framework naturally builds on other scholars' ideas. But the model used in *Shades of Gray* was specifically designed for the purpose of explaining continuities and changes in the history of older people in twentieth-century America. I shall present my argument initially as a set of three givens, upon which I shall then develop the rest of my argument.

First Given: The Core of "Modern America" Had Taken Shape by the 1920s

Most historians agree that a fundamental transformation of the structure and dynamics of western civilization began during the eighteenth century. Scholars emphasize different aspects of this transformation, but the cumulative impact of industrialization, technological innovation, bureaucratization, professionalism, urbanization, immigration, and the rise of novel scientific and philosophical perspectives are usually cited as key elements of "modernization." Initially, the process affected European nations (notably England) more profoundly than the United States (Stearns, 1975). America remained predominantly rural, preindustrial, localistic, provincial, and underdeveloped from its earliest colonization until at least the Revolution—and possibly as late as 1830. To varying degrees and at different rates, the new republic's demographic, economic, political, social, and cultural configurations were altered between the early 1800s and World War I (Brown, 1976; Jensen, 1978; Wiebe, 1967). By the 1920s, the United States had a coordinated and integrated political economy as well as a transcontinental style and pulse that made it a "nation" more than it had ever been before. This fact, more than any other single item, underscores the essential continuities between the 1920s and 1980s.

The modernization of America has been uneven and variegated.

Even though we shall concentrate on developments during the past six decades, it is imperative to understand that we are limiting our attention to one segment of a broad phenomenon that has been evolving for centuries. The origins of many things we will be discussing predate the twentieth century. Nevertheless, I think it reasonable to claim that "the core of America's modern state was a national political economy that acquired its basic form in the 1920s" (Wiebe, 1981: 760). This date signals a new stage in the development of a process that remains incomplete. Infrastructures became more complex and interrelationships more complicated over time. Rates of change within society and across major subdivisions continued to differ. New discontinuities and dysfunctions appeared. But the 1920s do serve as an appropriate baseline for our attempt to understand the most recent phase of modernization in the American experience.

Demographcially, modernization has involved at least four factors (Bogue, 1959; Grabill et al., 1958; Hendricks and Hendricks, 1981; Vinovskis, 1978). The first factor is a long-term drop in the birth rate. Census data indicate that, since the beginning of the nineteenth century, successive cohorts of native-born, white American women have been consciously determining the number of children they want to bear. Fertility rates for foreign-born and minority women have also fallen, though the timing and rate of the decline varied by ethnic and racial group. By the 1920s, all segments of the American population engaged in family planning. A second factor is the remarkable increase in life expectancy at birth. Most of this stems from a decline in the incidence of infant and childhood mortality during the second half of the nineteenth century, which is attributable to advances in medical technology, knowledge, and therapeutic interventions, as well as better public health, hygiene, and diet. Specific mortality rates varied by gender, race, nationality, class, and location; still, the children of all groups by the 1920s were likely to live longer than their parents. Third, America's population was aging. In large part, this was a result of declining fertility rates, but changes in mortality rates also contributed. Gains in adult longevity were noticed in the 1920s, but they have become more manifest and significant in recent decades. Finally, although Americans have always valued and formed nuclear families, the institution has undergone basic changes in size and structure, as well as in the allocation of power, resources, and production responsibilities.

Although outside agencies assumed greater responsibilities for many duties once managed primarily by families, such changes did not mean that the family diminished in importance. Most families ceased to make their own clothes or grow their own food, but the household itself remained a crucial economic unit. The family depended primarily on the breadwinner's income throughout the Industrial Revolution and into the twentieth century. The institution's role in transferring property and skills from one generation to the next remained intact. The relationship between the family and the larger community, in short, has always been multi-dimensional and fluid (Lasch, 1977; Gordon, 1979; Tilly and Cohen, 1982).

Economic trends, as well as demographic transitions, are intimately linked with the long-term process of modernization. The shift from an agrarian-rooted to an industrially based economy is probably the most familiar development. Associated with this change were the diminishing importance of farming as an occupation, the rise of middle-class professionalism, and a growing number of women in clerical and domestic positions. Managers made unprecedented efforts to consolidate bureaucratic activities so as to reach a national market for new products. This led to the growth of organizations that advanced the personal, collective, and financial interests of capitalists and workers alike (Chandler, 1977; Porter, 1973; Dubofsky, 1975; Nelson, 1975). New economic structures on the American landscape served as catalysts for novel social arrangements and distinctive popular beliefs.

One of the happier consequences of the growth of factory industry, mechanization, and labor productivity was the striking reduction in average work time. The normal work week in most occupations fell from about sixty hours to less than forty-five hours between 1880 and 1930 (*Recent Social Trends,* 1933: 828–29). The shortening of the work week, coupled with a general lightening of the work load, caused an increase in the average worker's appetite and capacity to consume goods (thereby further stimulating the mass production of basic necessities and luxury items). It also tended to heighten the desire of many workers to spend free time enjoyably (thereby making them a receptive market for merchandisers and entertainers). This increase in leisure time and the greater ability to spend it in pleasurable activities accelerated the development of athletic facilities and enlarged the market for automobiles, radios, household appliances, and movies. It spurred the development of private recreational parks modeled on the success of Coney Island (Kasson, 1978; Belasco, 1979). These developments, in turn, affected ideas about "work" and "leisure." Robert and Helen Lynd devoted a chapter of *Middletown* (1929) to answering the question "Why Do They Work So Hard?" Personnel managers increasingly worried about how to attract punctual workers and motivate employees on the job. Leisure ceased to be a preoccupation limited mainly to the rich and powerful. It became a "problem" for those who could not use it constructively. The realms of work and leisure thus took on new meanings as commentators began to wrestle with a new set of potentially conflicting interrelationships.

As the ramifications of the evolution of an increasingly complex, consumer-oriented economy were felt, important changes were also taking place in the polity. The gross anatomy of government closely resembled the system ratified in the Constitution in 1789. Alterations in its overall functions and levels of responsibilities, however, tended to increase its scope, cost, and importance in everyday life (White, 1948, 1958; Wilson, 1975; Keller, 1977). Government spending rose by 65 percent in per capita expenditures between 1915 and 1929 alone. Bureaucratic principles and procedures, which were making Big Business more efficient, were adopted in the public sector at all levels to make government more accountable and responsive to changing circumstances. Concurrently, the balance of power shifted from the state to the federal level. In part, this change resulted from the fiscal importance attributed to federal grants-in-aid for state-supervised programs. In part, the change reflected Washington's nascent role as a fact-finding agency. Above all, it underlined the most basic social trend of all: most of the truly profound challenges and problems shaping the republic's political economy transcended city, state, and regional boundaries.

Socially, America became more urban as it grew more industrial. From the beginning, there had been urban villages flourishing in the countryside. The nation's population increased twelve-fold between 1800 and 1890; cities over the same period grew eighty-seven-fold. Not until 1920, however, did more than half of the population live in "urban" centers, which the U.S. Census Bureau defined as places with at least 2,500 residents. As cities grew in size, they also changed in character, patterns, and structures. The cities' lures and discomforts—the urbanity and opportunities as well as the prejudices and inequalities, the advantages of technology and inadequacies of public services—increasingly defined the "standard of living" by which many Americans measured their progress and set their goals. Mass production, mass consumption, and mass media transformed people's tastes and relationships (Rodgers, 1978; Warner, 1972). By the 1920s, people living in nearly every section of the country were able, and felt the need, to be more in touch with developments that were fundamentally reshaping everyday life in the United States.

Culturally, this magnified a paradox deeply rooted in the national experience. On the one hand, middle-class life became more widespread and homogeneous (Fass, 1978; Sklar, 1970; Hofstadter and Wallace, 1970). The automobile—perhaps modern America's most apt icon—ceased to be a luxury and became the vehicle for geographic mobility and individual freedom. A nationwide cult of youth, who created fads and groped for new modes of expression with every season, flourished in high schools and on college campuses. The increased accessibility of higher education and the value placed on it were themselves symptomatic of the times. At the same time, long-standing prejudices festered in "modern" America. White, native-born Americans vaunted their Anglo-Saxon heritage as they vented their fears, anxieties, and anger against blacks, Catholics, Jews, and all others who were viewed as different, thus second-rate.

Before the Great Depression, public officals did not consider it part of their job to promote the interests of people who had traditionally been denied positions of power. Whether wittingly or unintentionally, government served "the people" by catering to organized interests (typically advocating the ideas of Big Business) and other clients who peddled fairly parochial goals. Neither state nor federal representatives bestowed special favors or extended compensatory (much less preferential) treatment to groups struggling to achieve their fair share of economic and social justice. Women did not gain the right to vote until 1920. Even then, government did not attempt to rectify the double standard that prevailed in the marketplace, courts, and other major social institutions. Jim Crow laws, which since the 1980s had denied blacks the right to vote and access to most public facilities in southern states, continued to flourish. *De facto* racial segregation prevailed in the north. Despite America's claim of being the world's "melting pot," ethnic and racial hostility were condoned. When the Ku Klux Klan revived after World War I, its membership denounced Catholics, Jews, and urban immigrants, as well as blacks. The government sharply curtailed the influx of immigrants during the 1920s.

Yet these very "outsiders," to varying degrees and in different ways, were embracing the beliefs and customs characterizing mainstream America. Most second-generation Americans, the sons and daughters of Oriental and Eastern European immigrants, unabashedly rejected or subtly played down traditional folkways in an attempt to assimilate. Their parents viewed their children's course of action with a mixture of pride, envy, fear, and uneasiness. Women mobilized the individual resources. Blacks, despite tremendous disadvantages, also made limited gains by trying to make "separate-but-equal" institutions work for them rather than against them. The forces of cultural integration thus counterbalanced the tendency of groups to preserve ethnic boundaries from within.

Historically, therefore, the process of modernization did not affect everyone the same way, Various segments of the population adapted to changes around them with divergent degrees of success. The Amish, Cajuns, Indian tribes, and Mormons, for instance, hewed to traditional mores as long as possible, despite "modern" advances and interventions made by the dominant culture. Others, such as entrepreneurs and professionals on the make, were at the cutting edge of change. Women, blacks, and immigrants very often felt and responded to the impact of social change in ways that diverged from the modal experiences of middle-class, white males. No group, however, was immune to the large-scale transformation of American society itself after World War I.

Second Given: The Fundamental Modernization of Old Age in America Took Place After 1920

I have just suggested that the processes associated with modernization had divergent effects on men and women, blacks and whites, native-born and foreign-born citizens, and city dwellers and farmers. The forces of social change also altered the meanings and experiences of particular stages of life.

I do not mean to suggest that the ascription of distinctive assets and liabilities to particular age groups is a by-product of the process of modernization. The allocation of social roles, responsibilities, qualifications, and prerogatives according to age-specific distinctions has a long tradition in western civilization (Eisenstadt, 1956; Maddox and Wiley, 1976; Keith, 1982; Achenbaum, forthcoming). Nevertheless, the nature and dynamics of age-consciousness and age-grading have changed dramatically over time. The sheer population growth, the broadening scope and magnitude of governmental bureaucracies, and the increasing complexity of macroeconomic structures have contributed to fundamental changes in the ways people define the life-cycle, especially its latter stage(s).

Upper-class households in Europe, contends Ariès (1962), "discovered" children and granted them a new sensibility before the Industrial Revolution. According to Kett (1977) and Gillis (1974), the concept of "adolescence" was invented and popularized on both sides of the Atlantic in response to the challenges and problems wrought by socioeconomic and cultural changes during the latter half of the nineteenth century. Furthermore, modernization affected the timing of major events in the life-cycle. Schools and universities became increasingly homogeneous: a child typically began his or her formal schooling by the age of six; few were still in the educational system by the age of twenty-five. In response to an ever-changing environment, men and women beyond the age of eighteen exercised greater control over when and whom they married. They consciously determined the number and spacing of their offspring (Elder, 1974; Modell, Furstenberg, and Hershberg, 1976; Demos and Boocock, 1978). As a result, the major turning points in the life course have become more and more uniform and predictable over time.

The elderly were among the last age groups to be affected by the new order (Achenbaum and Stearns, 1978). Numbers partly account for this lag: there were relatively few old people in early

American society. The new nation was literally a young republic. Less than half of the population was over the age of sixteen in 1790; the median age was 22.9 in 1900; it is slightly over thirty today. But demography alone does not explain why the process of modernization initially had less impact on the elderly than on younger age groups.

Economic modernization touched but did not radically disrupt the aged's place in society. Older workers throughout the nineteenth century continued to play a vital role in agriculture, politics, most professions, and traditional crafts. The proportion of gainfully employed elderly men declined very little in nineteenth-century America. Aged women, mainly spinsters and widows, earned money by serving as seamstresses or housekeepers, and by taking in boarders and lodgers. Working and saving for one's later years and relying on family, neighbors, and (as a last resort) local charity remained the prevailing ways of dealing with old-age dependency.

Political modernization (in terms of new state functions or new political groupings) did not impinge upon the modernization of old age until the latter part of the nineteenth century. Even then, its impact was felt first in Europe and then in the United States. Some scholars have suggested that rising democratic impulses led to the displacement of old people from political power (de Beauvoir, 1972; Fischer, 1977). The historical record does not confirm this hypothesis, however, save for brief revolutionary episodes. Governments did not offer categorical assistance to the aged prior to Bismarck's social insurance scheme (1889) in Germany. Old-age dependency basically remained a problem to be handled within the family circle or in the local community. The only major exception was the granting of pensions to military veterans and their widows. This practice did not involve any new concept of public responsibility toward the old. It merely elaborated the idea that the state owed its soldiers and sailors a debt of gratitude (Glasson, 1918; Cetina, 1977).

Although the early stages of modernization placed new emphasis on youth, progress, equality, and material satisfaction, this broad cultural reorientation had a minimal effect on perceptions of the elderly. Definitions of old age's chronological boundaries held fast from place to place over time (Roebuck, 1978; Freeman, 1979; Kastenbaum, 1979). Cross-cultural studies of the elderly reveal the persistence of conflicting attitudes toward the aged. There is no evidence indicating that the wide range of self-images among older Europeans or Americans changed significantly (Demos, 1978; Fischer, 1978; Stearns, 1978, 1980c; Philibert, 1968, 1974, 1979; Berg and Gadow, 1978; Moody, 1979). This is hardly surprising, since western civilization's posture toward the aged had never been uniformly benign and benevolent. Negative commentaries on old people's value and gruesome descriptions of their physical appearance and personal characteristics can be found in Homeric literature and Scripture. Nor is there evidence that the aged's life-style changed abruptly before the twentieth century. Profound modifications in behavioral patterns among the young and middle-aged in the United States and western Europe were not paralleled by revolutionary shifts in the elderly's household arrangements, marital patterns, or property relationships (Stone, 1977a,b; S. R. Smith, 1978; D. S. Smith, 1978; Achenbaum, 1978a; Laslett, 1977; LeRoy Ladurie, 1979; Stearns, 1977, 1981).

On the basis of existing historical evidence, therefore, it seems clear that the actual modernization of the elderly proceeded slowly. By "the modernization of the elderly," I mean two complementary and simultaneous developments. I intend to show that the continuing transformation of American society in recent decades has altered the nature and quality of late life. Yet the elderly have not been simply *acted upon*. Old people themselves have adapted to new developments and coped with setbacks in unprecedented ways. As a result, changes in the meanings and experiences of old age have become more evident during recent American history. Some of the distinctly "modern" characteristics of a graying society—especially the presence of a relatively large percentage of citizens over sixty-five who are not employed but rely on the intergenerational income transfers provided by both the public and private sectors—were not prevalent before the twentieth century. New ways of defining and dealing with the social "problems" of growing older have gained widespread acceptance fairly slowly. Only in the past seventy-five years have the aged as a group engaged in collective action, involving mutual aid, political activism, social protest, or some combination thereof. Let us consider each of these points in more detail.

1. *Demographic trends.* The aging of America's population base made the elderly more and more visible. Before the Civil War, less than 5 percent of all men and women were over the age of sixty. By 1970, 14.1 percent of the population was at least that old. There was a 59 percent increase in the number of people over sixty-five between 1870 and 1920, and an extraordinary 115 percent rise in the next fifty years. Indeed, the very old—those over the age of seventy-five—now constitute the fastest growing segment of this nation's population in relative terms, if not in absolute numbers.

2. *Changing images of old age.* Not only did Americans see more and more older persons within their midst, but they perceived their assets and liabilities in new ways. People increasingly characterized old age as a "social problem." By the end of World War I,

if not before, Americans no longer ascribed to the elderly duties and prerogatives that once had permitted them to fulfill socially useful and respectable functions (Achenbaum, 1974; Gruman, 1978; Dahlin, 1980; Haber, 1979). And while many of the individual woes of growing old had long been spoken of, commentators in the early decades of this century underscored the presumably "scientific" basis for viewing later life as a period of pathological deterioration, eccentric behavior, and painful irrelevance. Yet science alone was not responsible for making the aged appear obsolescent. The prevailing belief that societal change was occurring at markedly quicker rates devalued the cumulative worth of long years. Simultaneously, this belief enhanced the presumed ability of youth to adjust to ever-changing circumstances and to lead the rest of society to new horizons. Furthermore, the rise of large-scale organizations and the institutionalization of bureaucratic principles reduced people's need to rely on older Americans' expertise. These trends also accentuated the elderly's disadvantages. Demographers, economists, and other observers postulated that the aged's position would grow more and more precarious as America continued to evolve, particularly given its age-graded system for allocating roles and resources. The "modern" era, all signs appeared to indicate, was creating a situation in which "old age, merely by that name, is a synonym for poverty" (Kelso, 1929).

3. *Group action among the old.* The elderly themselves engaged in collective action to "salvage old age" for the first time during the early decades of this century. Older people in many large cities and rural communities started clubs and met informally for educational and social purposes. A spate of bestsellers, including Elmer Ferris's *Who Says Old?* (1933) and Lyman Powell's *The Second Seventy* (1937), also sought to mold more positive images of the elderly. Dr. Lillien Martin, a retired Stanford University psychologist, opened an Old Age Center in San Francisco and wrote books and articles describing how countless elderly Americans had benefited from her self-help regimen. Dr. William McKeever operated a "School for Maturates" in Oklahoma City. *Senescence* (1922), the last major study written by the eminent psychologist G. Stanley Hall, marshaled anthropological, clinical, and literary evidence to prove that older Americans could improve their situations by mobilizing their own resources and tapping their potential.

4. *New directions in old-age welfare.* As the elderly's plight attracted more attention and their overall economic situation grew more vulnerable, various groups expressed unprecedented interest in the issue of old-age dependency. Social workers, reformers,

scholars, business groups, and civic organizations in the private sector sought new ways to assist older Americans. An increasing number of private companies, notably in the transportation sector, provided monthly benefits based on an employee's age at retirement and length of service (Conant, 1922; Brandes, 1975; Graebner, 1980). Insurance companies sold old-age annuities. A rising generation of philanthropists earmarked funds for the elderly: Andrew Carnegie established a retirement fund for college professors; Benjamin Rose left a fortune to aid Cleveland's aged poor. Especially after the 1870s, the number of private old-age homes and informal support networks run by churches, unions, ethnic societies, and fraternal groups mushroomed. Agencies at the municipal, state, and federal levels also responded to changing circumstances. Most large, industrial cities provided nominal pensions for retired firefighters, police, and school teachers (Fogelson, 1981). Some states assisted their superannuated bureaucrats; the federal government inaugurated a retirement program for civil servants in 1920. Military veterans and their dependents, if they satisfied an increasingly more liberal set of criteria, often qualified for pensions and sometimes for free medical care and housing. After a few false starts, a growing number of states in the 1920s began to provide monthly assistance to those who met stringent age, residency, and financial requirements.

All these developments seem strikingly "modern." Nevertheless, it is important to appreciate their tentativeness and uneven impact in the 1920s. The most significant growth in the aged population occurred after 1920, not before. While most commentators agreed at the time that old age had emerged as a social issue of unanticipated magnitude, the nature of proposals for dealing with hardships in later years greatly depended on how serious various groups perceived the problem to be. Some called for bold action, but most doubted that radical measures were necessary. The majority, in fact, opposed any scheme for the elderly that might jeopardize the position of other age groups. Furthermore, although innovations in old-age insurance and assistance ultimately provided crucial precedents and organizational bases for more ambitious programs (both private and public), efforts to help the elderly remained piecemeal. Corporate retirement systems were inadequately funded. They covered a fairly small proportion of the labor force; usually workers' benefits were not guaranteed. Only eighteen states provided relief to the needy aged before 1931; the dollar amounts of that assistance fluctuated wildly. The federal government steadfastly rejected appeals for the creation of a national old-age relief program, a plan first proposed in 1909. Finally, one should not pretend that older Americans' community activities constituted a highly mobilized, sophisticated political force. A "gray lobby" eventually would emerge from grass roots coalitions, but prior to the Great Depression it simply did not exist.

The particularly "modern" features of the elderly's position emerged, therefore, in a society that itself had essentially modernized. The decisive modernization of older Americans themselves is a twentieth-century phenomenon. Indeed, one of the most fascinating patterns that we will study is that of the elderly's successes and failures in modifying behavior and outlook in light of socio-historical developments since the 1920s. The modernization of old age, as we shall see, was neither smooth nor unidirectional. Very often, the aged's private desires and collective ambitions meshed neatly with national priorities. At other times, however, older Americans competed with other segments of the population for limited resources. The elderly's sense of themselves or their needs did not invariably dovetail with the views of other commentators. Hence, we must be particularly sensitive to the ways in which the modernization of old age has both paralleled and diverged from the main lines of development in twentieth-century American society and culture.

Third Given: Old-Age Policies Formulated in "Modern" America Represent New Resolutions of Enduring Value Dilemmas

I have just indicated that an essential feature of the modernization of old age in twentieth-century America was the inauguration and elaboration of social-welfare policies to enhance the economic and social well-being of elderly people. These policies were sensitive to the rising proportion of older persons in American society, that age group's growing political strength, as well as the positive and negative impact of recent societal trends on the elderly's socioeconomic conditions. Yet the specific provisions of federal old-age policies during the last half-century are more than the result of actuarial estimates of dependency ratios, econometric calculations, bureaucratic machinations, and congressional deliberations. Although broad-scale economic and political developments, demographic and social trends, and constitutional and legislative precedents all clearly affected the evolution of policies, an assessment of these factors does not tell the whole story. Value choices made in a dynamic socio-historical context also have entered into the calculus. Hence, it is essential to schematize the manner in which contemporary value dilemmas are manifest in social programs affecting the aged.

Acknowledging the significance of values in old-age policies underscores an obvious point: the process of modernization in twentieth-century America has a normative dimension. The ways in which one views and comprehends the world today are filtered through values that have been nurtured by "modern" societal patterns and processes, which they helped to sustain. Basic societal institutions have been, and remain, value-laden. Personal attitudes and societal values change as historical circumstances alter, though not necessarily in the same ways.[2]

Because value choices pervade all aspects of life, their impact in the realm of policymaking can hardly be exaggerated. Sometimes, novel value preferences that were grafted into social policies resulted from new economic arrangements or political commitments. Sometimes, "modern" values precipitated new public policy agendas. Recent developments, moreover, have exposed profound contradictions in the ways Americans have attempted to adapt their national creed to ever-changing realities. "The more uncompromisingly we pursue the goal of equalizing individual opportunity, the more it appears to conflict with the theory of democratic pluralism. There is an ambiguity in the American value system which tries, on the one hand, to promote conformity to an American way of life, and, on the other, to demand of those who work at the bottom, that they alter their position within the social structure" (Rein, 1976: 193; Vickers, 1968). Such a normative conundrum embodies the messiness inherent in the modernization of America and the diverse impact of the process on this nation's population.

Despite their fundamental importance, however, values are not handled well in literature. Much of the current uneasines in talking about values in an analytic and dispassionate manner attests to the pluralistic and relativistic nature of the prevailing value system. Key terms are often confused. Researchers sometimes find it hard to disassociate their own values from those found in their subject matter. Others claim to be using a "value-free approach," which is laden with implicit judgments and untested hypotheses. Because the remainder of this volume is based on the assumption that societal

---

[2] Elaborating on this observation would require me to amplify all that has been discussed thus far. Within the "personality function" of the changing American household, for instance, were planted not just the germ of a family's stability but also the seeds for its disintegration. Philosophical family issues that affect all of us now—the choices people must make in relationships between parent(s) and child(ren), husband and wife, friends and neighbors—have always concerned Americans. This is not the first generation to face the repercussions of divorce, new sexual mores/pressures, and the tensions between work and play, or career and family. The tension between one's identity as an individual and one's identity as a family member is a central force in the American experience.

My reason for raising this theoretical issue here is mainly to underscore the significance of "values" in this historical analysis. In my opinion, most other "modernization" models fail to take questions of values seriously. In *Shades of Gray*, I am attempting to demonstrate the intimate relationship between the normative and structural components of recent American societal development.

values count, it is necessary at the outset to make clear my position on the relationships among old age, American values, and federal policies since 1920.

For my purposes, a "value" shall be defined as "any discrimination of importance as to priority or degree once made that is held over time" (Tice, 1978). A value differs from an "opinion," which tends to be volatile and ephemeral (Converse, 1964). It differs from a "belief," which need not entail an explicit or implicit choice. A value differs from a "norm" because the latter is by definition a proscription or prescription defining a specific mode of behavior; values may concern end-states of existence, as well as general kinds of behavior. A value differs from an "attitude," which refers to the way that a person (or group) sums up beliefs, opinions, and ideas about a specific object or situation (Rokeach, 1960). What makes a value distinctive is that it involves a long-standing choice. A "value system" refers here to an analytic device imposed by an investigator who is interested in exploring the connections among several specific value choices. It is a meta-structure that facilitates the study of how particular values cluster and interact in a complex and fluid manner at any given moment, as well as over time. Such an analytic construct helps both the researcher and the reader to focus on those—and often only those—values that have a bearing on the subject at hand. It enables them to understand why, in some instances, different groups of historical actors have defined their alternatives in roughly the same way, and thus made essentially the same choice. It also encourages the analysis of how and why fundamental shifts have occurred in certain value preferences expressed during the evolution of (American) culture and society. A "value system," therefore, highlights enduring patterns, decisive breaks, and covert or overt biases in normative choices.

And yet it is essential to note that such a construct can neither reduce basic tensions nor resolve inherent contradictions within any set of values under scrutiny. To be sure, Americans' continuing commitment to Judeo-Christian ideals and Enlightenment principles, to a democratic form of government, and to a capitalist economic system has enabled a civic culture to flower, which has been remarkable for its resilience and longevity. Nevertheless, inconsistencies and ambiguities have long existed in this country's value systems. This is because dominant American values at any moment reflect and result from the interplay of disparate historical vectors. Even among the nation's power elite, economic motives have rarely meshed perfectly with political ambitions and social desires. The potential for normative conflict and tension across the spectrum of society has been deeply rooted in America's heterogeneous population and uneven historical development. Beliefs associated with emerging forces of social change have perennially clashed with established norms and venerated ideals. Points of convergence and divergence between the values of "insiders" and those of "outsiders" have remained in flux, because boundaries defining the center and separating different social groups changed over time (Bell, 1976; Moore, 1982; Douglas and Wildavsky, 1982). Consequently, "modern" American values are a curious admixture of prevailing verities, premodern attitudes, anti-modern impulses, and those esoteric, sometimes deviant, values that may well presage the next set of mainstream views.

Given the variety of configurations that rightly can claim to represent twentieth-century American values, analysts rarely have discussed major patterns in the same way. Indeed, there are many ways to conceptualize the value system of modern America that have had an impact on the aged (Becker, 1973; Lasch, 1979; Neugarten and Havighurst, 1977). Following, I have identified a set of seven enduring, discrete, and complementary dilemmas that have been instrumental in the formulation and execution of federal old-age programs. (See the Technical Appendix for a more sophisticated rationale and defense of *this* particular construct.) The seven pairs are as follows:

- *Self-reliance / dependency,* which emphasizes the strain between the desire for self-sufficiency and personal initiative, on the one hand, and the need to recognize the limits to individual autonomy and the necessity of relying on other people, on the other. Throughout most of American history, people of all ages endeavored to affirm and preserve their independence. In a society that places a premium on self-reliance, it is not surprising to find successive generations extolling the trailblazer, the yeoman farmer, the solitary inventor, the daring entrepreneur, the pilot or astronaut circling the earth alone. Self-reliance has always been esteemed; those who could not make the grade were viewed with pity and disdain. However, "dependency" was recognized as a social reality. It was increasingly perceived as an inevitable by-product of broad-scale modernization. The tension between self-reliance and dependency has special significance for older people. Those who enjoyed good health and had economic resources sufficient to maintain an independent existence generally were not thought of as "old." In contrast, the aged "dependent" deserved special consideration. To be deemed dependent was to be viewed as different, however, isolated conceptually and socioeconomically from the mainstream of society.

- *Expectation / entitlement,* which suggests the tension between constantly defending or working for everything one can get and being guaranteed certain things because one is a human being or because of some plausible or legitimized precedent. Foreign observers and native critics have consistently seized upon American optimism and belief in progress as a fundamental national trait (Higham and Conkin, 1979). In this sense, Americans of all ages have tended to look forward, and to seek improvements in their individual and collective lot. Once certain gains are made and rights secured, in fact, they take them for granted. What one has at the moment becomes the basis from which one grasps for more. Yesterday's expectations typically are perceived as today's entitlements. For older people, benefits under federal programs constitute old-age entitlements. Expectations are based on these entitlements, as well as on the desire for additional benefits.

- *Work / leisure,* which confronts the realm of work and its meanings for an individual's identity, particularly when he or she is not duty-bound to be productive. The work ethic is deeply rooted in the American experience. In "modern" society, people often presume certain characteristics and assign a particular value to a person's worth primarily on the basis of his or her main task in life. Thus while leisure-time pursuits may actually be preferred to the job, work takes precedence over leisure. With few exceptions,. notably some of the very rich, this has always been true for people past the age of maturity. Indeed, prior to the twentieth century, the aged generally could not look forward to any more creative leisure time than younger people. When they ceased working, the old typically joined the ranks of the dependents; they rarely became part of the leisure class. In recent decades, the potential conflict between work and leisure has been lodged in retirement experiences. When, why, and how one retires reveals much about the tensions in this pair of values.

- *Individual / family,* which underlines the problem of balancing one's personal goals and needs with those of the family into which one is born and/or which one forms through marriage and procreation. Despite the individualistic implications of both national mythology and actual modernization experiences, overwhelming historical and sociological data indicate that the feats of individuality Americans celebrate are typically facilitated by a family background and network that give a person the confidence and support (and sometimes the negative incentive!) necessary to take the leap. The need for a sense of individual identity does not diminish with age, though family members and close friends become indispensable in late life. Policymakers, however, must decide whether they should provide income and social services on the basis of an elderly person's needs. An alternative is to allocate benefits to an older person in his or her familial unit. The choice between individual- or family-based assistance affects the nature, cost, and utility of any specific old-age program.

- *Private / public,* which describes the conundrum of whether to use personal, institutional, and corporate resources or to use governmental means (at any and all levels) to achieve desirable societal goals. By and large, Americans have preferred to rely on private institutions to achieve essential social and economic goals. Government's task, especially prior to the twentieth century, was to provide or enhance private opportunities through direct and indirect means. There have been sharply defined limits, moreover, to what Americans have wanted their government to do and what they have claimed it *should* do. Some wanted to restrict the functions of government to ensuring the nation's defense and internal order. Others saw government as a powerful social service organization and civil rights advocate. This value dilemma has affected the well-being of late life. For instance, coping with old-age dependency historically had been viewed as a private matter, until changes were wrought by the New Deal. Since then, benefits from the public sector have been viewed as a floor upon which to build up resources through savings and private pensions. The boundaries between public and private responsibilities to old people, however, have become fuzzier over time.

- *Equity / adequacy,* which refers to the policy conflict between ensuring fair treatment to all under the law and fulfilling the responsibility to help those most in need according to some prescribed minima. Americans over time have been more concerned with preserving and gaining equity than with promoting adequacy. This is consistent with the long-standing belief that the United States is, and should remain, a land in which equality of opportunity counts for more than any scheme with equality of result as an explicit objective. Indeed, compassion toward the needy old and liberalization of benefits toward the dependent of all ages have typically reflected the belief that something, but not too much, should be done for the poor. Efforts to raise levels of social adequacy capitalized on current or anticipated increases in equity. That is, a willingness to allocate a larger piece of the pie for welfare generally resulted from the fact that the pie itself had grown larger.

- *Novelty / tradition,* which characterizes the perennial choice individuals and groups make between looking for new, rational, possibly transient, ways of coping with life's risks and crises and relying on perennial, time-tested, widely accepted sources of support. Ever since Columbus claimed "the New World" for his Spanish benefactors, Americans have vaunted the novelty of their condition and made the quest for the new a central feature of their national tradition. This is not to say that experience, or more precisely the wisdom of years, counts for nothing. Nor is it to suggest that tradition has no home in "modern" America. "Premodern" values derived from Classical traditions and the Judeo-

Christian heritage persist. Anti-modernist impulses compete with the latest fads for public acceptance. But those institutional and human guardians of age-old values and long-standing mores must consistently and continually demonstrate that maintaining the old order is not antithetical to progress.

This set of tensions is not complete, but it does seem useful in describing and explaining major policy conflicts affecting the aged since the 1920s. The values are ones to which we are all committed and to which we all owe allegiance—differences in priority, divergent levels of intensity, and multiple loyalties and self-identities notwithstanding. Such interlocking of values implies ambiguity and conflict, but it does not necessarily signify mutual exclusivity.

Duality, in fact, is a crucial feature of America's value system. This becomes particularly evident the moment one begins to examine the rhetoric and philosophical assumptions underlying the evolution of federal programs for the aged during the last half-century. Thoughts about public issues have been connected overtly or covertly to ideas about private issues. Defining the family has often required decisions about specific roles that each individual in that unit was presumed to play. With varying degrees of explicitness, policymakers have related perspectives on self-reliance to notions about dependency. The struggle to gain new benefits for older Americans has required, among other things, careful justification of these benefits in light of past precedents and sensitivity to normative constraints. Thus the key problem in balancing the juxtaposed, potentially contradictory, dysfunctional, anomalous relationships of many of our cherished beliefs in any given instance has been to maximize what one value represents without vitiating, or repressing, what another important value represents. As we shall see, Americans rarely have been successful in accomplishing this goal.

Part of the reason that old-age programs are riddled with inherent contradictions is that the American value system has been, and continues to be, both pluralistic and dualistic. Especially in the policy arena, one can trace historically how legislators and administrators, their staffs and consultants, interest groups, and the informed or aroused public sought to "satisfice" (Simon, 1955) demands advanced by different groups that advocated radically different lines of action. Sometimes, contradictory demands came from coalitions expressing strong value support for two or more positions. It thus is appropriate to invoke the metaphor of a kaleidoscope: the chips remain basically the same, but an incremental turn here or there gives a vastly different appearance to any particular pattern.

"Shades of gray" indeed characterizes the changing relationships among old age, American values, and federal policies. Rarely have

Americans had to make black-or-white choices. The refractions of temporal and cultural context since 1920 have caused old-age programs to change. But the shifts have not been as direct or clear as one might predict. For this reason, the premodern antecedents of our contemporary values are as important to understand as recent developments. The modernization of the American experience in general, and of its older population in particular, has colored our policy alternatives. Different shadings of value dilemmas have cast new light on old options. Fresh policy initiatives necessitate new normative decisions, and vice versa. Policy outcomes embody the layers of compromises and constraints inherent in a dualistic, pluralistic, dynamic value system.

Accordingly, I propose to reconstruct the evolving interrelationships among major socioeconomic trends, pivotal aging policies, and dominant American values during the past six decades in the following manner. Chapter 2 examines major developments occurring between the onset of the Great Depression and the end of World War II. I suggest that the passage of the Social Security Act constitutes a watershed in the history of old age in America. As such, it serves as an appropriate baseline for assessing all subsequent developments. Chapter 3 analyzes the consolidation and elaboration of New Deal programs amidst postwar affluence in the late 1940s and 1950s. Chapter 4 explores whether the Great Society constitutes a watershed in American social (welfare) history. Chapter 5 reviews the drift of events during the late 1960s and 1970s. Chapter 6 recasts the major themes by offering a tentative assessment of the historical significance of Reaganomics. The volume ends by making a forecast about the possible shades of gray on the political horizon in aging America.

Doris Ulmann's photograph "Old Man and Woman, Waiting" (ca. 1930) suggests why a "New Deal" for older America became so necessary in the depths of the Great Depression. [Courtesy of The Library of Congress.]

Chapter

2

A New Deal
for Aging
America

American historians frequently use the geomorphologic metaphor of "watershed" to mark important divisions in our national experience. To some, a historical watershed divides the flow of events associated with one era from those of the next. To others, a watershed is a significant period of change within the fluid process of long-term historical evolution itself—the temporal analog of a large river basin that gathers major tributaries and then spews forth new currents and streams. The metaphor's ambiguity sometimes makes it an imprecise interpretative device. Invoked too often, it can overstate the degree or frequency of change; it can underplay fundamental continuities from one generation to another. Worse, it can create a false sense of dislocation and alienation from historical roots (Cunliffe, 1968). Yet historians continue to use the watershed metaphor despite its imperfections: it affords them a useful way to accentuate crucial moments in our past during which established patterns ceased to predominate or were transvalued, junctures at which divergent trends emerged on the historical landscape or began to dominate it.

This chapter invokes this metaphor in order to set the tone for all that is to follow. I believe that the Roosevelt years (1933–1945) were a decisive turning point in American history. More precisely, the period constituted a watershed in American values and federal policies affecting the aged. Because the Great Depression was such a profound economic crisis, it put into a new context the intellectual developments and structural trends that had been transforming American culture and society for decades. It fomented fresh, sometimes unprecedented, efforts to redefine or reconcile long-standing tensions within the American value system by forging a new set of social policies: the passage of the original Social Security Act in 1935 together with its important 1939 amendments constituted a critical moment in the development of categorical programs for the nation's current and future aged. But rehearsing the legislative history and interpreting the significance of the New Deal for aging America is only half the story. The meanings and experiences of being old in the United States were not altered just by the enactment of new federal legislation. They also were affected by the outbreak of World War II in Europe, the events leading up to Pearl Harbor, and this country's commitment to win a war waged in two far-flung theaters. Insofar as the priorities and exigencies of war caused changes in key elements of America's political economy and cultural life, they directly, indirectly, and often unexpectedly changed the elderly's place in society.

The Great Depression and World War II redefined the relationship between the federal government and the American people, and altered many attitudes and patterns of behavior across all age groups. These events, however, did not lead to a radical break with the past. They did not have a uniformly decisive impact on all aspects of American life. Franklin Roosevelt's administration did not coincide with the first or even the most important watershed in our national experience. Nonetheless, the period did witness necessary and significant alterations in our social fabric, including basic shifts in the rhetoric and realities of growing old. As such, the era stands as a useful starting place from which to measure subsequent transformations of values and policies that have shaped this aging nation during the "modern" period.

Americans Experience a Great Depression

The stock market crash is usually the first image that comes to mind when we think about the Great Depression. Stock prices fell a staggering $14 billion on October 25, 1929. American Telephone and Telegraph lost $449 million and the net worth of United States Steel (the traditional bellwether) declined $142 million in a single day. Between October 1929 and June 1932, U.S. Steel fell from 262 points to 21, Montgomery Ward (then the nation's biggest retail chain) from 138 to 4, and RCA from 101 to 2.5. Overall, the common stocks price index dropped from 260 to 90. Most of the early losers were speculators who had recklessly played the "bull market" during the summer of 1928. As time went on, thousands of brokers and investors, who had committed money modestly but confidently in American capitalism, also lost savings and with them a major source of their security (Patterson, 1976: 198–203). Wall

Street's woes eventually extended across the nation. Nearly five thousand banks, with aggregate deposits exceeding $3.2 billion, had folded by September 1932. Ninety thousand businesses failed. Other corporations prevented bankruptcy by limiting output (merchandise exports dropped from $5.2 billion in 1929 to $1.6 billion in 1932), by slashing wages (the average weekly wage for production workers dipped from $25.03 to $16.73 in the same period), and by laying off workers (the national unemployment rate rose from 3 percent to 25 percent, the highest it has ever been). Farmers were as hard pressed as industrial workers. The farm products index between 1928 and 1932 dived from 105 to 51; the gross income realized by farmers had fallen from $13.9 billion to $7.1 billion by mid-1932.

The Great Depression was neither the first nor the only sharp downturn in American economic history. Slowdowns and adverse conditions frequently crippled manufacturing, agricultural, commercial, and mining interests in different regions of the United States during the nineteenth century. The country had endured panics in 1819, 1837, 1857, 1873, and 1893. The pattern continued in the twentieth century: there were recessions in 1907–1908 and immediately after World War I. Yet "while the intensity of falling prices and monetary contraction was not at all unprecedented, the intensity and duration of unemployment was new and shocking" (Rothbard, 1962: 1). For the first time in their lives or memories, a sizable proportion of the presumably prosperous and self-sufficient middle class personally underwent the tragic experiences of dependency. Bread lines formed. Families were forced to huddle together in shacks on vacated lots because they had lost their homes. Others skimped in ways their parents had not had to do. In the depths of the Depression, eighteen million Americans sought emergency relief in order to subsist. Unquestionably, the number who really needed help surpassed that figure. It was estimated in 1932, for instance, that 80 percent of Philadelphia's 280,000 unemployed received no relief whatsoever (U.S. Congress, Hearings on H.R. 4120, 1935:19).

The economic crisis, not surprisingly, occasioned a reassessment of the national creed. Americans did not suddenly abandon their traditional beliefs because of the hard times. Conditions, nonetheless, did accentuate tensions within America's dominant values. The widespread unemployment, for example, made most Americans appreciate the benefits of gainful occupations more than ever and widened the distinction drawn between working and not working. Blue-collar and white-collar employees gladly accepted pay cuts and part-time positions in order to keep their jobs. As factories shut down, businesses closed, and farms went bankrupt, many displaced workers were willing to do menial jobs—anything—so that they could put morsels on the table. Countless thousands left home in search of jobs. The number of hobos soared; in 1931, one hundred thousand men and women applied for skilled positions in the Soviet Union. According to estimates made by the Farm Security Administration, more than five hundred thousand farmers with family members totaling 1.5 million took to the roads in search of work. This did not mean, however, that "leisure" became unspeakable in the American idiom. More than ever before, Americans turned to recreational activities in order to pass time pleasurably and to escape their worries. Nearly two-thirds of the population saw a movie once a week. The number of people possessing radios rose nearly threefold in the 1930s. "Monopoly" became the most popular game of the decade. While most Americans took momentary solace in their fantasies, leisure did not assuage their guilt about being out of work. Nor did hard times diminish people's responsibility to their kith and kin. To be sure, evidence indicates that there was a rise in abandonment and wife abuse, and young adults postponed marriage or consciously limited the number of their children. Yet on balance, the Depression years sustained the primacy of the family and corroborated the father's role as chief breadwinner and household head. The celebration of domesticity was a major theme in comic strips and movies, as well as in bestsellers such as *Life with Father* and *The Grapes of Wrath*. Domesticity was also reaffirmed in public opinion surveys and prevailing practices of employers who routinely denied jobs to married women whose husbands worked and who made no apologies for sex discrimination in hiring or salaries.

Besides underscoring the value people placed on work and their family's well-being, the adversities brought on by the Great Depression also forced a profound reevaluation of American "individualism." Unemployment, said observers at the time, weakened self-esteem and induced guilt to a greater extent in the United States than elsewhere, because of the perennial American emphasis on self-reliance.[1] That one-fifth of all men who wanted to work still could not find jobs as late as 1938 painfully demonstrated that "rugged individualism" had fallen upon rugged times. Even the citizens of "Middletown," who publicly claimed to believe that an individual got what he or she deserved in the long run, seemed to be worried, sore, and frustrated about their lot and their future. Elaborating on this theme after a second research trek to Muncie, Indiana, in the mid-1930s, Robert Lynd wrote,

> A prevalent mood among sophisticated persons today is a sense of helplessness in the face of the too-bigness of the issues we confront.

[1] It should be noted that recent research indicates that this was not a uniquely American response. According to Garraty (1978), unemployed workers in European countries that had elaborate socialist welfare systems expressed the same sorts of feelings of inadequacy that Americans did.

This is no new experience for human beings. . . . But the sense of the big- and out-of-handedness of our contemporary world is neither illusion nor merely another expression of this recurrent restlessness of man in civilization. . . . We feel ultimately coerced by larger forces not controllable within our immediate area of personal concentration (1939: 11–12).

As no other event had quite done before, the Depression experience required Americans to recognize limits to individuals' control over their personal and collective destinies. Circumstances forced people to acknowledge their dependence on others. Dreams of boundless prosperity and the images of pioneers carving out a niche in the frontier—the stuff that had inspired mainstream America and waves of immigrants for decades—hardly meshed with the harsh realities of the day.

Government Responds to the Economic Crisis

Even though the economic crisis of the 1930s made a collectivistic approach to solving a nationwide societal crisis more palatable to a growing segment of the population, it hardly follows that Americans were immediately, or irrevocably, prepared to overturn the fundamental economic, political, and social bases of their society and culture. In fact, quite the opposite is true. Herbert Hoover believed, as did other thoughtful leaders inside and outside government circles, that America's capitalist system itself was essentially healthy. It *had* been rocked by instability abroad and excessive speculation within. But once the private sector got its operations in order, predicted the President, the economy would remedy its own troubles. Thus, Hoover repeatedly promised imminent economic recovery and urged his fellow citizens to exercise "responsible individualism" (Romasco, 1965; J. H. Wilson, 1979: 112–21). He preferred jawboning and moral suasion to legally binding, mandatory guidelines or extensive public works activities. Hoover sincerely believed that "voluntaristic associationalism" between industry and labor, as well as increased relief efforts at the state and local levels, would suffice to turn the tide. By the latter part of 1931, however, all indicators revealed that the economy was grinding to a halt. Despite presidential protestations, major industries slashed wages and cut production. Funds available to private charity groups were rapidly depleted as demands for assistance grew. Realizing that the federal government had to take more decisive steps, Hoover created the Reconstruction Finance Corporation, which gave loans to large banks and insurance companies on the brink of bankruptcy. He hoped that this "trickle-down" approach would have a ripple effect throughout the economy. The President also signed the Emergency Relief Act (1932), which provided a limited number of federally funded jobs. To the end of his term, however, he steadfastly ignored public clamor and refused to authorize direct federal assistance to the needy. He rejected his advisors' counsel that he endorse even bolder steps of control at the federal level.

Hoover was not a heartless reactionary who simply failed to appreciate (or worse, subbornly renounced) the powers available to a president. After all, Hoover had received widespread praise for his efficient, humane supervision of America's relief efforts in Europe after World War I. Through his experience as an agency head in the War Industries Board (1917–1918), he discovered the extent—and to him as well as to many of his peers, the dangerous degree—to which a centralized authority could intervene within a capitalist society. (Ironically, Hoover's current reputation is better than ever, precisely because he *did* understand that the federal government is not the source of all wisdom and that its powers must be limited.) Nevertheless, when he at last moved beyond voluntarism and began to mobilize resources at his disposal, his actions were belated and paltry. Efforts to engineer a dramatic improvement in the economy foundered. The President's stubborn reluctance to move beyond the sagacity of lifelong beliefs in the face of unexpectedly dire circumstances exacerbated the Depression. His unwillingness to enlarge the powers of his office, coupled with the failure of the captains of American industry and business to stimulate a quick recovery, probably accelerated the changing balance of power between the private and public sectors. Indeed, Hoover's inability to solve the nation's problems, despite his assiduous application of time-tested political tenets, had the unintentional effect of predisposing Americans to welcome the forceful use of federal power that his Democratic opponent promised to employ if elected president.

Franklin Delano Roosevelt carried all but six states on election day, 1932. During the four months before he took office and then during the "First Hundred Days," Roosevelt and his advisors pieced together an extraordinarily wide-ranging legislative package, which he confidently predicted would ensure a "New Deal" for all Americans. Unlike Hoover, Roosevelt was willing to experiment boldly, to tinker with programs until they finally accomplished their stated aims. Working closely with congressional leaders and independent consultants, he proposed legislation and created bureaucracies designed to promote relief, recovery, or reform in nearly all areas of society. The mind-boggling array of "alphabet agencies" should not distract one from the cumulative significance of the New Deal enterprise. Each new law, each new administrative body, each new ruling augmented the visibility and power of the federal government in

American life (Karl, 1963). The prevailing relationship between private concerns and public affairs was upset as more and more authority to shape the nation's future was vested in public officials. Simultaneously, the balance of power within the public sector tilted more discernibly toward Washington, and away from city halls, county seats, and state houses. Only at the national level, the Depression experience appeared to demonstrate, could issues that were nationwide in scope be addressed. Hence, in the minds of Americans, the federal government seemed less and less remote. Most people no longer viewed it simply as a dispassionate arbiter of the last resort. Increasingly, citizens viewed Washington as a dynamic catalyst for social action, the dominant partner involved in everyday affairs as well as in matters of nationwide importance.

This profoundly important redirection in the power structure of the United States was designed and tolerated in order to achieve a very conservative goal: the preservation and enhancement of democratic and capitalist traditions. That this nation's political system did not collapse in the midst of economic turmoil of the 1930s—as did the governments of Italy and Germany—demonstrates the basic faith in the American system evinced by leaders and the public at large. Roosevelt and his advisors persistently rejected fascist, communist, and socialist alternatives because these forms of government seemed alien to them. Indeed, viewed as an economic scheme, the New Deal clearly was intended to restore and invigorate capitalism for the welfare of all citizens. Officials intervened in the marketplace, subsidized prices, and regulated practices largely to prevent the recurrence of another economic catastrophe. They intended to reduce inequities and abuses that were thought to have caused the Depression in the first place.

Furthermore, the New Deal rarely departed radically from past political practices. To be sure, the Tennessee Valley Authority was designed to be a federally authorized experiment in social democracy, with reconstruction of the region supervised by local citizens. Yet other efforts at grass-roots democracy, such as the Resettlement Administration and the Farm Security Administration, failed because of underfunding, political opposition, and gross misjudgments about the scope of the problems they were established to solve (Lilienthal, 1944; Leuchtenberg, 1963; Baldwin, 1968). And despite his periodic experiments with planned social management, Roosevelt never instituted a "fully articulated system of Planning where national and rational perspectives would necessarily come to bear on every public decision" (Graham, 1976: 65). Rather, the federal government acted, reacted, and interacted in an ad hoc, piecemeal manner, typically on behalf of groups that had the political leverage to draw national attention to an issue.

The primary responsibility of the federal government, as it evolved in the New Deal experience, was to serve as a broker that recognized the political legitimacy of all organized interest groups. Washington attempted to reconcile, or at least to appease temporarily, the conflicting demands placed on it. In a sense, the institutional arrangements created in the 1930s to mediate among competing elements in society were simply a modern version of a view already articulated under very different circumstances by James Madison in the *Federalist Papers* (1787–1788). Madison brilliantly demonstrated in Federalist No. 10 that democratic governments must recognize and defuse the influence of "factions"; Roosevelt wanted the Capitol to be more responsive to and reflective of the large-scale institutions and associations that had been shaping American society. But New Dealers broadened Madison's concept of democratic rule: they recognized that the concerns of hitherto disenfranchised or politically impotent elements in the population had to be considered, if this was truly to become a government of "the people." Hence, Roosevelt's administration helped the unorganized gain a voice at the federal level. For example, the National Labor Relations Act of 1935 (Wagner Act) advanced the unionization of unskilled workers and regulation of collective bargaining. Despite its accomplishments in reshaping labor-management relationships, however, the Roosevelt administration actually helped unrepresented and underrepresented groups gain access to power only to a limited degree. Often governmental efforts on behalf of blacks, Indians, and Mexican-Americans were meager and begrudging (Weaver, 1935). At best, the New Deal made the maximum participation of all segments of society an implicit, potentially attainable goal, not an explicit political fact of life.

The rise of interest-group liberalism as the prevailing political system in the New Deal augmented the power and prerogatives that the federal government wielded. Besides curbing the private sector's free rein, the new political calculus generated at least two new principles that were to become major parameters for policy development (Conkin, 1967; Ekirch, 1969: 105–25). First, Roosevelt clearly upheld the belief that protecting individual rights was a democratic government's chief responsibility. But the President also recognized the need to take collective action on behalf of individuals who shared common disadvantages or deserved special consideration. Rendering categorical assistance, in this context, became a means of promoting and guaranteeing an individual's basic civil rights. In so doing, the New Deal deliberately downplayed the factors of self-reliance and independence extolled in nineteenth-century and early-twentieth-century American definitions of individualism and in the exaltation of the mythic yeoman farmer. Rather, the Roosevelt administration emphasized that people achieve their true identity in a cooperative, group-oriented setting.

In reality, of course, political infighting took precedence over inter-group cooperation. Special interest groups and lobbyists competed with one another for national recognition and federal bounty. The "politics of incrementalism"—the strategy of achieving broad policy goals in a gradual, step-by-step manner—increasingly became the way Washington did business.

The acknowledgment of the limits of self-reliance and the acceptance of the value of interest-group liberalism led to a second new principle of policymaking: the federal government, to promote the general welfare, had an obligation to ensure a measure of economic security for *all* citizens. Few discounted the important incentives and benefits that belief in "equality of opportunity" had contributed in the past. The application of this principle had served to advance individual and corporate efforts to attain financial well-being for many, and even affluence for a few. More than any previous president, however, Franklin D. Roosevelt echoed and reinforced a growing popular sentiment for more extensive federal intervention. The Depression experience, to an extent true of no earlier economic crisis, stirred support in the United States for measures to protect against the "equality of inopportune disasters" that characterized "modern" society. Consequently, the specter of insecurity due to circumstances beyond one's control could not be ignored, or dismissed as irrelevant, in the search for liberty and pursuit of happiness. It had become an issue of fundamental importance.

Addressing the Aged's Current and Anticipated Needs

Perhaps the situation of the elderly best illustrates the emerging political order and evolving social values of the 1930s. Older Americans possibly suffered more than any other age group. Unemployment figures for those over sixty-five were higher than those for young and middle-aged workers. The nest eggs set aside for emergencies—savings, nearly paid-off mortgages, and contributions to various insurance plans—broke to bits in the crash. Charitable societies could not provide relief to everyone. Friends and family, who were strapped themselves, could not afford to help the elderly, even if they so desired. The precise extent of old-age dependency became a moot point. Hard times "increasingly convinced the majority of the American people that individuals could not themselves provide adequately for their old age and that some sort of greater security should be provided by society" (Douglas, 1936: 6–7). As more and more people suffered prolonged hardships and the aged's predicament became indisputable, Americans expressed fewer reservations about the immediate need for federal relief for the aged poor and some sort of retirement insurance for the aging.[2] Thus, in the gloomy context of a Great Depression that exposed the weakness and inadequacy of prevailing means of relieving and preventing old-age dependency, demands for federal action became so strident that they could no longer be ignored.

The aged themselves organized the largest grass-roots pressure group. By late 1934, Dr. Frances E. Townsend of Long Beach, California, had rallied hundreds of thousands of frustrated older Americans behind his proposal that all persons over sixty be given $200 monthly on the conditions that they not be gainfully employed and that they spend their pensions within thirty days. Within a year, Townsend had claimed to have five million supporters and at least sixty members of Congress sympathetic to his cause (Putnam, 1970; Piven and Cloward, 1971: 100–101; Neuberger and Loe, 1936). Others endorsed Upton Sinclair's plan to make people on relief self-supporting and to grant pensions worth $50 to all Californians over sixty who had resided in the state for at least three years. Still other groups advocated less utopian panaceas. The American Association for Old Age Security, founded by Abraham Epstein in 1927, sought to broaden its constituency by joining the fight for unemployment insurance as well as for old-age provisions. Union officials, notably the leaders of the American Federation of Labor, reversed earlier stands and called for concerted efforts at the state and federal level to protect workers from financial hazards due to unemployment, disability, and old age. Pressure mounted in all quarters.

Just because all of these different groups called for changes in the status quo, however, does not necessarily mean that they shared common philosophies, values, or strategies. Supporters of publicly funded unemployment insurance disagreed, among other things, over which people within the ranks of the "unemployed" deserved and/or required assistance (Lubove, 1968; Nelson, 1969; Garraty, 1978, especially ch. 9 and 10; Berkowitz and McQuaid, 1980).

---

[2] Bear in mind that the really significant connection between the economic crisis and the passage of Social Security is *not* that the Depression initiated a rapid deterioration in the aged's status. We have already seen that older Americans had been vulnerable for decades to changes in the economy over which they had little control. Nor can we reasonably argue that implementing a public social security program at the national level required a depression as a precondition. Alternative schemes for a federal retirement plan had been debated for at least two decades. Organized pressure for some sort of scheme had increased significantly between 1927 and 1932. There also had been a noticeable decrease in political and philosophical opposition to federal intervention in this country even before Franklin D. Roosevelt took office. And, while the American approach to social security for the elderly was striking in both its timing and its two-pronged method, other countries, including Great Britain and Canada, had already established programs that influenced policymakers in this country (Heidenheimer et al., 1975).

Similarly, commentators in the late 1920s and 1930s did not agree in their assessments of the needs of the "aged." Some contended that every older American should be assisted. Others proposed limiting relief to those who could prove that they were poor. Still others believed that a potential recipient's marital status and number of kin (who might be able to help out the older person) should be taken into consideration. Just as different groups had divergent targets of relief in mind, so too they disagreed about the best way for the federal government to proceed. The American Association for Labor Legislation (AALL), for instance, had been calling since the end of World War I for protective old-age insurance plans to be funded through collective bargaining demands and business cooperation. Abraham Epstein saw social insurance not simply as a cushion against the vicissitudes of modern life but also as a way to redistribute income (Pratt, 1976; Leotta, 1975). Such lack of consensus on these and other issues, even among those who thought that Washington should venture into this arena in the first place, forced policymakers to make tough choices that they knew would disappoint all factions one way or another.

Disagreements within the fledgling "gray lobby" and between the Left and Right were not the only factors that made it difficult to get a social security measure enacted, particularly one ambitiously designed to satisfy immediate needs and to achieve long-range goals. After all, Roosevelt had been urged by fellow Democrats to endorse several assistance measures introduced into Congress between 1932 and 1935, proposals that bore some resemblance to the old-age relief program he had secured while serving as governor of New York. But the President chose to wait until the economy had begun to recover and until the first round of public and congressional debate had identified the salient issues and placed the debate over possible options into sharper focus. Even when Roosevelt and his advisors decided to act, the administration was keenly aware that it would have to surmount serious obstacles that had thwarted earlier attempts to involve the federal government in any public-relief system or in social and unemployment insurance schemes. Members of Congress who opposed any federal intervention, or who espoused the views of the Townsendites, or who clung to particular features of prior bills that had no chance of passage, would have to be swayed to support the President. The Supreme Court would have to be persuaded of the measure's constitutionality, a particularly ominous task since the Justices had just invalidated the federal government's Railroad Retirement Act. Compromises, in short, were inevitable on philosophical, legal, political, social, and economic grounds. Drafting a successful Social Security bill would require juggling a variety of issues in a hot-house environment.

By June 1934, Franklin D. Roosevelt surmised that the moment had come for the federal government to take decisive steps. "If, as our Constitution tells us, our Federal Government was established, among other things, 'to promote the general welfare'," declared the President, "it is our plain duty to provide for that security upon which welfare depends . . . . Hence I am looking for a sound means which I can recommend to provide at once against several of the great disturbing factors in life" (Roosevelt, 1934: 4). Roosevelt recommended that the legislation be national in scope and that the states and the federal government share responsibility for its implementation. The actual legislative history culminating in the president's signing of the Social Security Act on August 14, 1935 has been discussed elsewhere, and need not be repeated at length here (see Achenbaum, 1978b: 130–38, and the references cited on p. 210 at note 12). Under Title I, the federal government offered to share equally with a given state the amount of money allocated by that state's legislature to care for those destitute persons over sixty-five who met the broad eligibility criteria set by that jurisdiction. Eligibility rules and benefit levels varied considerably from state to state, but ultimate responsibility for this old-age relief program rested with the federal government: an elderly applicant could appeal to Washington if he or she felt ill-treated by a state or county bureau.

The New Dealers' response to the aged's economic plight did not stop here. Policymakers established an old-age insurance scheme (Title II) at the same time, in order to reduce the incidence of pauperism among the elderly in the future, and thereby limit the subsequent costs of maintaining the relief scheme instituted under Title I. Originally, plans called for raising funds for an Old-Age Reserve Account by taxing a certain proportion of an employee's salary and collecting the same amount from his or her employer. After January 1, 1942, people over sixty-five who had contributed a sufficient proportion of their earnings to the Old-Age Reserve Account would then be eligible to draw pensions, which were based on their prior contributions. (As will be shown shortly, the philosophy and the funding mechanism initially set forth in Title II were changed in 1939 by an important set of amendments. Thus, even before the first old-age insurance pension was ever collected, key features of the original legislation were amended so as to achieve an even larger set of policy objectives.) A national Social Security Board was established. This body was charged to study the most effective ways of providing economic security for the aged through social insurance and to make recommendations, when necessary, about ways to improve the overall system. It is important to note that the Social Security Act also dealt with the needs of those who were not old or in need of some sort of retirement insurance. The original bill inaugurated a controversial federal-state system of unemployment insurance. Other titles allocated matching grants-in-aid to states to provide monies for dependent mothers and children, the blind, and public health services.

The Normative Foundations of Social Security

The Social Security Act, obviously, was a profoundly important, complex document. Creation of the bill required melding familiar and innovative but sometimes contradictory ideas into a reasonable policy. The resulting statute presented a delicate balance of programs pieced together in the spirit of pragmatic compromise against a backdrop of national urgency. Often, diametrically opposed concepts were fused together. For this reason, it is instructive to discuss the Social Security Act in terms of the value construct set forth in the previous chapter. In so doing, we shall discover two important things. First, the measure altered relationships within and among prevailing value dualisms. Second, it created new philosophical conflicts, which quickly developed a momentum of their own.

Public / Private

The very enactment of the Social Security Act signaled a fundamental shift in old-age policies. Government assumed a vastly broader, often unprecedented, responsibility for an area of social welfare that historically had been left primarily to the individual, the family, the free market, and various private groups, with public agencies (traditionally at the local or county level) playing an ancillary role. In the process, Washington became a key mover in the public arena.

The Social Security Act set into motion a new dynamic interplay among various levels of government and the public and private sectors. The old-age assistance provisions under Title I actually gave the states considerable leeway in deciding in what amounts and under what circumstances they would offer relief to the needy aged. Indeed, an attempt to set national standards for "subsistence compatible with decency and health" met opposition in Senate hearings. Because it seemed to contravene states' rights, the provision was dropped in the final version of the bill. (That seven states still had not enacted any program as late as 1937 suggests that a state could opt to do nothing!) Hence it should not be surprising that eligibility criteria and benefit levels varied greatly from place to place from the very start. The measure affected other existing arrangements as well. For example, a section of Title I specifically precluded giving monies to elderly residents of almshouses. There is evidence to suggest that this provision hastened the demise of that dreaded institution. But since the Act said nothing about people in "rest homes," Social Security indirectly fostered the growth of private, old-age domiciliary care.

Though the federal government's involvement could hardly be denied, its power was neither absolute nor universal. The fact that Washington was assigned a role in relieving and preventing old-age poverty did not necessarily diminish the responsibility of other groups. Indeed, the creators of Social Security themselves practiced the politics of incrementalism. They hoped to prove the validity of certain philosophical principles within carefully prescribed parameters and to demonstrate the viability of their programs with sharply limited target populations before they attempted to address the poverty problem in all of its ramifications. In other words, they deliberately left the situation fluid. There was much room for maneuvering and for altering the relative scope of power of the various public and private agencies that were promoting financial security for older Americans. It was also possible to revamp or even scrap procedures whose limitations seemed to outweigh their merits. What could not be challenged, after several Supreme Court rulings in the late 1930s, however, was the duty of the federal government to deal with the elderly's plight as a vital aspect of "general welfare."

Expectation / Entitlement

As a result of the Social Security Act, old age—defined for administrative purposes as the attainment of age sixty-five—for the first time became a criterion for participation in several important programs at the federal level.[3] Title I guaranteed to all people over sixty-five the right to appeal their case to a higher authority. Public relief in old age ceased to be a gratuity; it became a right that could be legally enforced. Title II initially established an insurance

---

[3] Considerable confusion surrounds the reasons why age sixty-five was selected as Social Security's administrative baseline. It was *not* picked because Count Otto von Bismarck originally had chosen it. Actually, seventy was the retirement age designated by German policymakers in 1889 for the world's first social security plan; officials reduced the age to sixty-five in 1916. Nor was it a matter of demography: people did not universally assume that age sixty-five signaled the onset of old age; other years also were cited. Rather, sixty-five was a compromise date that made sense on two levels. The figure was midway between eligibility criteria (sixty, sixty-two, sixty-five, seventy) already being used in various state old-age programs. From Washington's perspective, moreover, establishing a program to which only people over seventy were eligible would be too limited in scope; helping everybody over sixty, on the other hand, seemed prohibitively expensive.

plan for employees in industrial and business sectors that was expected to decrease the likelihood of financial hardship upon their retirement. Hence, during the New Deal, the elderly as a group at last became entitled to legitimate consideration in federal policy circles that had long been denied them. As a political constituency, the aged could expect to get more, and be expected to demand more, if only because older Americans now were the actual and potential beneficiaries of a categorical program that was national in scope.

And yet, while the aged clearly had now become "entitled" to special consideration, this fact alone hardly vitiated the tension between entitlement and expectation. It merely changed some of the issues to be debated. Not every older person benefited directly or immediately from the passage of the Social Security Act. To extend rights earned by select groups of older Americans to the entire elderly population would require further legislative action, which would be prompted by new political demands. Title I, after all, did not uniformly cover all the aged poor; eligibility rules were subject to certain broad guidelines, but precise criteria varied from state to state. Likewise, Title II did not initially apply to farm workers, government employees, military personnel, or clergy, among others. (At first, according to estimates by the Brookings Institution, only 60 percent of the work force was covered.) The architects of Social Security justified such exclusions on administrative grounds, pointing out that it would be too cumbersome and too expensive to cover everyone at once. However plausible these reasons may have seemed from a bureaucratic perspective, the system ignored employees who "lost" earnings, credits, and benefits they otherwise would have received as members of other employment groups. Blacks and Mexican-Americans were especially penalized by this ruling, because of their heavy concentration in agricultural occupations. Policymakers clearly assumed that coverage someday would be universal. Various segments of the aged population shared this hope. But expectation is not entitlement.

Much had been achieved by the enactment of a law that entitled specific groups of older Americans to rights that had been guaranteed by Congress and upheld in the courts. Yet much remained to be done. Guaranteeing the first rights and distributing the first benefits constituted a laudatory achievement in a long and often frustrating struggle to gain and protect Americans' financial well-being in old age. The struggle, however, was not over. Full coverage was a policy desideratum, not an accomplished fact. Few doubted that future efforts to liberalize existing benefits and to broaden coverage would continually force policymakers and interest groups to defend past entitlements and to fight for more.

Equity / Adequacy

By placing its old-age insurance and assistance programs under separate titles, the 1935 version of the Social Security Act attempted to compartmentalize its "adequacy" and "equity" provisions. Title I was basically an adequacy measure. The provision of relief to those in need in later life certainly represented an effort to address at least some of the economic woes of a group deserving help. Contemporary critics (and later commentators) may judge the effort to have been "inadequate" by any one of several criteria, but the initiative was a genuine attempt to provide minimal assistance toward relieving the financial needs of the aged poor. Conversely, Title II was primarily concerned with "equity"—that is, giving people a fair return on their contributions, according to rules that applied to everyone in the same way. The notion of free use of one's own property, as in household equity or venture capital, was not implied here. Insofar as insurance rests on the principle of guaranteeing a prescribed benefit that is based on a specific premium, Title II, as the government-sponsored old-age insurance plan, was meant to be equitable.

From the start, however, it became clear that the issues of equity and adequacy could not be separated so neatly. The potential for conflict between the two values, in fact, quickly materialized in the use of both Titles I and II. For instance, because no uniform eligibility criteria and no benefits scale were established in old-age assistance programs, the federal government's attempt to promote social adequacy sometimes created gross inequities. Federal aid under Title I was an inducement, not a mandated pledge, for public welfare programs in the various states. Thus elderly Americans who were equally poor were not treated equally. Among other things, the extent of relief varied: whereas the sum that poor, older Mississippians could expect to receive in 1936 was $3.92 per month, a resident of California could expect to receive ten times that amount.

Furthermore, the equity principle underpinning the old-age insurance program was altered before the first Title II benefit was ever paid. Social Security amendments in 1939 continued to correlate monthly benefits with the amount of money a wage earner had contributed over time. But the amendments also promised to award payments to a wage earner's "dependents" (usually a wife and young children) even in the event of that wage earner's death. Hence, under the amended old-age insurance program, the wage earner was protecting his family as well as himself. Those who had not "earned" benefits through gainful employment could receive them anyway, if they could demonstrate a legally acceptable relationship with someone who had made sufficient contributions.

Thus, in a variety of ways, the demand for equity counterbalanced the concern for adequacy in Social Security (Hohaus, 1938; Pechman et al., 1968). The 1939 amendments elaborated on the original intentions and provisions of the 1935 act, and in so doing placed equity and adequacy into dynamic equilibrium. The act was not simply a welfare package; it was not exclusively an insurance plan. It was intended to be both simultaneously. Therein lie both the grounds for the system's future evolution and a prime reason for subsequent misunderstanding of its purposes (Schiltz, 1970). One could not emphasize the equity component at the expense of the adequacy component, or vice versa, without fundamentally affecting the equilibrium in the program itself, as it existed in 1940, when monies were distributed for the first time under both the old-age insurance and the assistance provisions.

Self-Reliance / Interdependence

The Social Security system recognized the utility of individualistic and collectivistic approaches to the old-age problem without preferring one over the other. Both Titles I and II were premised on the need for interdependence in dealing with the common vicissitudes of life. Taxes paid by the more fortunate were to be used to relieve the indigent. Contributions from the earnings of employees still in the labor force went to those who had become old enough to collect on their own prior contributions, so that the system operated primarily through intergenerational transfers. Initially, however, benefits disbursed through the Social Security system provided little more than a floor upon which to build for one's later years. It would have been difficult, even the under the best of circumstances, for people to live exclusively on this income source. (This remains true today, of course.) From the start, other types of provisions—savings, private insurance and pension plans, assistance from family and friends—have been needed as supplements. The designers of Social Security never intended otherwise: once economic conditions improved, they assumed that people would resume making provisions for their old age and that corporate involvement in welfare capitalism would be expanded. Hence, the affirmation of interdependence in preparing for later years did not negate the concurrent need for self-reliance (Brown, 1972).

Individual / Family

The financial integrity of the Social Security system rested on the ability of the state and federal governments to collect, either through taxes or payroll contributions, payments from employees and their employers. Since the program was financed by individuals, it makes sense that benefits should also have been allocated on a case-by-case basis. In consonance with the principle of equity, for instance, monthly insurance benefits under Title II were calculated on the basis of a potential beneficiary's prior earnings. Furthermore, benefits under Title I went directly to needy persons, as did benefits to the blind and disabled. These individual-oriented features of the system, however, did not preclude a concern for the family. The actual old-age assistance provisions stipulated by the states under Title I treated familial responsibility for the elderly differently—in some cases, it was a criterion; in others, it was not. Under some titles of Social Security, moreover, the benefit group was the family unit, not the individual. The original measure furnished monies to single mothers with dependent children, thereby acknowledging the need to maintain a family unit's integrity. The 1939 amendments to the old-age insurance program, moreover, shifted emphasis from the employee as an individual to the employee as the breadwinner of a family (Bane, 1939). Hence, depending on the particular title, the Social Security Act addressed either the needs of the individual or those of the family. Does this suggest a certain ambivalence on the part of policymakers? Did they intend to give greater weight to individual needs than to potential family problems? Or, were they oblivious to the potential conflicts and choices that their policies might cause people to face? A case can be made for this third possibility.

When the initial legislation was enacted in the 1930s, there was little controversy within official circles or in society at large over whether government income-support programs should be designed to help the individual *or* the family. In part, this reflects the fact that nearly 76 percent of the work force was male and that most men supported a family. In fact, an overwhelming percentage of all households in 1940 included both a husband and a wife. Less than 2 percent of all men and women over fourteen were divorced (Vickery, 1978: 124–5; U.S. Bureau of Census, 1976: 15, 71). The image of the family that influenced policy—one in which an adult male worked for a living while the adult female stayed home and raised the children—was not a universal reality, but it was sufficiently pervasive to seem uncontroversial. As a result, prevailing public attitudes and demographic realities made it less likely that value tensions would occur in this area then than now. The debate that one day would pit the needs of the family unit, in its multitudinous forms and variations, against the needs of the individual had not yet become a major issue.

The first studies of the potential impact of federal programs on intergenerational attitudes about children's obligation to care for their parents, in fact, did not register a significant swing one way or the other. Insofar as the existence and availability of public old-age assistance provided a "certain liberation for kinfolks, usually heavily burdened by their own economic problems, and the provision of greater happiness, self-respect, and joy of life for a larger number of men and women" (Klein, 1938: 610), Social Security may have reduced tensions across age groups while ensuring a measure of financial protection. Other evidence indicates, however, that older people's anxiety was heightened over the concern that the state might deny them relief on the assumption that children would support them (Dinkel, 1944; Hart, 1941). By its very enactment, in other words, Social Security might have created a set of tensions that had not hitherto existed.

Work / Leisure

The wording of various provisions in the Social Security Act underscores the extent to which policymakers operated on the assumption that work and leisure were antithetical conditions. And yet, insofar as various titles might appear to suggest a value preference for either work or for leisure at specific stages of life, they did so only in the context of other considerations—such as a concern for a proper balance between equity and adequacy. This interplay among value choices thus muted the potential effectiveness of the provisions as an explicit and direct instrument of social control that might have induced older Americans to stay on the job or quit working.

A wage earner had to work a certain period to become eligible for benefits under the old-age insurance program. This requirement was not burdensome, since most people expected to work for nearly five decades anyway. The issue as it affected wage earners over sixty-five is a bit more complicated. Commentators since the 1930s frequently have claimed that Social Security was designed chiefly to get older workers out of the marketplace in order to give younger adults a chance for employment.[4] Evidence exists to corroborate this

---

[4] This interpretation of the Act as an employment tool is still espoused by scholars. See the impressive social control thesis presented by William Graebner (1980). My own research makes me skeptical of this reading of the evidence, however. Had it been the desire of the policymakers to require employees over sixty-five to quit their jobs, they could have articulated a more explicit rationale and designed a more efficacious instrument, probably by altering existing tax codes. Other considerations apparently influenced their thinking. It is essential to remember that government planners during the 1930s were quite cost-conscious as they struggled to relieve unemployment, improve the economy, and assist needy segments of the population simultaneously through one omnibus piece of social legislation. A careful reading of the congressional testimony suggests that, regardless of their personal views on the worth of

notion. Dr. Frances Townsend's plan, for instance, was premised on the assumption that the elderly should not be working but rather spending money to spur the economy. This Townsendite bias was espoused by influential members of both houses of Congress. It seeped into various drafts of the legislation, particularly those crafted by Barbara N. Armstrong, who served on the Committee on Economic Security. By the time the measure reached the White House for the President's signature, however, the rationale for Social Security benefits was that they were intended to replace lost earnings, not to force a majority of older workers to leave the labor force (Cohen, 1957). Consequently, architects of both the 1935 version and 1939 amendments to Title II rejected proposals requiring workers to retire in order to qualify for old-age benefits. They did so not because they preferred work over leisure in old age (or vice versa), but because the full dimensions of that issue had to be addressed in the light of other value-laden policy choices, especially those involving questions of adequacy versus equity and the individual versus the family.

In short, provisions of the old-age insurance program were not used to initiate a compulsory retirement scheme at the national level. An earnings limit was imposed, consistent with the view that benefits under the title should compensate for earnings forfeited in retirement and not supplement currently earned income. This ceiling was established not to penalize the elderly who wanted to work, but to make certain that the overall wage structure was not depressed through the subsidization of older people's wages. Thus, as far as the federal government was concerned, elderly workers could decide for themselves whether they could afford to quit working or whether they preferred to stay on the job. As we shall see in the next chapter, this option was increasingly limited by a new factor—the growth of mandatory retirement policies in the private sector. In 1940, however, the percentage of the work force actually affected by private-pension programs that enforced rigid retirement clauses was not great.

Tradition / Novelty

Historians, social scientists, policy analysts, politicians, and other commentators have been debating the "real" meaning of certain

---

older workers, most witnesses did not want to provoke a pell-mell exodus of older workers from the labor force, which might have cost more in both the short and long run than it was worth. In those crucial 1939 amendments, moreover, the social-welfare dimensions of Social Security clearly took precedence over considerations of social control. Those who interpret the retirement provisions of Title II without commenting upon the changes that were legislated even before the first retirement benefit was distributed miss the true breadth of the title's concerns (for a more elaborate development of this latter argument see Achenbaum, 1980).

provisions and the overall significance of the Social Security Act for nearly five decades. This is hardly surprising, since policymakers and legislators at the time melded together new ideas and old practices, conservative objectives and liberal strategies. The formative years of Social Security were greatly influenced by happenstance. A distinctive mix of personalities, ideas, and institutional constraints, as well as competing societal priorities, affected its development. The significant actors—appointees of the executive branch, members of Congress, lobbyists, critics, older people, and the public at large—perceived reality in different ways. They represented quite distinctive constituencies. They used, misused, and abused their power to different ends with varying degrees of efficacy. All of this is fairly obvious, and it should not distract us from the most important point of all: federal old-age assistance and insurance programs were novel steps in social-welfare legislation.

The passage of the Social Security Act in 1935, even if one ignores the 1939 amendments, represents a watershed in the history of old age in the United States. The Act embodied an unprecedented concern for the elderly by the federal government. This concern was institutionalized by the creation of the first nationwide organizational framework to assist older Americans. Henceforth, the public sector would play an increasingly larger role in providing options both for the aged and for aging adults, who had to make preparations for their later years. In addition, for the first time the aged as a group had gained a voice in setting national policies and priorities. Older men and women were increasingly perceived as a bona fide interest group, with demands that had to be considered. By the end of the 1930s, their impact on government depended not on whether they were given a chance to present their case, but on how well they competed against others in claiming an ever-growing share of the federal budget.

The Impact of World War II on Aging America

As responsibilities widened and spending increased at the federal level in the late 1930s and early 1940s, lobbyists expected to gain more and more for their constituencies. Supporters of the fledgling gray lobby were quite willing to engage in the politics of incrementalism in order to capitalize on New Deal gains. Key members of Congress and chief administrators on the Social Security Board routinely pressed for greater coverage and benefit increases. The Wagner-Murray-Dingell bill introduced in 1943, for instance, proposed a national old-age assistance program to replace the mechanism established under Title I, recommended that farmers and domestic workers be covered by the old-age insurance system, and called for an ambitious health insurance scheme. Proponents of such measures justified them in terms of the country's present economic requirements and future needs once the war had been won. Arthur J. Altmeyer, who headed the Social Security Board, argued:

> Because of the economic dislocations which may characterize the aftermath of the war, it is important to provide greater security against economic risks to workers and their families by remedying these deficiencies and strengthening our social insurance system before that time. The enlarged excess of contributions over disbursements which would accompany the early phase of social insurance expansion would reduce current purchasing power and serve as a potent force in the fight against inflation. Investment of the excess of Government obligations would make corresponding sums available to the Treasury. These investments would aid in financing the war just as do war savings bonds purchased by individuals. Thus, a measure can be taken now which will provide the basis for a better society after the war and at the same time will serve the economic and fiscal needs of the moment (1942: 5).

Despite such cogent arguments, those who advocated liberalizing the social-welfare agenda for aging America set forth in the 1930s made little headway once the nation became preoccupied with the exigencies of waging war. No new programs were established. Existing Social Security contributory taxes and benefit rates remained constant during the war, even though increases had been scheduled.

The impasse in Social Security initially appears to corroborate the liberals' plaint at the time that World War II had effectively ended the New Deal. After Pearl Harbor, military objectives took top priority. The American economy and all elements of society had to be mobilized to combat the enemies menacing on two fronts. Even the President was declaring by 1943 that "Dr. New Deal" had been replaced by "Dr. Win-the-War." Those who had expected the war effort to revitalize the social-reform thrust thus were sorely disillusioned. Historians sometimes echo this theme in their interpretations of the fate of the New Deal after 1938. A convincing case can be made, however, for a more sanguine interpretation of the impact of World War II on the development of American society and culture.

Wartime experiences exercised a profound and (on balance) positive influence on the country's economic, political, and social institutions. The United States escaped many of the horrors of World War II—it was one of the few nations in the conflict whose homeland was not physically invaded and whose cities were not destroyed; American casualty rates were lower than those of its allies and enemies. Millions of Americans, whose employment opportunities were dim and whose economic status had remained precarious in spite of all of the recovery and relief programs instituted in the 1930s, now benefited from the job openings and high earnings made possible by the need to assemble goods and equipment to win the war. As productivity soared, so did wages, profits, and economic prospects. Political arrangements forged in the early years of the New Deal were strengthened by the war effort at home. The powers of the presidency were greatly augmented. The federal bureaucracy expanded its ties with business executives, union officials, and the leaders of various interest groups (Polenberg, 1972). Other favorable social consequences of the war went beyond the gains achieved through reducing unemployment and stimulating productivity. Historian Geoffrey Perrett claims that

> . . . enormous new groups of government beneficiaries came into existence; that barriers to social and economic equality which had stood for decades were either much reduced or entirely overthrown; that the old pyramidal class structure of the United States was cast onto the rubbish heap of history and a genuine middle-class nation came into existence; that access to higher education became genuinely democratic for the first time; that the modern civil rights movement began then; that the greatest gains in longevity occurred then; that the only basic redistribution of national income in American history occurred then; and that an entirely new role in the world was taken on (1973; 11).

Even if Perrett overstates his thesis by exaggerating the extent and degree to which so many socioeconomic trends converged in this particular six-year interval, his basic point remains valid nonetheless. World War II did *not* cause the relationship between federal policies and American values to diverge from the trajectory plotted by the New Deal braintrust; if anything, it accelerated trends already in motion during the 1930s.

The status of older Americans changed as conditions for the rest of society improved. Data collected by the Social Security Board indicate, for instance, that the gradual but long-term decline in labor-force participation rates among men over sixty-five was interrupted by the needs of the wartime economy. Officials noted that skilled workers postponed retirement and deferred benefits under Title II's insurance provisions. Some previously retired workers rejoined the work force. Disability, hypothesized labor economists and government researchers, accounted for the decision of some older wage earners to retire from their jobs instead of contributing to the war effort (Paschal and Koellner, 1942). Such evidence tells us two important things about how social policies for the aged meshed with other forces shaping society at the time. First, it is clear that the existence of Social Security did not diminish older workers' employment prospects during World War II. Even though some members of the legislative and executive branches wanted the Social Security system's old-age insurance benefits to serve as an inducement to force workers over the age of sixty-five out of their jobs, changing economic circumstances created a wide gap between possible intended outcomes and the actual results. The overwhelming (even if short-term) need for skilled and unskilled employees during the war made the aged a far more valuable resource than they had seemed in the midst of the Great Depression. Since the law did not *require* them to stop working, older workers behaved like younger members of society. Those who had skills and talents to offer contributed to the patriotic cause as they saw fit. This leads to a second point. The war underscored the extent to which the economic well-being and welfare needs of the elderly depended upon the state of the political economy and current level of national income. Social programs for the aged thus were not simply a response to their presumed problems and actual entitlements—they also were greatly influenced by current national priorities, prevailing ideas about older Americans' assets and liabilities, and the perceived relationship of the aged to other segments of society.

Indeed, as most Americans during the Roosevelt years realized, having enough money to live and being able to pursue meaningful activities were necessary but not sufficient preconditions for well-being in old age. "The time has come," a writer in *Harper's Monthly* noted, "when for social security we must think about the problems of the aged in terms of what they really need" (Helton, 1939: 459). For this reason, various private foundations and public agencies sponsored research designed to provide a better understanding of the elderly's needs and desires. Investigations before World War II concentrated primarily on the biological and medical aspects of growing older. In 1937, the Josiah Macy, Jr., Foundation, coordinating its efforts with the Union of American Biological Sciences and the National Research Council, organized the first American conference on aging at Wood's Hole, Massachusetts. The proceedings were published a year later in an influential volume, *The Problems of Aging,* edited by Dr. E. V. Cowdry. Distinguished social scientists, such as Talcott Parsons, began to do research in the area, publishing their results in leading scholarly periodicals. Concurrently, private hospitals opened clinics to offer coordinated medical and social services for the elderly. The federal government soon joined efforts to promote the systematic examination of questions related to aging issues. In 1940, the National Institute of Health, an arm of the Public Health Service, established (with seed money from the Macy Foundation) a unit whose chief aim was to serve as a clearinghouse for studies in the fledgling field; the Surgeon General also appointed a National Advisory Committee on Gerontology. A year later, the Public Health Service sponsored a conference on the mental health needs of the elderly.

Such research initiatives did not cease with the attack on Pearl Harbor. The number of professionals and experts interested in the problems of aging was not large, but they were making great headway. By 1942, for instance, biomedical researchers and clinicians had progressed enough to establish the American Geriatrics Society. A year later, the Social Science Research Council appointed a committee on Social Adjustment in Old Age. A small cadre of scholars and administrators established the Gerontological Society in 1945 and published the first issue of the *Journal of Gerontology* in January 1946. In that issue, Lawrence K. Frank, a Macy Foundation official, claimed that the purpose of these efforts went beyond a desire for academic credibility or respectability. Evincing an ever greater concern for the "almost brutal neglect or callous dismissal" of older Americans, he argued, was essential if America was to stop its tragic "wastage of human resources." In his opinion, the extent to which policymakers and concerned citizens placed the individual needs and collective problems of its eldest members on the agenda as they made plans for the future was undeniably "a crucial test of our democratic faith" (1946: 1–10).

Frank was not alone in seeing the challenges and opportunities of an aging society as one of the major issues confronting the United States. In the midst of World War II, President Roosevelt looked forward to new freedoms in the post-war era: "We have accepted, so to speak, a second Bill of Rights under which a new basis of security and prosperity can be established for all—regardless of station or race or creed" (Braeman et al., 1975: 301). The first Bill of Rights had sought chiefly to protect individual liberties and political freedom *against* excessive governmental infringement. Roosevelt's vision of a second Bill of Rights was no less majestic in scope. Among other things, he hoped to guarantee to all Americans the right to work, to earn decent wages, to own a home, to gain access to decent medical care and education, and to enjoy a comfortable old age. He intended, moreover, to establish a new basis for individual and national security *through* the aegis of the public sector. This ambitious set of objectives became the overriding goal of the New Deal intimated in the depths of a Great Depression and now elaborated in the midst of a world war. Roosevelt wanted to have the federal government coordinate, and if necessary regulate, collective efforts to ensure personal happiness and well-being. But by the end of World War II, it was not clear whether Americans truly wished to achieve such a noble goal. Until Americans made that profound choice, the ultimate fate of the aged's New Deal hung in the balance.

The title of this 1954 photograph, "Foster Grandparent," is quite apt. More often than not, older men and women were tangential to the pursuits and concerns preoccupying middle-class Americans after World War II. [Courtesy of the Library of Congress.]

Chapter
3

American Affluence and Its Manifest Destiny

To the men and women coming home from war in 1945 and 1946, and to the loved ones who awaited their return, nothing mattered more than the chance to regain a sense of "normalcy" in their lives. The past fifteen years had wrought profound dislocations in society and had disrupted the natural course of personal events. In those years, the country had suffered its most severe and long-lasting economic crisis. It had endured a harrowing threat to western democracy mounted in both east and west; that confrontation finally lifted the nation out of its depression, but not before it had claimed a staggering number of lives and casualties. Indeed, World War II ended with the incineration of one hundred thousand people in Hiroshima and forty to seventy-five thousand more at Nagasaki. Most homes in those two large cities were instantly destroyed by an incredibly devastating weapon. The awesome, awful clouds produced by these explosions ushered in a new era. American life might once again become normal, but it could never be the same.

Yet even without the advent of the nuclear age, American society and culture probably could not have recaptured the tenor of pre-Depression days. By mid-twentieth century, the United States attained, for better and for worse, the seemingly "manifest destiny" its people had so long desired.[1] To an extent unrivaled anywhere, most Americans appeared to be living well in a nation whose economic growth seemed boundless. By 1945 America had inherited

[1] "Manifest destiny" was a term coined by an editor in 1845 who denounced other nations' policy of "hampering our power, limiting our greatness and checking the fulfillment of our manifest destiny to overspread the continent alloted by Providence for the free development of our yearly multiplying millions" (quoted in Bailyn et al., 1981: 430).

from Europe the duties and privileges of being western civilization's prime defender and finest champion. Given the affluence at home and tremendous influence overseas, Americans viewed themselves as the distinctive product of a brave, new world, a social fate alternately celebrated and deplored. With a mixture of admiration, envy, mistrust, and fear, others looked on the United States as the world's leading purveyor and chief beneficiary of the blessings of the "modern" epoch.

At first glance, the concerns that dominated the years between 1945 and 1960 seem far removed from those of the 1980s. Present-day domestic and international crises make it hard to take seriously any longer Americans' claims to a unique place in the world order. The prophecies proffered about "the flowering of an American century" have become a source of embarrassment to some and of nostalgia to others. Cynics and critics disparage the pretentiousness of the post-war American dream, though that dream still serves as a rallying point for those too young to remember subsequent nightmares or too committed to the halycon vision to give it up quite yet. Nevertheless, there is another way to interpret the period, a way that looks for long-term continuities and changes that have occurred during the last half-century.

Viewing the history of post-war America as the result and manifestation of the process of modernization not only elucidates many of the prevailing trends of the 1940s and 1950s, but also helps one see how many of the current challenges and choices were created by decisions and developments made in those important years. The period was not a watershed in the same sense that the preceding era had been. One cannot point to profound economic dislocations, the creation of new political movements, the rise of strikingly novel social patterns, or the emergence of revolutionary cultural beliefs. Yet the historical terrain is hardly barren. Large-scale social, political, demographic, economic, and diplomatic trends that took shape or prevailed immediately after the war remain salient today. Americans continue to grapple with problems and adapt to constraints that bedeviled their predecessors three decades ago. In retrospect, it is clear that the normative foundations of the country's value system underwent subtle transformations that were not always comprehended at the time. Indeed, much that we will discuss in this chapter deals only tangentially with the aged *per se*. Yet to truly appreciate the impact of recent events on this aging nation, we must first analyze the historical milieu that gave a special quality and tenor to life in post–World War II America.

Post-War America: An Overview

Statistics barely capture the dazzling surge in productivity and prosperity that ensued as the economy readjusted to peacetime needs. The gross national product—the total value of selected goods and services produced—stood at $100 billion (in current dollars) before the crash of 1929. In 1945, after four years of wartime prosperity, the GNP reached $212 billion. Incredibly, that figure had more than doubled by 1960. The GNP of the United States surpassed one trillion dollars eleven years later. The growth record was marred by short recessions in 1949, 1953–1954, and 1959, but the quarter-century after World War II constitutes the longest segment of uninterrupted prosperity this country has even enjoyed. America's extraordinary productivity, moreover, was accompanied by a striking decline in unemployment. The jobless rate averaged 4.6 percent in the 1950s and hovered around 5 percent in the 1960s.[2] Most Americans believed that the unemployment problem had been reduced to manageable, or at least socially tolerable, proportions. They thought that nearly everyone who wanted to work could do so.

Many ingredients went into America's spectacular economic growth. The new prosperity was intimately related to basic changes in the nation's population structure. Certainly the most widely discussed alteration in America's age structure was the "baby boom." Since 1800, when the average fertility rate was 7.0 births, there had been a steady downward trend. A nadir was reached in 1936, when the figure stood at 2.1. As the adverse effects of the Depression diminished (especially after the war), the birth rate rose, reaching a high of 3.8 in 1957 (Gordon, 1979: 115). The reason for this reversal is fairly straightforward. Couples who had postponed having children, or had deliberately reduced the number they would have, now felt they could afford to have as many children as they wanted. The baby boom had profound economic implications. A growing market for comfortable new three-bedroom homes in the suburbs ensured boom years for the housing and automobile industries. Parents routinely voted for tax levies in order to upgrade the quality of public education. They spent as much as they could afford on enriching their children's experiences. New-found prosperity and rising expectations spurred greater and greater consumption of material goods.

Although having children seemed to be a national obsession at mid-century, it is worth noting that the increase in fertility rates did

[2] These aggregate figures, it should be pointed out, mask significant pockets of unemployment among blacks and other minority groups, as well as among unskilled and transient laborers. It is also worth mentioning that our unemployment record was not as good as that achieved by many European nations. Swedish, British, and German economists at the time considered anything anything over 2 to 3 percent unacceptably high (Garraty, 1978).

not wholly mask the growing numbers of older people. In 1920, 7.5 percent of the population was at least sixty years old; in 1940 and 1950, the figures were 10.4 percent and 12.1 percent, respectively. Perhaps even more significantly, breakthroughs in medical technology were enabling the older population, especially women, to live longer. By 1950, in fact, more than a fifth of all Americans over sixty were at least eighty years old (Achenbaum, 1978: 60–61). The aging of the overall population structure was not unprecedented: the demographic reality had been observed and discussed since the beginning of the century. But, as we shall see, the accelerating growth in the number of elderly adults touched nearly every aspect of American society and culture.

The nation's affluence was also stimulated by various changes in economic modes of production, organizational structure, and institutional goals. The spread of automation, the invention of the computer, the growing use of sophisticated technologies and new machinery, all cut labor costs and improved productivity. Companies that built and maintained the nation's infrastructure—in ways as diverse as constructing roads or manufacturing structural steel or improving sewage treatment—flourished. So did firms that catered to middle-class Americans' seemingly insatiable desire for interesting fads and leisure pursuits, new or improved household conveniences, and ready-to-eat meals. Technological advances transformed the daily operations of the country's corporations, which, more than ever before, had become the pivotal unit of the American economy. Over half the net income reported by all firms in 1958 was earned by less than 1 percent of all companies (Degler, 1975). America's international corporate giants were in the best position to grow even more powerful. They had the facilities and the vast amounts of capital and income necessary to modernize plants, take big risks, and diversify into new areas. The economic pacesetters also benefited from their heavy investments in research and development, very often with funds appropriated by the federal government.

Washington's role in fueling the nation's post-war affluence hardly can be exaggerated. Consider its help to veterans. Men and women home from the war received preferential treatment when they returned to the civilian labor force. Those who improved their career opportunities by obtaining a college education benefited from the generous tuition and housing benefits of the G.I. Bill. The Serviceman's Readjustment Act also made available insured mortgages and relatively cheap business and farm loan credits. By 1961, the Veterans Administration had approved 5.6 million housing loans for veterans of World War II and the Korean War (Gilbert, 1981: 23). Obviously, such federal support had a ripple effect throughout the economy. And the national government did not limit its concern to veterans and their dependents. Federal officials enunciated an ambitious policy agenda. The Employment Act of 1946, for instance, committed Washington to pursue a goal of full employment. It also authorized a Presidential Council of Economic Advisors and established a congressional Joint Committee on the Economic Report. Subsequent measures expanded federal involvement in the economy. By making changes in the tax code and permitting new ceilings on the deficit, public policymakers could stimulate growth or cool the economy, as circumstances warranted.

Throughout this period, a substantial proportion of the federal budget was allocated for defense purposes. Lucrative contracts to major corporations, universities, and think tanks spurred developments in weaponry and military equipment while stimulating the economy. Increased collaboration among business executives, engineers and technicians, academic researchers, and government officials led, in turn, to new systemic priorities. "The conjunction of an immense military establishment and a large arms industry is new in the American experience," observed Dwight D. Eisenhower upon leaving the presidency in 1961. "We recognize the imperative need for this development. Yet we must not fail to comprehend its grave implications. Our toil, our resources and livelihood are all involved; so is the very structure of our society" (Blum et al., 1981: 807). Eisenhower may not have realized just how prescient his valedictory remarks were, but he plainly was correct in identifying a different thrust in the nation's political economy.

The emergence of a "military-industrial complex" clearly had both international and domestic ramifications. Although Americans at the time acted as if domestic and foreign affairs operated in separate spheres, the two actually were closely related. The United States was the acknowledged leader in efforts to promote democracy and to safeguard the free world. To this end, it endeavored to contain communism through strategic defense alliances with nations in Europe, Latin America, Southeast Asia, and the Middle East. Every administration tried to reduce the Soviet Union's influence in an endless sequence of "cold war" incidents and crises. By providing military aid and various types of financial assistance overseas, the United States hoped to restore and stabilize once strong economies. It sought to accelerate the development of economic resources in pro-western, third world nations. In so doing, it was simultaneously training a foreign labor force that could produce durable goods more cheaply than was possible at home; it was also creating new markets for its own finished products. There was at least one other connection between America's national and international interests. The need to be fair and just prompted an intense, urgent self-consciousness about the meaning of the American experiment—its accomplishments, its deficiencies, and its prospects. Ensuring that American life actually conformed to its self-image—one to which foreign observers had contributed—became a national priority.

In sum, three factors—the growth at both ends of the population structure, the emergence of a new stage of advanced industrialism, and the nation's widening influence abroad—reduced the likelihood that Americans could return to their pre-Depression ways of life, even if they had so desired. Continuing changes in the social fabric, moreover, set the stage for alterations in the country's value system between 1945 and 1960. The optimism for which the era is best remembered did indeed prevail. Often, though, the ebullience was tempered by deep discontent and diffuse anxieties. Sometimes public confidence was shaken by crises at home or abroad. Indeed, the complex interaction of demographic realities, cultural developments, and socioeconomic trends greatly affected the dynamic equilibrium within and among the seven value dualisms that we have studied.

Working Easier and Playing Harder

Working meant something very different in post–World War II America than it had meant earlier in the century. New technologies and more efficient modes of production were altering the nation's employment structure. In 1940, roughly a third of all workers in the United States were rendering services or handling the goods that the other two-thirds were producing. Sixteen years later, 50 percent of the labor force was engaged in this so-called tertiary sector of the economy (Degler, 1975: 174, 180). Most of the people in this category were described as "white-collar workers," to distinguish them from the blue-collar workers who were engaged (in a non-supervisory capacity) in mining, farming, and manufacturing.

By and large, working conditions improved over time. The average working week was shortened from 44 hours in 1940 to 41.5 hours in 1956. There were exceptions, of course. Professionals who set their own work schedules and corporate executives ambitious to reach the top routinely put in sixty to eighty hours a week. Highly skilled persons who belonged to especially powerful unions, on the other hand, rarely had to work more than thirty-five hours a week unless they wanted to increase their take-home pay. (By 1960, manufacturers were paying employees who worked more than forty hours a week double or triple their hourly wages.) Even without overtime, average wages and salaries rose, outstripping the rate of inflation prevailing then. Nevertheless, the new, advanced industrial order was not without its drawbacks. The rising demand for workers who possessed certain skills, coupled with the introduction of labor-saving devices, created a new kind of structural unemployment. There were simply fewer places in the labor force for unskilled workers. Although social researchers and popular commentators were sensitive to this problem, another matter concerned them even more deeply. Paradoxically, at the very moment that the typical worker's environment was improving, worker discontent was surging.

"Underneath virtually all experiences of work today," observed the esteemed sociologist C. Wright Mills, "there is a fatalist feeling that work *per se* is unpleasant" (1951: 229, 235). Teams of industrial psychologists surveyed workers' satisfaction with their jobs. Among other things, they discovered that satisfaction appeared to be related to income. Absenteeism, boredom, and sloppiness were found to be highest among semi-skilled workers who performed the same monotonous tasks day in and day out, and whose prospects for advancement were slim. In order to increase job enthusiasm, industrial managers and personnel heads attempted, in Mills's words, "to conquer work alienation within the bounds of work alienation." Almost all employees by the end of the 1950s enjoyed paid vacations, a privilege that had been extended to less than 40 percent of the work force in 1940. Vacation time itself increased from one to two weeks' duration. Savvy bosses routinized morning and afternoon coffee breaks, which they once had derided as boondoggling.

Although efforts to reduce on-the-job boredom helped, most Americans sharply distinguished between "work" and "leisure." The distinction itself was not new, to be sure, but the emphasis placed on leisure as the essence of one's *real* life was extraordinary. By the 1950s, the average American was spending more time outside of the home and a larger proportion of the monthly budget on eating out, recreation, travel, and sports than ever before. An incredible array of new appliances and conveniences—ranging from power lawnmowers, electric knives, processed and packaged foods to disposable diapers—gave men and women more free time. Television became the evening's chief entertainment in millions of households. Publishing paperback books, which had been virtually unknown in 1939, became a major cultural industry. More than thirty thousand titles were in print by the 1960s. Increasingly, Americans defined their status in terms of their job but assessed the quality of their lives by how they spent their leisure time.

The rising emphasis placed on leisure, particularly among middle-class workers, made "retirement" an increasingly significant and pervasive phenomenon. To be sure, other factors contributed to the nature and timing of the retirement decision. Nearly every survey of retirement in the 1950s indicated that an employee's overall health and physical capacity greatly influenced his or her decision to stay on the job: the lower an older worker's occupational status or income, the more likely it was that that individual had been forced to retire because of chronic illness or physical disability or because he or she did not feel well enough to continue working (Stecker, 1955; Steiner and Dorfman, 1957). The reemergence of corporate and union pension funds, most of which had gone bankrupt during the Great Depression, also accelerated the growth of retirement in post-war America.[3] The number of workers covered by private pension plans mushroomed from 3.7 million in 1940 to 19 million in 1958, or 28.5 percent of the civilian labor force. An additional 4 million employees were covered by government-sponsored programs (Shock, 1957: 60; Gordon, 1960: 578). This meant, of course, that the number of men and women who would have to stop working because of formal retirement systems was bound to increase significantly in the future.

But the biggest incentive for retirement probably arose from the workers themselves. Americans looked forward to a time in their lives when they would have discharged most of their responsibilities to their children and could take it easy, without the looming threat of poverty. Retirement was increasingly viewed as a well-deserved and earned release from the instrumental chores of work. According to one contemporary survey, for example, only 32 percent of all steel workers and 49 percent of all skilled craftspersons wanted to work past the age of sixty-five. From a "conception of retirement as protection from the hazards of old age in an industrial society," noted Wilma Donahue and her associates in an article that magisterially summarized current trends, "has grown a positive conception of retirement as a period of potential enjoyment and creative experience which accrues as a social reward for a lifetime of labor" (1960: 361; see also Maddox, 1968). Fortunately, workers' actual experiences in retirement generally conformed to their sanguine expectations. Many who retired from white-collar positions claimed to be at least fairly satisfied with their lives: they liked the chance to travel and to pursue their hobbies, and some said that they cultivated new interests. And while retired workers noted that they had to be careful about their expenses, the combined income generated from Social Security, private plans, annuities, and savings, among other

---

[3] It is important to note that the resurgence of interest in retirement programs in the private sector was the result of several converging factors. First, the extension and expansion of Social Security benefits spurred interest in supplemental retirement benefit schemes. Second, a series of Supreme Court decisions and National Labor Relations Board rulings in the late 1940s made pension plan provisions a bargaining point in labor contract negotiations, as well as a legitimate way for management to impose wage freezes (Drucker, 1976: 6–7; Friedmann and Havighurst, 1954: 183).

sources, provided enough to cover necessities and justify an occasional luxury. Retired Americans had become the nation's new leisured class.

Yet the convergence of mandatory retirement programs and new opportunities for leisure was not universally celebrated (Tibbitts, 1954: 77–78; Michelon, 1954: 371–78). A large number of workers claimed that they could not afford to retire. Income security was not always their prime consideration. Nearly two-thirds of all department store salespeople, for example, wished to continue on the job even though they could afford to quit. Those who had to cease working because of poor health or disabilities probably could not extol the pleasures of retirement with as much enthusiasm as someone in better health. Others, especially men and women who enjoyed their jobs, found the transition to forced vacation traumatic. Many social scientists found, in fact, that adjusting to retirement was made all the more difficult by the role ambiguity ascribed to and experienced by retirees and by the relative novelty of the phenomenon among middle-class Americans: "Perhaps the fundamental problem of the aged in industrial societies is that they have no definite place in the social structure. That is, there are no regular, institutionally sanctioned responsibilities for their care and social participation which square with both traditional values and the requirements of an industrial system" (Moore, 1951: 530; see also Parsons, 1954). To remedy this situation, writers urged those about to retire to take on new responsibilities in social, religious, and political associations. They encouraged the pursuit of challenging hobbies and emphasized the support to be found in peer-group associations. A few organizations offered assistance. For example, in 1957 the United Auto Workers established a national direct service network of counseling and referral services. It provided its membership with benefits and educational opportunities linked to a variety of community-based and consumer-action programs (Havighurst, 1952: 11–17; Steiner and Dorfman, 1957; United Auto Workers, 1980).

The attempt to afford men and women the chance to continue engaging in society was consistent with a broader movement to refurbish the image of old age in American culture at large. Ironically, this endeavor also provided new evidence that might have led people to question whether retirement was necessarily beneficial for every employee or business concern. Research conducted in industrial and business settings during the 1950s, for instance, documented that older workers were highly reliable and useful: overall, their low absentee rates and steady output made them very attractive employees. Such studies might have undermined the prevailing belief that older workers should quit working because they were worn-out and inefficient (Welford, 1951; Mark, 1957: 1467–71). To a limited extent, they did. Corporate executives at Metropolitan Life Insurance, the R. J. Reynolds Co., and other firms, not wishing to lose competent personnel whose expertise they still valued, took bold new steps in the human resources area. They experimented with special measures such as the gradual tapering off of one's career, the creation of "flexi-jobs" and the employment of older persons in part-time positions or consulting activities—ideas still considered fairly novel and relatively untested three decades later (*U.S. News and World Report,* 1958: 88).

It is crucial to recognize, however, that both critics and supporters of retirement were operating on the assumption that leisure took precedence over work in late life. Few called for the abolition of mandatory retirement schemes. Age discrimination in employment hiring and training practices remained rampant. The central problem identified at the time was how to guarantee that older employees who chose to quit working would not suddenly find themselves destitute. Since savings tended to be relatively minimal and most workers were still not covered by private pension schemes, the public sector probably had to provide funds sufficient for a good retirement. It is now time to see if this in fact was the case. We must determine whether there was a discernible shift in government's response to the needs of older Americans.

Public Expenditures and Private Ambitions

Government's role, especially at the federal level, continued to expand after World War II. Before the 1930s, federal spending had never exceeded 3 percent of the gross national product, except during wartime. Most of this money had been used for the armed services and veterans' benefits. Although overall expenditures dropped sharply after peace was declared, federal domestic spending rose significantly, surpassing 5 percent of the GNP in the 1950s (Owen and Schultze, 1976: 325–29; Clecak, 1977: 69). If one examines public spending patterns closely, the picture becomes more complex. Two trends merit special attention. First, the proportion of money allocated for social-welfare expenditures fluctuated in relation to government outlays for all purposes. There was no steady increase or decrease at any level of government. In fact, the proportion of all federal dollars going to social welfare in 1929 (27.5 percent) was virtually the same as that in 1960 (27.1 percent); at the state and local levels, the proportions rose from 41.2 percent in 1929 to 60.6 percent in 1960 (*Social Security Bulletin,* December 1967: 12–14). Second, fundamental changes occurred in the relative amount of money allocated to various programs within the broad area of social welfare. In 1929, for instance, more than 60 percent of all social-welfare expenditures went to education; only 10 percent went to social insurance and public assistance programs. Not surprisingly, public relief became the largest category during the Depression. After World War II, education once again became predominant, but in 1957 social insurance allocations exceeded all others for the first time. Thereafter, social insurance programs became an increasingly costly and crucial item in the federal budget.

This increase in expenditures for social insurance indicates that the public sector's response to the needs of the elderly population was growing. Why? The major reason was the maturation and liberalization of various categorical components in existing programs. There was a gradual expansion in the size and cost of the federal social insurance program as more and more groups, previously excluded from participating and receiving benefits, were "blanketed in." The 1950 amendments to the Social Security Act required farmers, domestic workers, and civilian employees not covered by the federal government's own retirement program to make contributions under the provisions of Title II, the old-age insurance program. In 1954, 1956, and 1960, participation became compulsory for all self-employed professionals and military personnel. It became elective for ministers and members of religious orders not under a vow of poverty as well as for those state and local officials whose agencies chose to join (*Social Security Statistical Supplement,* 1973: 15). The number of beneficiaries grew as the proportion of the population participating in the program expanded. In December 1940, about 222,000 Americans received cash benefits under Title II; by December 1960, the figure had surpassed 14.8 million. Although most of the beneficiaries were elderly, official records indicate that at least one-sixth of all recipients in any year between 1940 and 1960 were under the age of sixty-two (*Social Security Bulletin,* February 1978: 65). Furthermore, benefits were raised and eligibility criteria liberalized—usually in election years, but not without concern for prudent management of fiduciary matters. Hence, the federal government's old-age insurance attained an ever-growing legitimacy during its first quarter century of operations, as more and more Americans perceived it to be a responsible agent for their future welfare.

Indeed, the reciprocal relationship between old-age assistance (Title I) and old-age insurance (Title II) described during the original hearings of the Social Security Act seemed to be working. As experts had anticipated, the proportion of Americans receiving old-age assistance benefits under Title I was steadily declining as the proportion of workers and their dependents eligible for money under the old-age insurance program was rising. From this perspective, 1951 definitely was a turning point of some note. In February 1951, the number of persons receiving benefits under Title II exceeded the number receiving benefits under Title I for the first time; six months later, the amount of insurance benefits surpassed the amount of assistance payments. Responsible officials during the Truman and Eisenhower administrations used such evidence to help sustain the conviction that public assistance for the aged would continue to diminish in the years ahead (Cohen, 1952: 154; G. Steiner, 1974: 48–50). They also cited statistics demonstrating that current beneficiaries under Title II were receiving a fair return on their investment. In most instances, it was noted, recipients actually got back far more than they had contributed. Although the reasons for this windfall were not generally articulated at the time, they are not difficult to figure out, given the *modus operandi* of Social Security and the overall state of the economy. As the proportion of the work force required to participate in the program expanded, the total number of contributors grew at a faster rate than the number of people eligible for benefits. As the economy boomed and incomes rose, the system itself took in larger and larger amounts of revenue, without making a noticeable dent in individual contributors' take-home pay.

This does not mean that the Social Security system had eliminated old-age poverty by the end of the 1950s. On the contrary, experts inside and outside official circles documented that a sizable number of older Americans were in desperate circumstances. The Social Security Administration reported that 35.2 percent of all Americans over sixty-five had inadequate incomes in 1959. Using data gathered in the same year, James Morgan and his associates at The University of Michigan estimated that 48 percent of all families headed by an aged person were potential welfare recipients, compared to 28 percent of all families in the total population (1962: 194). Critics charged that these statistics exaggerated the extent of deprivation in the United States during the 1950s by ignoring some crucial sources of income, such as part-time jobs or failures to report all earnings. It also was possible to manipulate the statistics by altering the scope of the target population. For example, according to census data, the incidence of poverty in families with an aged head dropped from 57 percent to 47 percent between 1947 and 1960; during the same period, however, the percentage of poor families with an aged head *rose* from 27 percent to 34 percent (Fishman, 1966: 23–24; 32–35). Such biases notwithstanding, it seems fairly clear, looking at the situation in the 1980s, that public efforts to promote "social adequacy" remained woefully inadequate. The question becomes: Why?

Equity First—Adequacy If It Does Not Cost Too Much

There are at least two closely related explanations for the comparative lack of success in advancing social adequacy by means of public intervention. On the one hand, the federal government took little initiative, since presidents did not accord a high priority to this issue. Truman was sympathetic to welfare measures: he pushed for federally funded health care among other things. But Truman faced a Congress in which the balance of power was fragmented. A coalition of states-rights Democrats and Republicans were usually able to block or delay bills intended to expand the realm of governmental activities (Marmor, 1973: 74). Eisenhower was fairly hostile to public welfare issues, even though he appointed the first secretary of the newly formed Department of Health, Education and Welfare. On the other hand, it seems unfair to blame the legislative and executive branches entirely for inaction. Elected officials apparently were deliberating in a manner in conformity with the American public's desires. A sizable portion of the electorate, pollsters reported, tenaciously clung to their perennial skepticism about the trustworthiness of public officials. In particular, they wanted to limit the amount of power to govern that was vested in agencies. Voters did not mind bureaucratic officials efficiently monitoring social programs already established, but voters did not wish them to expand the scope of welfare functions. Even the elderly, who might have benefited most directly from new public initiatives, did not advocate a radical change in existing arrangements (Free and Cantril, 1967: 20, 30, 178; see also Dos Passos, 1944: 4; Morgan, 1962: 10–11). Americans of all ages seemed to prefer that public officials take steps to reduce dependency rather than expand efforts to relieve poverty. Government, it was widely believed, should promote financial incentives and educational programs that would encourage people to work. Thus, Americans underscored their traditional belief that welfare capitalism should spring ultimately from the activities of individuals working in the private sector. Insofar as the scope and cost of public responses to the elderly increased, therefore, this growth was not at the expense of private responsibilities.

By extending this line of reasoning, we can tie together the value dualisms discussed so far. The concerns of the public and private spheres do not appear to have been in as much conflict in this period as they had been during the New Deal era. Instead, government and industry seem to have been preoccupied with very different issues between 1945 and 1960. The public sector was promoting old-age insurance while placing less emphasis on relief measures. Similarly, the private sector concentrated on questions of equity. Efforts to ensure a measure of social adequacy were not abandoned. But neither did such initiatives threaten the overriding importance placed on guaranteeing a fair return—ideally, a handsome profit—on investments of money and energy in an era of seemingly boundless prosperity. In this heady, ebullient economic atmosphere, the public and private sectors tended to assume complementary rather than adversary positions. Without retreating from the pivotal role it was accorded in the New Deal, yet without augmenting its dominance, the federal government endeavored to stimulate business and industrial growth in every way possible, thereby aiming to benefit the American worker as well.

Arising from this seemingly harmonious set of public objectives and private interests at the societal level, however, was a conflict that provoked tensions within another set of juxtaposed values which we have been tracing. The fundamental dilemma facing middle-class Americans in the post–World War II era, according to many observers, was not the choice between work and leisure, nor the potential incompatibility between public interests and private desires, nor the possible problems inherent in simultaneously satisfying calls for equity and adequacy. Rather, the most elusive problem Americans had to address was that of balancing the needs and wishes of individuals against those of the groups to which they belonged. The potential for conflict between individuals and groups was age-old, but contemporary conditions had sharpened the crisis to an unprecedented degree. Indeed, the ubiquity and preeminence of large-scale institutions increasingly seemed to threaten the very identity of every individual in the United States.

Self-Reliance and Interdependence

Many social scientists writing after World War II believed that the sweeping changes occurring in society were altering basic features of the American character. One of the most insightful, provocative elaborations of this theme was *The Lonely Crowd* by David Riesman, Nathan Glazer, and Reuel Denney. The quintessential American, in their opinion, was the "other-directed" personality typified by the new middle class of salaried professionals and bureaucrats in white-collar occupations. Other-directed persons seemed shallower than the archetypal, inner-directed, nineteenth-century "self-made man." Such people, argued Riesman and his associates, were more uncertain of themselves and their values and more likely to adopt the tastes, prejudices, and beliefs of peers:

> What is common to all other-directed people is that their contemporaries are the sources of direction for the individual—either those known to him or those with whom he is indirectly acquainted, through friends and through the mass media . . . . The goals toward which the other-directed person strives shift with that guidance: it is only the process of striving itself and the process of paying close attention to the signals from others that remain unaltered throughout life (1950: 21).

Other-directed personalities verged on being pathetic figures. Unable to rely on their own instincts with any degree of confidence, yet often alone because of self-doubts, such individuals lived in a condition of diffuse anxiety. They wondered if they were receiving the approval of the group or really deserved it anyway. In a similar vein, William H. Whyte's *The Organization Man* (1956) explored the training, ideologies, and life-styles expected of those who worked in the bureaucratic mazes of the nation's large institutions. Whyte concluded that having a job in any of the big organizations—corporations, government, universities, charitable groups, labor unions—proffered security and a comparatively high income. But it also necessitated that the employee give up the hopes and ambitions that had motivated earlier generations of workers.

Needless to say, it is easy to exaggerate the extent to which self-reliance was crippled during the 1950s by a mindless capitulation to organizations and peer groups. After all, the very fact that *The Lonely Crowd* and *The Organization Man* were widely discussed and became bestsellers suggests that white-collar Americans were not oblivious to the conformist pressures of modern life. Furthermore, novelists as diverse in style as J. D. Salinger, Saul Bellow, and John Updike all won critical acclaim for works that focused on the protagonist's desire to be himself or herself and to overcome institutional constraints. Nice tough guys like John Wayne and Gary Cooper were the big films stars and Fess Parker's Davy Crockett became a hero to millions of children, because they all knew right from wrong and were willing to put their lives on the line for their principles. A yearning for self-expression enabled artists such as Jackson Pollock to win critical praise. The general public applauded efforts by James Dean and Marlon Brando to approach "reality" through a "method" style of acting energized by their emotions. Adolescents swooned over Elvis Presley as he rose to stardom swinging his hips in ways that rocked and shocked.

Nevertheless, while the realm of art, drama, and literature might be a suitable place to articulate moral concerns and to express one's innermost thoughts and emotions, it was not, from most Americans' perspective, the "real" world. Since a return to the unrestrained individualism of the nineteenth century was neither feasible nor desirable, most critics called for greater self-assurance amid the pressure to conform. Riesman's prescription for the personal malaise he diagnosed, for example, was adherence to the model of an "autonomous man," who had all the virtues and none of the defects of the inner- or other-directed personality:

> If the other-directed people should discover how much needless work they do, discover that their thoughts and their own lives were quite as interesting as other people's, that, indeed, they no more assuage their loneliness in a crowd of peers than one can assuage one's thirst by drinking sea water, then we might expect them to become more attentive to their own feelings and aspirations (1950: 307).

Riesman's ideal type was not necessarily a beatnik, and definitely not a revolutionary, but rather a rational, ethical person who eschewed trite ideas, mundane tastes, and conventional morality; he or she wanted to be a unique individual in a highly interdependent culture. Nor was this ideal limited to specific age groups. In an article on aged personality types, Riesman posited that "autonomous" aging— "accretions of wisdom with no loss of spontaneity and ability to enjoy life" (1954: 379)—could enable the elderly to live independent of structures imposed upon them by disability and societal conventions.

Riesman's interest in the process of aging and his characterization of old age as a period of further self-realization and growth were not idiosyncratic. The expectations and experiences of elderly individuals received far less attention in the media and in scholarly circles than did the distinctive features of infancy, youth, and middle age, but there were notable advances in the field of gerontology. A loose coalition of physicians, clinicians, psychologists, biologists, and behavioral and social scientists formed the Gerontological Society in 1945 to exchange research findings and promote professional visibility. In addition to those who made the study of old age their primary field of inquiry, a rising generation of medical and social researchers examined the socioeconomic and psychological dynamics of late life as part of their ongoing investigations into other topics (Calhoun, 1978). Analysts typically borrowed concepts and research designs from other disciplines. M. L. Barron (1953), for instance, proposed that the aged be viewed as a minority group. Although researchers quickly seized on the differences between the old and other racial or ethnic minorities, Barron's formulation nevertheless spurred inquiries that challenged prevailing conceptions of senescence. Indeed, most of the research undertaken after 1945 was revisionist in scope and results. "The concept of aging which we are outgrowing," observed Clark Tibbitts, "is based on an assumption of general organic, functional and psychological deterioration, beginning in middle age and proceeding rather rapidly until it becomes disabling and fairly incapacitating" (1952: 6). Yet if there was a growing sense that existing hypotheses about the aging process were inadequate, no single theory dominated the field of gerontology in its formative years. Perhaps the most significant developmental model set forth in the period was formulated by Erik Erikson. The ultimate challenge of human existence, according to Erikson (1963), was resolving the conflict between ego integrity and despair: those who had successfully grappled with this choice in late life were prepared to face death with resignation.

Other investigators offered different perspectives on the relationship between the aging individual and the larger world. In a collaborative venture (1953) and independent studies, Havighurst (1954) and Albrecht (1951) argued that a definite relationship existed between an older person's activity and the ease with which he or she adjusted to old age. Staying involved in daily activities, they argued, helped to sustain morale. In direct opposition to this "activity theory of aging," Elaine Cumming and William Henry's *Growing Old* (1961) asserted that the disengagement of the aged was a universal and inevitable phenomenon, equally beneficial to the well-being of the elderly and the smooth functioning of major social institutions. The notion of "disengagement" was pathbreaking. Not only was it the first theoretical construct formulated by social gerontologists, but it also was the catalyst for considerable debate among researchers, which in turn led to more subtle investigations.

As academics debated the nature and dynamics of senescence, a variety of groups sought to deal with the needs of the current old and address the challenges associated with an aging society. We have already discussed the public sector's contribution in helping older individuals obtain a measure of financial security. At the same time, Washington evolved slowly into a major clearinghouse for information on the elderly—a function underscored by its sponsorship of the first National Conference on Aging in 1950. The private sector played a key role, too, which went beyond underwriting pension programs for retired workers (Pratt, 1976; Calhoun, 1978). Educational centers, inspired by the activities at several midwestern universities, pioneered adult learning curricula and encouraged service, research, and training programs. Older people mobilized resources to create special-interest groups such as the American Association of Retired Persons and the National Retired Teachers Association. Thanks largely to the generosity of the Ford Foundation, public and private health, recreation, community-action and social-work agencies joined forces in 1950 to form the National Council on Aging (NCOA). It is significant that these innovative efforts to promote the well-being of aged individuals were facilitated by new organizational arrangements. The potential conflict between the individual and society, paradoxically, was ofttimes best handled in an institutional setting. The aged, like younger members of society, very often succeeded in attaining a new sense of individual identity by creating and participating in large and sometimes impersonal institutions intended to promote their collective well-being.

Indeed, counterbalancing the appeal of being an "autonomous" individual at any age, much less becoming a "rebel without a cause," was the aged's desire to belong. As Whyte so brilliantly demonstrated, the ways that the "organization man" was trained in college and on the job, how he lived, worshipped, and played away from work, and what he hoped to get out of life all promoted the celebration of togetherness. Ironically, the potential tension between the individual and the group was assuaged in part by pleasures afforded by the very institutions that demanded loss of autonomy.

Family and Individual

Among other things, the appeal of togetherness helped to sustain a cult of domesticity, which emphasized the welfare of the family—sometimes at the expense of individual well-being. More than ever before, it seemed, Americans yearned to enmesh themselves in the tender trap of marriage and parenthood. And once those steps were taken, other changes in life-style—especially for women—were sure to follow. Homes in the suburbs were inhabited mostly by wives during the day. Endless rounds of PTA meetings, Little League games, scout fund-raising drives, church-group meetings, dancing lessons, and car pools were the hallmarks of middle-American bliss. The divorce rate continued to mount, but Americans typically felt sorry for, or at least uncomfortable around, those who were single past thirty. Hence remarriage remained the norm, especially for men. Government statistics conformed, in fact, that a much larger proportion of life at all three major adult stages—reproductive, middle, and late—was being shared by married couples than had been the case in the 1940s (Carter and Glick, 1970: 64). Even the family dislocations caused by job transfers and promotions usually occurred not at the request of the individual breadwinner but at the behest of the company. In most instances, however, moving merely meant trading one familiar situation for another similar to it, and shortly thereafter, another, and then, in a while, yet another. The need to be geographically mobile on the trek to the top of the corporate ladder reinforced the commonly held view that the family was, ultimately, the only unit that counted.

It is temptingly easy to ridicule the benign milieu of "Father Knows Best" and to smirk at the hapless Ozzie Nelson, two of the most popular television programs during the 1950s. Both series consistently illustrated and endorsed white, middle-class, suburban values. It is distressing to recall that Lucille Ball, the zany star of the *I Love Lucy Show,* consistently resolved her weekly predicaments by resuming her status as a housewife. But the emphasis placed on ideal family types was not shallow. In part, it reflected a conscious desire of men and women whose own childhood security had been shattered in varying degrees by the Great Depression and World War II to give themselves and their children things their parents once could only have dreamt about. In part, it represented a deliberate effort to create a tranquil haven from concerns of the marketplace and dangers associated with the nuclear era. Finally, the family fulfilled a key traditional role, which now seemed all the more important: it provided a supportive context in which to instill personality traits deemed instrumental for life in advanced industrial society. Thus, far from declining in significance, a loving and secure family still epitomized the essence of the American dream.

Curiously, the aged's relationships with children, grandchildren, and other relatives received very little attention amid all the writings on family life in the 1950s. The surprising paucity of information probably reflects society's preoccupation with conjugal units which had children at home. Grandparents rarely figured in this picture. Old people played supporting roles in television shows, movies, and bestsellers, if they appeared at all. The aged continued to exercise their strong preference for maintaining independent residences as long as possible. Few suburban dwellings in Levittown and across America had enough rooms for three generations. (A review of 1950 census data in fact reveals that a significant minority of men and women past the age of sixty-five lived alone. The increasing number of single-member households is much discussed by demographers and policymakers nowadays, of course, but it received scant attention thirty years ago.) Furthermore, there was a tendency in the scholarly literature to view elderly relatives as "problems" or to discuss their role in the family in fairly negative terms (Beard, 1949; Burgess, 1957). This problem-oriented perspective was frequently reinforced by contrasting current household arrangements with the image of the extended family that was presumed to have flourished in a golden age of yesteryear.[4] Some social scientists, however, did investigate older Americans' perceptions of the family and their actual contact with relatives. The composite portrait that emerged from this research is more sanguine than one might expect. On the basis of their interviews with older subjects, Townsend (1957) and Shanas (1962) reported that "modern" life had not necessarily diminished the frequency or quality of intergenerational contacts. The elderly could, and did, turn to their families for companionship, support, and comfort. Exchange patterns, moreover, were reciprocal, not one-way. After surveying the latest findings of the period, Streib and Thompson concluded that a "realistic appraisal of the older person's familial relationships not only should emphasize the misfortunes of the older person who feels excluded by the conjugal pattern but also should emphasize the opportunities which some older persons may enjoy because of independence from entangling financial alliances" (1960: 486). The family, in short, was a dominant influence in people's lives over the entire life-cycle.

Novelty / Tradition: The New Secular Religion

Just as the family prospered in post-war affluence, so too American religious sects and churches were blessed with a resurgence of pious observance and remarkable institutional growth. A 1958 Bureau of Census survey indicated that less than 3 percent of all those interviewed reported having no religious preferences. The figure for people over sixty-five was slightly smaller than the statistic for the population as a whole. Other popular opinion polls and scholarly research underscored an unwavering belief in the existence of God among the elderly and corroborated the stable and significant impact of religious beliefs on an older person's self-image (Maves, 1960: 698–701; Moberg, 1965: 78–87; Riley et al., 1968: 495; LeFevre and LeFevre, 1981). Avowed religious convictions clearly affected the vitality of organized religion. Data on church membership reveal that the proportion of the population belonging to a formal religious group rose form 47 percent in 1930 to 69 percent in 1960. Amazingly, 96 percent of all Americans surveyed by the

---

[4] We now know that this characterization was inaccurate on several counts. Among other things, historical demographers have demonstrated that there were few extended family dwellings in early modern American history. And even though some of the problems besetting contemporary families are novel, what is striking is the number that parallel crises in past times. Because such insights did not inform the research undertaken after the war, most investigators were unable to recognize the bias they were inadvertently introducing into their analyses (Gordon, 1978).

Census Bureau in 1957 reported affiliation with a specific denomination. On the basis of longitudinal data, there appears to have been an overall rise in church attendance over the life-cycle. Regular worship patterns for Americans rose after the age of twenty and then persisted through the seventh decade, when chronic illness, poor health, and/or transportation problems forced a steadily increasing number of older people to stay home. (Churches and synagogues rarely made special arrangements for older members of their congregations. Clerical and lay leaders devoted most of their attention to satisfying the needs of middle-aged, middle-class parishioners.) The late 1940s and 1950s also witnessed an extraordinary acceleration of church building. Americans spent $26 million for this purpose in 1945, and never less than $409 million in any year during the 1950s. More than one billion dollars (in current amounts) was spent in 1960 alone (Ahlstrom, 1972: 952–53). This growth was not limited to mainstream denominations. The rapid growth of fundamentalist churches during the post-war era indicates that millions of Americans, including poor whites and migratory blacks, earnestly sought salvation through revivals and adherence to age-old traditions. Indeed, the trust Americans placed in their clergy in 1953 far surpassed their confidence in business and labor leaders or government officials. In the 1940s, religious leaders had ranked a distant third.

This renewal of religiosity did not reflect a deepening theological sophistication among most Americans. To be sure, the trenchant ideas of Reinhold Niebuhr and Paul Tillich, who were confronting the problem of finding a creative form of human freedom in a basically unreceptive universe, were often discussed in sermons and editorials. But far more attention was commanded by the uplifting messages of Bishop Fulton Sheen, a witty and effective media personality; of evangelist Billy Graham, who converted millions in tent revivals and radio broadcasts; of Dr. Norman Vincent Peale, who recharged the morale of Americans with the "power of positive thinking"; and of Anne Morrow Lindbergh, whose bestselling *Gift from the Sea* was directed to housewives. In fact, theologian Will Herberg claimed in *Protestant, Catholic and Jew* that religion had lost its theological content for many. Celebrating the American experience, he contended, had become "the characteristic American religion, undergirding life and overarching American society despite indubitable differences of religion, section, culture, and class" (1956: 77). The new symbols of this enlivened civic religion were manifestly abundant. The phrase "under God" was added to the Pledge of Allegiance in 1954; two years later, "In God We Trust" became the country's official motto. Humanists appalled at such a crass debasement of religion and atheists who fought political piety through the courts were looked on by most God-fearing citizens with disdain or contempt. Americans had truly found a "comfortable pew" in a land of plenty.

Entitlement / Expectation: Middle-Class America Pursues the Good Life

The self-satisfied civic moralism that characterized most religious sentiments carried over into the realm of politics. In their hallmark study of the political attitudes of *The American Voter*, Angus Campbell, Philip Converse, Warren Miller, and Donald Stokes of The University of Michigan discovered that the American public had a surprisingly unsophisticated view of political matters:

> When we examine the attitudes and beliefs of the electorate as a whole over a broad range of policy questions—welfare legislation, foreign policy, federal economic programs, minority rights, civil liberties—we do not find coherent patterns of belief. The common tendency to characterize large blocs of the electorate in such terms as "liberal" or "conservative" greatly exaggerates the actual amount of consistent patterning one finds. . . . Very few of our respondents have shown a sensitive understanding of the parties on current policy issues (1960: 543).

Just as most Americans' religious orientations lacked the high sensitivity to ethical dilemmas that one might have expected church-going to produce, so too political debates were strikingly free of conflict over philosophical issues—this despite this genuine interest Americans evinced in fulfilling some civic responsibilities. (Some 75 percent of all eligible persons reported having voted for a presidential contender in 1956, and 66 percent had cast a ballot in congressional races!) On the basis of most analyses of voting behavior between 1948 and 1960, it appears that most people voted on the basis of party affiliation. Partly loyalty, in turn, was typically determined by parents' preferences, a person's own responses to the New Deal experience, and the opinions expressed in the media or by peers.

Extrapolating from such data, observers tried to explain why elderly Americans were typically more "conservative" than younger voters. Commentators mentioned the possibility that the aged's political orientation might be linked to their physiological and psychological condition. Most, however, pointed out that the current generation of voters over sixty-five was socialized politically when the Republicans controlled the national government and state houses in all regions except the South, where conservative Democrats dominated the scene. Like other voters, then, the aged generally adhered to their original affiliations (Stouffer, 1955; Cottrell, 1960; for a review of trends since the 1950s, see Campbell and Strate, 1981). It did not seem likely, analysts reported, that older Americans would abandon their views in order to coalesce around some age-specific issue. The Townsend movement, which had clearly rallied the support of older conservatives and radicals in the 1930s, still existed, but it was no longer a potent force. The so-called gray lobby—including such special-interest groups as the National Council on Aging (NCOA) and the National Retired Teachers Association/American Association of Retired Persons (NRTA/AARP)—opted for mainstream political activities to express the views of its constituents. No other senior-citizen lobby was created to serve as a counterpoint to the Republican and Democratic parties. These parties presumably satisfied the demands and goals of the aged (Holtzman, 1954).

In order to appeal to all age groups, the major political parties themselves opted for the "vital center." Their platforms left room for both individualism and social welfare, for government regulation of the economy and encouragement of private enterprise. That such emphases might really be incompatible was not stressed. Instead, political commentators admired the system's ability to balance divergent opinions without threatening the integrity of the political process. The greatest dangers to democracy, it appeared at the time, arose from the spread of communism and the possibility of subversive infiltration in our midst. The Hiss trial, McCarthy hearings, communist aggression in Korea, and the Soviets' repressive rule of eastern Europe dominated the news. Such threats mobilized Americans into joint action rather than dividing them. On balance, international crises associated with the Cold War enabled Americans to think that it was "us" against "them" in the issues that really mattered.

One of the most striking features of American political and social culture after World War II, in fact, was the extent to which the public overwhelmingly endorsed its current way of life. Historians reinterpreted the national experience in order to emphasize its commitment to the liberal, capitalistic, democratic tradition in good times and bad. Daniel Boorstin (1953) argued that "the genius of American politics" lay in the country's extraordinary success in avoiding ideological disputes that could divide the people. Even social critics acknowledged the difficulty they had in getting Americans to attend to social problems. "The end of ideology" debate sparked by Daniel Bell in the late 1950s rested on the assumption that there was a "disconcerting caesura" among western intellectuals, who for a variety of reasons no longer found socialism appealing yet could not formulate a viable alternative to the status quo (Bell, 1960). On the surface, then,

Americans seemed self-content. Most people appeared oblivious to tensions among the values they so enthusiastically supported. Perhaps they were too busy to notice.

Expectation / Entitlement: Clouds on the Horizon

Although the public sensibility of the 1950s appears on the surface to have been unified, the feeling of contented tranquility amidst affluence was far from uniformly shared. "The good life" which so neatly coincided with "the American way" was a distinctly middle-class vision. Other groups found slim pickings at the great American banquet. The discrepancy between "what is" and "what should be" was most evident in the differential opportunities and relative statuses accorded blacks and whites, although other non-Caucasians suffered comparable discrimination. Hence, beneath the placidity of consensus lay a perennial if ofttimes ignored conflict. Blacks wanted, expected, and periodically demanded entitlements to the very things that whites took for granted.

That racial conditions were deplorable could hardly be questioned. The Swedish sociologist Gunnar Myrdal in his monumental two-volume study, *An American Dilemma* (1944), claimed that most white Americans were inured to the situation. Black Americans seemed powerless to change the status quo. The seeds of change, however, were being sown at the very time Myrdal was compiling his materials. World War II accelerated the drive by minorities to secure equal rights in opposite but complementary ways. Insofar as blacks got some long-awaited rewards for their wartime contributions, they wanted even more—their fair share. Insofar as they were denied basic privileges and benefits, their bitterness at the system mounted (Buchanan, 1977). Another major turning point was reached in 1954, when the Supreme Court unanimously overturned the "separate but equal" principle in *Brown* v. *Board of Education of Topeka*. The Justices heard evidence indicating that segregation made equal education impossible and caused severe psychological damage to both black and white students. Hence, the Court ordered the states to proceed with "all deliberate speed" to integrate schools. Though progress was painfully slow, the judicial system's willingness to fight actively on behalf of the underprivileged provided one powerful way for this nation to establish equitable moral and social standards for all its citizens.

Their hopes roused by the Supreme Court decisions, blacks began to protest the social caste system by provoking incidents that could be adjudicated in the courts. Probably the most famous incident was the 1955 arrest of Rosa Parks in Montgomery, Alabama, for refusing to sit at the back of a public bus. Her arrest led to a year-long boycott of the bus system, mobilized by the Rev. Dr. Martin Luther King, Jr. Blacks did not ride buses until the Supreme Court ordered the city to integrate its transportation network. King then organized the Southern Christian Leadership Conference (SCLC) to fight segregation through nonviolent civil disobedience. King's SCLC, older groups such as the National Association for the Advancement of Colored People (NAACP), and newer groups such as the Congress of Racial Equality (CORE) and the Student Nonviolent Coordinating Committee (SNCC) mobilized support in the black community—and increasingly in the white community as well—to struggle for civil rights at the grass-roots level.

Yet in the 1950s blacks did not manage either cooperatively or separately to galvanize nationwide support for their cause. At the national level, the forces resistant to change in race relations were formidable. Long-standing prejudices were deeply rooted in the American experience. Conservative politicians in the legislative and executive branches believed that things had already gone too far too fast and were reluctant to press for additional gains. Internal rivalries within the black community complicated efforts by dissipating energy and diffusing issues. Other priorities in the late 1950s—such as Sputnikitis—seemed more urgent to mainstream America. Hence, the mounting struggle for black rights forces us to rethink the fundamental significance of the 1950s in the shaping of advanced industrial America. At one level, the movement belied (or at least tempered) the self-confident complacency sweeping the country after World War II. Yet, it was also an anomaly before 1960, because it raised questions and concerns that differed from the self-doubts and anxieties that preoccupied most white Americans at the time. From the perspective of the 1980s, however, both black resentment and white dubiety, while expressed over divergent issues, were by-products of expectations fueled by affluence.

A mood of critical national and individual reappraisal, in sum, clouded an otherwise sunny horizon in post-war America. As Daniel Bell presciently declared, "America at mid-century is in many respects a turbulent country, oddly enough, it is a turbulence born not out of depression but of prosperity . . . the American experience demonstrates that prosperity brings in its wake new anxieties, new strains, new urgencies (1960: 34; see also Dickstein, 1977; Miller and Nowak, 1977: 242). The discontent and doubts were genuine, even if not widely shared to any depth.

Furthermore, it seems clear in retrospect that the stage was set during Eisenhower's second term for the new wave of federal initiatives associated with the "Great Society." Despite his disappointment with the Supreme Court decision in *Brown* v. *the Board of Education,* the President sent troops to Little Rock in 1957 to enforce school desegregation. In the same year, Congress passed the first Civil Rights Act in more than eighty years. The federal government's financial commitments to secondary education and grants to colleges and universities increased; funding for manpower (re)training grew. The passage of the Kerr-Mills Act (1959), which expanded publicly funded health-care services for the aged poor, was an important breakthrough in efforts to grapple with the challenges and opportunities of an aging society. Such initiatives sometimes ran counter to prevailing sentiments in society at large and clashed with official governmental postures concerning the role of Washington in everyday life. Yet from this terrain would soon emerge a set of historical conditions and actors that had the power to inspire new and grander goals that would benefit all segments of society, particularly the aged. In the 1950s, one can discern premonitions of things to come, but no real appreciation of their significance.

With Harry S Truman looking on, President Lyndon Baines Johnson signed Medicare into law on July 30, 1965. The health needs of older America "fit" into the Great-Society mold.

Chapter

4

The Grand
Expectations of
a Great Society

The 1960s—more precisely, the fifteen years between 1957 and 1972—were an extraordinary period of ferment in American history. The burgeoning of governmental activity, the challenging of conventional morality and norms, not to mention the burning, the shooting, and the looting, all symbolized a society in upheaval, one swirling in changes and confrontations unlike those experienced in the late 1940s and 1950s. A new generation—the children of the Great Depression—assumed control of the country's major political, economic, and social institutions. They wanted to leave their own distinctive mark on society. In response to the vague uneasiness and mounting anxiety lurking beneath the superficially placid affluence of post-war America, they sought to reform and re-form this nation, so that it would more faithfully correspond to its venerable ideals. A coalition of Democrats and liberal Republicans in all three branches of government attempted to forge a "Great Society." For some, the times seemed ripe for completing the New Deal agenda. Others hoped to usher in America's golden epoch in which promoting "the quality of life" and waging "a war on poverty" would become pressing national priorities. The aged, as one of the nation's more visible and increasingly powerful constituencies, were perceived to be likely targets of new initiatives. Many over sixty-five surely expected to benefit from this reform impulse.

The 1960s were a momentous, even critical era in American history, yet the great expectations of the time did not culminate in the founding and elaboration of a new political or social order. A reformist drama that "for one brief shining moment" had opened to the strains of *Camelot* closed with an administration whose reign could have appeared comical, had the stakes not been so high and the denouement not so disgusting. In order to appreciate fully why the 1960s did not constitute a watershed in contemporary American history, we must reconstruct the structure and dynamics of the times on several levels. Accordingly, in this chapter, we shall examine the societal context in which the Great Society legislation was created and review the major provisions of the "war on poverty," paying particular attention to the relationship of American values and federal policies to older persons. In the next chapter, we shall see how an overpowering combination of domestic events and international crises in the 1960s and 1970s disturbed the liberal-reform experiment, leaving a legacy that was both unsettled and unsettling.

A Call to Arms

In 1958, John Kenneth Galbraith published *The Affluent Society*. The distinguished Harvard economist was impressed by the dazzling rise of productivity in the United States since 1945 and was awestruck by the society's ability to reshape national priorities. Americans, he claimed, were quite capable of producing and consuming an endless number of automobiles, televisions, kitchen appliances, depilatories, and deodorants, among other creature comforts. They were less eager, however, to spend money on public services (such as municipal transportation and housing) and public institutions (such as hospitals and recreational centers) designed to improve the overall standard of living. Hence, most Americans evinced little interest in ensuring that government, with whom responsibility for the *common weal* lay, would attend to the needs of those millions who lacked what the rest of society took for granted (Galbraith, 1958: 81). This obsession with personal (private) ambitions at the expense of the common (public) interest, according to Galbraith, underscored the persistence of conventional attitudes and political beliefs. These attitudes made more sense when poverty, inequality, and economic peril were inescapable facts of life. In the context of "modern" socioeconomic conditions, however, such a posture demonstrated a failure to appreciate the extent of poverty and deprivation amid conditions of seemingly boundless prosperity. Ironically, he noted, this predicament could occur only in an opulent society, because only in such an environment do the poor constitute a minority.

Galbraith did not elaborate on the extent of poverty in America in the 1950s, but there was ample evidence that a sizable minority of Americans were impoverished. The 1960 census, for instance, showed that an eighth of the population lived in families with annual incomes less than the upper amount of eligibility stipulated in state public assistance laws. Leon Keyserling, a liberal economist, contended that 23 percent of the nation's households were poor; the conservative American Enterprise Institute conceded that the figure was not less than 10 percent. Using 1963 Census Bureau sample statistics, experts at the Department of Health, Education and Welfare estimated that 18 percent of the population lived in families that lacked an income sufficient to cover minimal nutritional and housing needs (Levitan, 1976). Insufficient income also seemed directly related to the high crime and delinquency rates in urban areas. For those who found government reports too dry and economists' debates too technical, Michael Harrington, then a free-lance writer and contributing editor to *Dissent,* wrote *The Other America* (1963). Invoking vivid language and shocking illustrations, Harrington argued that poverty in the United States was real but invisible to middle Americans.

> Poverty is a culture in the sense that the mechanism of impoverishment is fundamentally the same in every part of the system. The vicious circle is a basic pattern. It takes different forms for the unskilled workers, for the aged, for the Negroes, for the agricultural workers, but in each case, the principle is the same. There are people in the affluent society who are poor because they are poor; and who stay poor because they are poor (1963: 157).

Extending Galbraith's thesis, Harrington claimed that many poor people were not covered by social legislation, that others failed to take advantage of existing benefits, and that in still other cases the coverage was so woefully inadequate that it did not make a difference. In order to remedy this deplorable situation, Harrington urged his readers to press for a comprehensive set of new public programs that would extirpate the culture of poverty.

Thus, at the very moment that Daniel Bell was proclaiming "the end of ideology," scholars and reformers were preparing the intellectual foundations for a new utopian quest. They envisioned an American society in which economic and social resources would be used to help all citizens realize their fullest potential. The publication of works such as *The Affluent Society* and *The Other America,* however, was a necessary but not a sufficient catalyst for reform. The discovery that Americans were ill, ill-clad, ill-fed, and ill-housed in times of prosperity, not just in times of depression, was deeply disturbing. But such knowledge, compelling though it might have appeared to thoughtful commentators such as Galbraith and Harrington, needed to be politicized. Advocates could not change the status quo simply by calling for greater commitment to promoting welfare. It was necessary for those who wielded power, particularly those in high official positions, to use such arguments to effect changes.

As it happened, the new ideas about government's responsibility for the poor, which were percolating between 1958 and 1963, had an almost immediate impact. During the 1960 primaries, John Fitzgerald Kennedy became painfully aware of the desperate conditions in many parts of the country, especially in Appalachia. The Democratic nominee pledged on the campaign trail:

> The war against poverty and degradation is not over. . . . As long as there are 15 million American homes in the United States substandard, as long as there are 5 million American homes in the cities of the United States which lack plumbing of any kind, as long as 17 million Americans live on inadequate assistance when they get older, then I think we have unfinished business in this country (quoted in Schlesinger, 1965: 917).

Kennedy's allusion to a "war against poverty" received scant attention at the time, but it at least signaled a recognition that "something 'broad' was required." Lacking a grasp of the dilemma, the President feared economic disruption if he acted too precipitously. Hence during his abbreviated term of office Kennedy only marched to the brink of war. He mainly tackled isolated facets of the problem. In 1961, for example, he scored a relatively easy political victory with the first Area Development Act, which provided financial and technical aid to depressed areas. A year later, a bipartisan coalition enacted the Manpower Development and Training Act, which was designed to help the unemployed. In 1963, Kennedy directed his staff and professionals in various executive agencies to prepare a comprehensive study on poverty (Donovan, 1973: 23–25). An assassin's bullet, however, prevented him from setting forth a full-scale anti-poverty program.

It thus fell to Lyndon Baines Johnson to take the next step. Sharing his predecessor's belief that more had to be done for needy Americans, Johnson quickly imposed his own inimitable brand of political rhetoric in an effort to define the issues and establish policy objectives. In his first State of the Union address, the President solidified initiatives already underway by promising to "shortly present to Congress a program designed to attack the roots of poverty in our cities and rural areas" (Donovan, 1937: 26; Lampman, 1971: 12; Sundquist, 1969: 6–8). Although reducing poverty had been an implicit goal of presidents since Franklin Delano Roosevelt, this was the first time that an incumbent had declared "an unconditional war on poverty" to be a national priority. The "war" in fact was one of the few "performance" goals enunciated during the Johnson administration. So enthusiastic was he about using the federal government's resources to go beyond the economic and social-security parameters set forth by New Dealers that Johnson repeatedly stated his desire to improve "the quality of life" through legislation. The President used the phrase for the first time in a campaign speech on October 31, 1964. Although Johnson did not invent the concept of enhancing "the quality of life," he widened the potential scope of federal activities by using that particular expression.[1] Concern for "the quality of life" was not merely a less shop-worn synonym for "welfare." It connoted an interest in the psychological well-being of an individual, not merely in his or her financial circumstances (Rescher, 1972: 60–61; Campbell et al., 1976: 5–9). If Washington were to be in charge of ensuring goods and services that satisfied but ultimately embraced more than one's economic needs, then it followed that any "war on poverty" Johnson waged could not be limited to financial matters: it had to embrace a whole range of activities and areas in which government traditionally had not intervened.

Still, the impetus for the "war on poverty" legislation that Johnson's administration proposed between 1964 and 1966 cannot be explained solely in terms of a President's dreams of a "Great Society." It is doubtful that any significant legislative agenda could have been enacted so quickly had the political climate not been right. Calls for greater governmental responsibility for poor people had been issued widely since World War II, yet very little had actually been done, other than to extend existing programs. By 1964, however, executive concern for broadening the scope of federal activities was being fueled, possibly intensified, by public demands and expectations.

Probably the most important pressure applied on government figures was generated by civil rights activists. Through escalating nonviolent civil disobedience, a coalition of blacks and whites demonstrated that poverty was a shameful anomaly in an otherwise affluent nation. They emphasized again and again that there was an obvious relationship between the denial of civil rights and the persistence of poverty. Especially as the movement pressed northward, the stark connection between deprivation and racial inequality became all the more obvious. Indeed, the pace of protest accelerated after February 1960. Sit-ins and demonstrations began to attract media

---

[1] Johnson was not alone in attempting to define the "quality of life" in terms that went beyond the issue of financial security. Since 1957, there had been major research surveys into the public's perceptions of what was necessary for a "good life" and their opinions about the government's responsibility and ability to satisfy people's basic desires and needs, conducted at The University of Michigan and the National Opinion Research Center. Around the same time, academics and public program administrators began to develop what they hoped would be a comprehensive and coherent set of "social indicators" for evaluating both economic and noneconomic facets of contemporary life and for gauging the impact of recent changes in the political economy on various segments of society (T. W. Smith, 1981).

attention. The movement reached its most dramatic moment in August 1963, when two hundred thousand activists marched on Washington. From the steps of the Lincoln Memorial, A. Philip Randolph, age seventy-four, introduced the Reverend Dr. Martin Luther King, Jr., who told the throngs on the mall (and the millions who were watching on television) that he had "a dream": "One day on the red hills of Georgia," he prophesized, "the sons of former slaves and the sons of former slave-owners will be able to sit at the table of brotherhood" (quoted in Patterson, 1976: 419; see also Levitan, 1968: 14–15; Dickstein, 1977: viii). As the audience responded to King's stirring speech by singing the Baptist hymn "We Shall Overcome," few who witnessed the event doubted that this utopian vision with religious overtones, which could unite blacks and whites in a common cause, had a political significance that transcended the rhetoric and emotions of the moment.

This political impetus was not restricted only to those who identified or sympathized with the demands that the federal government guarantee basic civil rights for all races. Voter behavior in the 1964 election signaled an unmistakable mandate for change. The previous election had been a contest between markedly different campaign styles and personalities. Still, the results were incredibly close, in large measure because both candidates cautiously adhered to centrist positions. In 1964, there was "a choice, not an echo," in which two effective campaigners presented radically different agendas. Barry Goldwater called for a sharp reduction in domestic spending and a more aggressive foreign policy. Johnson, in contrast, pledged peace abroad and outlined a broad domestic program that would require far greater governmental activity. Indeed, most commentators assumed that a Democratic victory would set the stage for a concerted attempt to fulfill promises made to various special-interest groups, including the elderly. Johnson's victory had been anticipated, but few expected him to win by so large a margin: the incumbent won 61.4 percent of the vote and carried all but Arizona and five southern states. Democrats also piled up huge majorities in the Senate (68–32) and the House (295–140). Few political observers argued that the 1964 election resulted in a voter realignment comparable to the one forged by the New Deal. Some thought, though, that it was a "crucial election," insofar as *issue politics* seemed to replace *party politics* as the primary influence on mass political behavior (Huntington, 1975: 21; Nie et al., 1976). Presented with a dynamic, ideologically distinguishable campaign, the electorate responded differently from the way they had in the 1950s: they expressed their political preferences in a manner more deliberate and coherent than many observers had thought possible.

The demand for increased federal government action, as certified at the voting booth, signaled more than the voters' desire to alter the status quo. It also demonstrated an extraordinary trust in government. Commenting a year later on the 1964 returns, Robert E. Lane, a well-known Yale political scientist, concluded that "there has been a growing state of confidence between men and government, perhaps especially men and politics during the Age of Affluence. This argument takes on light when it is placed against the increased life satisfactions and self confidence" (1965: 895). Lane was not alone in hypothesizing that the economics of opulence were producing a new politics of affluence. As increasing numbers of Americans enjoyed a rising sense of well-being, it was said, people were steadily trusting one another and seemed more optimistic about the future. This posture presumably made them more willing to assist those perceived to be less fortunate.

Thus, by 1964, a variety of essential cultural and structural factors had made conditions propitious for a fundamental shift in American society. The current economic prosperity simultaneously improved the public's overall outlook and magnified the disparity between the haves and the have-nots. People increasingly reacted to the existence of significant pockets of degradation amid affluence with varying degrees of dismay. Commentators of all political persuasions generally concurred that the psychological, social, and political ramifications of abject need and "relative poverty"—a condition more difficult to define but no less important to address—required immediate action just as much as the economic manifestations did. In this context, an activist president did not have to persuade an unaware public that greater federal activity was needed. Johnson had received his mandate at the polls. The American people shared his great expectation that a war on poverty could be waged and won quickly.

The Great Society: An Overview

Once Johnson had decided to make the war on poverty the cornerstone of his administration, he directed Sargent Shriver to coordinate preparation of a comprehensive legislative package to present to Congress. The choice of Shriver was excellent. As a Kennedy relative, he could rally and retain the support of many of the slain president's staff. Shriver encouraged the Council of Economic Advisors, composed largely of Kennedy appointees, to continue developing a staff report on poverty along the lines John Kennedy had recommended. Shriver also relied heavily on the ideas of the Juvenile Delinquency Committee, headed by Robert F. Kennedy. In addition, Shriver energetically solicited the opinions of key personnel throughout the executive branch. He recruited Adam Yarmolinsky from the Defense Department, Daniel P. Moynihan from Labor, and James Sundquist from Agriculture to serve on his task force (Donovan, 1973: 29–31; Schlesinger, 1978: 416, 638). Experts in various other departments and agencies had proposals to offer and bureaucratic interests to protect. Wilbur J. Cohen, then the assistant secretary for legislation in HEW, made sure that his recommendations received careful consideration. So too did officials from the Bureau of the Budget, Commerce, Interior, Justice, the Small Business Administration, and the Housing and Home Finance Agency. The Shriver task force also turned to influential thinkers outside of government circles for specific program concepts.

Paradoxically, the presence of such keen minds and the availability of unprecedented resources did not readily lead to a consensus about the nature of "poverty" or the best way to tackle the problem. Despite all the input being offered, surprisingly few scholars, community leaders, or public officials had studied poverty in all of its ramifications. Consultants such as Michael Harrington took part in early deliberations, but, according to staff recollections, they had little impact on the policies that eventually were formulated (Yarmolinsky, in Sundquist, 1969: 38, 49; Schlesinger, 1978: 638; Moynihan, 1968: 1, 68). Most of those who prepared Johnson's anti-poverty legislation were familiar with fairly narrow aspects of the problem. They were technocrats whose expertise was limited to managing governmental operations or measuring Washington's political barometer. Hence, some discussed poverty as if it were confined to poor whites who lived in Appalachia. Staff members who recognized the racial dimensions of being poor frequently limited themselves to the plight of southern tenant farmers and ignored those trapped in northern ghettos, or vice versa. Even attempts to define the potential target population in terms of income—a strategy greatly boosted by the abundance of income data collected at the federal level—were stymied by the nascent conviction that the poor had little in common except low income, Harrington's culture-of-poverty thesis notwithstanding. Consequently, those who proposed poverty policies held quite divergent views. Possibly the only way that some common understanding as to the nature of poverty could have emerged would have been through intensive and extensive case studies and through testing of alternative methods of fighting poverty over a three- to five-year period.

But policymakers could not wait five years to act, even if they had so desired. In January 1965, the President was convinced that "ol' Landslide Lyndon" would be "Lameduck Lyndon" in eighteen months. Seizing on this election as a demand for broad, immediate domestic reform, he ordered his aides to get his proposals up to the Hill as soon as possible. He secured promises from his allies in Congress that these measures would receive quick, favorable action (Patterson, 1976: 430; Yarmolinsky, 1969: 348–50). Not only did Johnson want a program fast, but he also insisted that his program, whatever its components, be designed to produce quick, dramatic results. Hence, policy formulators were encouraged, and sometimes pressured, to abandon categorical assistance schemes that typically had a gradual, incremental effect on remedying a problem. Instead, they were urged to take big risks in addressing aspects of poverty that affected various constituencies within a given community. It was not enough to relieve or ameliorate the consequences of poverty. Programs were to get at the root of the problem at the local level. Such risks did not seem reckless at the time: after all, winning the war on poverty was now a national priority. Financial support sufficient to ensure victory seemed to be available.

The foremost goal of the Great Society legislation was to increase poor people's employment opportunities. Education and job training were deemed the best vehicles for helping the needy to obtain and keep decent-paying, relatively satisfying employment. The anti-poverty campaign was launched with the Economic Opportunity Act (1964), which established an independent federal agency to serve as a catalyst for mobilizing public and private resources and to represent poor people's rights. Among other things, the measure directed the creation of a domestic peace corps (VISTA); a Job Corps, which sought to improve the lives of school dropouts by training them in a residential setting away from the ghetto; a Neighborhood Youth Corps for jobless teenagers; Operation Head Start, a project aimed at emphasizing opportunities by giving pre-school training to children; Upward Bound, a program to encourage bright slum children to go to college; and New Careers, to fund paraprofessional training for the disadvantaged. As the titles of these diverse programs suggest, the primary focus of the Office of Economic Opportunity (OEO) was on toddlers, teenagers, and unemployed persons who should be entering the work force. By increasing the educational opportunities and vocational experiences available to children and youth, officials hoped that the intergenerational "cycle of poverty" could be broken. A rising generation, properly trained and motivated, could help themselves make it into the mainstream. They would surmount the inequality of opportunities into which they had been born. They could reasonably expect (and be expected) to reap the advantages of American life and to embrace attendant middle-class values. Once this group bore children, they presumably would make every effort to ensure their offspring a supportive home life and useful education.

No one expected the Economic Opportunity Act to be an instant panacea. Providing jobs and skills clearly addressed a major cause of poverty. This strategy, however, was not designed to provide income and services to people who desperately required immediate assistance. Hence, a second phase of the war on poverty was launched. The federal government attempted to help the poor by improving their accessibility to nutritious food, decent housing, and satisfactory medical care. Most successful of all the endeavors was the Food Stamp Program (1964). This measure expanded the purchasing power of the needy by permitting low-income families to use stamps (obtained at a substantial savings over their face value) for buying food. The Housing and Urban Development Act of 1965 was designed to upgrade the living conditions of the poor by introducing rent supplements for low-income tenants in specified units. It also authorized public housing agencies to lease private dwellings and provided reduced interest rates on loans for rental units built specifically for the poor and the elderly. The federal government's entry into health-care areas was particularly noteworthy, because it had been steadfastly opposed since the New Deal. The passage of Medicare and Medicaid made access to a publicly funded institutional network an acknowledged right for the nation's aged and needy. Other efforts to deliver and promote good health care at the national level included a nurses' training program, initiated in 1964. Aid for medical schools and needy medical students was increased in 1965 and 1968. Funds were also provided to staff mental retardation facilities, expand birth control programs, and build treatment centers for drug addicts and alcoholics.

Washington, in essence, attempted to get around the then politically volatile issue of underwriting gargantuan income-support programs by providing in-kind transfers to those who met mandated income eligibility requirements. Officials at the national level were keenly aware that in inaugurating a host of new welfare and medical-care programs they should consider community as well as individual needs. For if poverty were truly to be eliminated, argued many experts, the environment in which it festered also had to be improved.

Accordingly, President Johnson signed the Appalachian Redevelopment Act in March 1965, which authorized $1.1 billion for the thousand-mile-long region that cut through eleven states. The Public Works and Development Act, enacted five months later, earmarked $3.3 billion over the next five years to encourage the economic development of depressed urban areas. Many key provisions of the war-on-poverty legislation harked back to the grass-roots democracy schemes of the 1930s. Yet they also transcended New Deal parameters by mandating that the poor themselves have a voice in determining how monies were to be allocated in their areas. OEO's Community Action Program, for instance, established community-based agencies to mobilize the poor and to determine what sorts of legal services, adult education programs, and neighborhood health centers they needed. The poor were also assured leadership roles in the 1966 Demonstration (Model) Cities and Metropolitan Development Act.

The heightened sense of united action and renewal which Johnson and his analysts hoped to engender extended beyond geographical communities. It also encompassed various ethnic and racial groups in American society. Indeed, Johnson's actions on behalf of black equality, especially when compared to those of all his predecessors, were truly extraordinary. In rapid succession, laws were passed to outlaw discrimination in almost all public realms. A high watermark was reached with the passage of the Civil Rights Act of 1964. The measure guaranteed blacks (and women) voting rights, entitlement to equal employment, and unprecedented access to social and cultural facilities. The Voting Rights Act of 1965 enhanced the federal government's ability to protect southern blacks' franchise and to register minority voters. This provision, in turn, enabled blacks to help themselves by voting into office candidates who were sympathetic to their needs and willing to consider their demands. Blacks also benefited indirectly from federal initiatives and increased spending commitments in other areas. The National Defense Education Act of 1964, as well as the Elementary and Secondary Education Act and Higher Education Act of 1965, while not designed primarily with black needs in mind, nevertheless gave predominantly black schools access to public aid systematically denied them for decades.

A Great Society for Elderly Americans

Black Americans were not the only segment of the population singled out for special consideration. The needs of older people also were reviewed in light of the new political calculus. Like blacks, America's elderly population was perceived as a group whose collective problems merited social attention if the United States was truly to achieve a Great Society. Government officials, administrators, academics, and spokespersons in other key sectors of society believed that direct federal intervention could enhance the well-being of a whole category of people, even one lumped together by chronological age. However, few in public office expected the plight of the aged, unlike that of blacks, to be much improved by war-on-poverty measures. Thus while one can cite cases in which programs such as VISTA recruited retired teachers and senior citizens within impoverished communities to serve in various capacities, such instances are exceptional. Job-related and work-training programs for the elderly were not actually among OEO's original planks, because officials presumed that the aged were typically unable to work. In fact, the old-age problem itself was viewed as a special category. The needs of older Americans could not be ignored in addressing the culture of poverty, but they were to be treated as tangential.

The woes of being old, officials generally agreed, differed in two important respects from those of poor people who were growing old. "Fear of illness and lack of sufficient money are uppermost in the long list of worries that plague most of the nearly 18 million older Americans," declared Health, Education and Welfare secretary Anthony J. Celebrezze in the first annual report of the President's Council on Aging (1963) (*Science News Letter,* 1963: 339). Such an assertion accorded so neatly with the still prevalent conception of old age as a period of decay, wracked by debility, chronic disease, and destitution, that it scarcely needed documentation. Yet the necessary documentation was readily available. Negative descriptions of old age did have a basis in empirical reality. Data collected by the Social Security Administration and private groups indicated that people over sixty-five, as a group, were more sickly and less affluent than any other age category. There was a distressing relationship between low income and poor health. Seemingly irrefutable evidence indicated that the elderly lacked sufficient health insurance to pay for their high doctor bills and hospitals stays. Many lacked enough income to cover other monthly living requirements. Sociologists and economists reported that most men quit work not because they could afford to do so, or were being eased out, but because they were in poor health or disabled. Furthermore, available statistics revealed a surprising racial differential among the aged poor. A much larger portion of the white poor (23 percent) than of the nonwhite poor (8 percent) were over sixty-five. This suggested that whereas poverty tended to be a life-long problem for minorities, whites generally managed to avoid financial hardships until they lost their jobs or the income of the family breadwinner. At that point, they had to get by on inadequate savings and pensions, while they struggled with mounting medical bills.

Precisely because the major health and financial problems confronting the elderly seemed directly related to the fact that they were old, government officials decided to devise special categorical programs for older Americans. This approach was very different from those taken to remedy the conditions of poverty in youth and middle age. As the President's Commission on Income Maintenance Programs (1969) reported, "The poor will remain poor once they retire, and others who retire may become poor in their old age. Opportunities for the aged poor to make any improvement in their own lives are remote and unrealistic. Only public programs can make a difference in their incomes" (quoted in Marmor, 1971: 9; see also Orshansky, 1965). Defining the old-age problem in this manner had profound policy implications. Heretofore, officials discussed public assistance programs as stop-gap measures or, at most, as supplementary measures designed to complement benefits accrued through welfare and retirement plans in the private sector. Now public programs were being given unparalleled responsibility for making a critical difference in guaranteeing well-being in later years.

Indeed, federal programs on behalf of the elderly took two new directions in the 1960s. On the one hand, the federal government committed itself to doing more for the aged. As a result, Washington found itself under mounting pressure from special-interest groups to broaden its agenda for older Americans. As the growing gray lobby became more savvy on Capitol Hill, as politicians became more responsive to the demands of their elderly constituents, as existing old-age networks in the private and public sectors broadened their operations, as the media devoted more and more attention to the "problems" of age, and as civil rights activists saw that their posture on race relations had unmistakable ramifications for dealing with inequities in generational resources and opportunities, the needs of the elderly became a major item on the liberal reform agenda. On the other hand, the federal government's efforts to assist the aged also magnified the sometimes subtle, sometimes patent discriminations that had been written into public policies since the passage of the original Social Security Act. Legislative guidelines often excluded the old from programs that emphasized education and employment as means of breaking the poverty cycle. Similarly, programs for the aged were viewed as distinct from mainstream anti-poverty programs. Thus the image of older Americans as fundamentally different from other members of society was accentuated by Great Society legislation. As we shall see in following sections, the categorical distinction drawn between the "aging" and the "aged" sometimes caused seemingly straightforward measures to become ambiguous or dubious in intent, thereby confounding efforts to help the elderly help themselves. For the moment, however, it is necessary to point out that treating the aged as a needy and deserving group did have salutary effects.

The decision to focus on the elderly's health-care needs, for instance, increased the likelihood that some sort of federal health insurance program would at last be enacted in the 1960s. As we have seen, various presidents had been calling for a nationwide public system since at least the 1930s. Certain groups—notably the American Medical Association, the Chamber of Commerce, the American Dental Association, the Health Insurance Council, and the American Pharmaceutical Association—lobbied against any national program. Organizations such as the AFL-CIO, the National Farmers Union, Consumers Union, and the American Association of Social Workers usually could be counted in the ranks of insurance advocates. Political pressures were so great, however, that most measures proposed at the state or federal level never came to a final vote (Somers and Somers, 1967; Hirschfield, 1970). Then, in 1951, Oscar Ewing (who was head of the federal agency that shortly thereafter became the Department of Health, Education and Welfare) proposed that hospital insurance be provided for all people eligible for Social Security benefits. Ewing stressed, sensibly enough, that the aged needed some type of health protection if they were indeed to attain a measure of economic security. This proposal received little attention at the time, but efforts henceforth were channeled into designing a national health insurance program for the elderly segment of the population, the group which most Americans agreed had the highest health costs and least disposable income (Marmor, 1973).

It is significant that policy experts after 1951 looked for ways to build various health-care options into the bureaucratic apparatus and financial mechanisms institutionalized in the Social Security system. The strategy proved useful: Social Security enjoyed considerable popular support and had a reputation within and beyond official circles for being an efficient and effective administrative unit. Yet the idea of integrating a nationwide medical program to the Social Security network had the potential disadvantage of predisposing policymakers to be more concerned with expanding existing programs than with designing a health-care delivery system that addressed the age-specific needs of the people it was supposed to help. Systemic priorities and constraints sometimes mattered more than the flesh-and-bones problems with which real people were coping.

Various health-care proposals were introduced throughout the Eisenhower administration. Nevertheless, it was not until 1960, when election-year politics overcame the perennial obstacles, that any major steps were taken. In that year, Congress increased grants-in-aid to states offering medical payments to old-age assistance recipients. More importantly, it inaugurated the Kerr-Mills Medical Assistance for the Aged program, which provided new funds earmarked for those who were not on public relief, yet still were unable to pay for necessary medical treatment. John F. Kennedy, in one of his first messages to Congress upon entering the White House, urged that a hospital insurance program for the elderly be added to the Social Security system. Bills to effect this executive proposal were introduced by Senator Anderson of New Mexico and Representative

King of California. During the rest of Kennedy's term, Congress debated various drafts of the Anderson-King measure as well as alternatives proposed by other politicians and lobbyists. Not until Johnson's landslide victory and the election of a very liberal 89th Congress, however, was the environment at last conducive for decisive federal action.

Working closely with administration specialists such as Wilbur J. Cohen and policy experts in the private sector, Congressman Wilbur Mills, who chaired the House Ways and Means Committee, drafted a bill combining ingredients of three different health-care proposals (including one endorsed by the American Medical Association) that seemed to enjoy the most support on the Hill. The keystone of the package was the most recent version of the Anderson-King bill, a hospital insurance plan providing insurance benefits to recipients of Social Security, protection against the costs of hospitalization to those covered by the federal railroad-retirement program, and coverage of nursing home care for all persons over sixty-five. This became Part A of Public Law 98-97, Medicare. Part B of Medicare was a voluntary and supplementary plan, which initially cost the participant only $36 a year. It was intended to cover payments for services by physicians and surgeons as well as for diagnostic tests, ambulance services, prosthetic devices, and the rental of medical equipment that an elderly patient might need. At the same time that Medicare was passed, a variation of the AMA's proposal was enacted as Medicaid.[2] President Johnson, seizing on the historical significance of the moment, flew to Independence, Missouri to sign Medicare into law on July 30, 1965, in the presence of Harry S Truman, who in 1945 had unsuccessfully recommended a government health insurance plan. The symbolic gesture was particularly apt, for the aging former President personified the very target population that Medicare was designed to assist.

Leaders in the executive and legislative branches during the 1960s were not content merely with fulfilling New Deal hopes. Besides providing coverage to older Americans for some of their medical expenses, the architects of the Great Society made promises to the elderly that went far beyond anything envisioned before. In passing the Older Americans Act in 1965, Congress established a new social contract for the aged. Most of the measure's titles institutionalized recommendations and demands set forth at the 1961 White House Conference on Aging and at special hearings held by the Senate Special Committee on Aging in 1964. Among other

[2] Medicaid was a federal-state program that financed medical service for public welfare recipients of all ages and those who were deemed medically indigent. It expanded the scope of the Kerr-Mills Medical Assistance for the Aged Program. The measure was designed to mesh with the guidelines of Title I programs under Social Security.

things, the Act established an Administration on Aging in the Department of Health, Education and Welfare; authorized financial grants for community planning, services, and training programs; and provided formula grants to states for community services and demonstration projects, as well as for the establishment of state agencies on aging. More significant than these new public organizations, however, was the declaration of objectives set forth in Title I:

> The Congress hereby finds and declares that the older people of our Nation are entitled to, and it is the joint duty and responsibility of the Governments of the United States and of the several States and their political subdivisions to assist our older people to secure equal opportunity to the full and free enjoyment of the following objectives:
> (1) an adequate income in retirement. . . .
> (2) the best possible physical and mental health. . . .
> (3) suitable housing. . . .
> (4) full restorative services. . . .
> (5) pursuit of meaningful activity. . . .
> (8) efficient community services, including access to low-cost transportation. . . .
> (9) immediate benefit from proven research knowledge. . . .
> (10) freedom, independence, and the free exercise of individual initiative in planning and managing their own lives . . . (U.S., PL 89-73; see also Butler, 1975: 329–30).

This is an extraordinary statement. The Act promised unprecedented public commitment to improve the quality of life for all senior citizens. By extension, it ultimately embraced the needs of all Americans. In my opinion, Title I is potentially more revolutionary in scope than any other war-on-poverty measure. For the Older Americans Act did not limit itself simply to covering matters of income and health, or even to ensuring application of OEO's community-action thrust to the aged. This measure presumed that it was the duty of government to facilitate individuals' pursuits of "meaningful activities" and to maximize their options. If the government was really serious about fulfilling such pledges to older Americans, a new era in American society truly had dawned.

How are we to judge Congress's intent in articulating such a vision? Had lawmakers really moved beyond the goals of the 1930s? Or, was this merely a tantalizing restatement and extension of the logic and objectives implicit in the politics of incrementalism? One way to evaluate the rhetoric is to compare it to reality—to assess the actual impact of the Older Americans Act on improving the elderly's real standard of living. But as we shall see in Chapter 5, the results of such an examination would be greatly distorted by national and international crises that unexpectedly altered the momentum and dashed "the promise of greatness" vaunted in the early 1960s. Thus it might be more valid to reexamine the seven value dimensions that have provided the analytic framework for this study. If we were to discover a radical reworking of basic terms or a profound shift in emphases, then we would be justified in claiming that the Great Society was a turning point in the history of American values supporting federal old-age policies.

Values Reflected and Deflected in Great Society Programs

Before we investigate the normative repercussions of the Great Society on "modern" values and aging Americans, two preliminary observations should be made. First, changes in each of the seven value dimensions appear to have had a cybernetic effect on the entire normative structure. The Great Society was not simply the New Deal reshuffled. The overall program moved beyond the parameters established in the 1930s. Public officials introduced some new terms and fresh priorities. The times demanded, and facilitated, bolder steps in the areas of civil rights and social-welfare activism. Assumptions were made, aspirations articulated, and demands heard that reflected soaring expectations and a self-confident presumption that money and commitment made all good things possible. But, a second comment must immediately be added. Changes in the normative rationale underpinning the public policies promulgated in the 1960s did not resolve tensions and difficulties already manifest in America's value dualisms. Rather, new concerns and issues often masked, or ignored, long-standing contradictions. They did so, unfortunately, without demonstrating a coherent course of action or pointing to a well-marked set of objectives.

Public / Private

There can be no doubt that the public sector's mandate to press for a more just society vastly outstripped the role taken by the private sector. It no longer sufficed for the public sector to supplement community and philanthropic initiatives or to ameliorate worker compensation programs established in business and industry. Concurrently, the relative responsibilities of various levels of government were changed as Washington moved into fields in which state and local offices previously had held dominant, if not exclusive, sway.

The remarkable augmentation in the federal government's

sphere of duty resulted from the convergence of two different but indisputable historical trends (Cox, 1966: 96, 122; Lampman, 1971: 67, 74–75). First, by the early 1960s, both the legislative and executive branches were ready to take advantage of latent powers, which the Supreme Court had adjudicated to be constitutionally vested in the federal government, to address long-ignored social problems. Were this the only salient force affecting the policy arena, the flurry of civil rights activities between 1964 and 1966 might be interpreted as an inevitable response to the call for vigorous constructive public initiatives sanctioned by *Brown* v. *Board of Education* in 1954. Yet it is highly dubious that the other branches of federal government would have accepted this judicial invitation to intervene in new areas had it not been for a second factor. In the early 1960s, people began asking more of the federal government. Not only was Washington given a message to act after the 1964 election returns were counted, but it was also expected to ensure that its efforts achieved the stated goals. Thus the government's forays into the areas of health, education, and welfare were not a bald usurpation of power. They resulted from a deliberate policy choice on the best way to deliver essential services to American citizens. Officials decided that their duty could not be effectively discharged just by giving cash. They felt that they also had to provide medical care, pre-school and compensatory educational programs, and job training, as well as support for legitimate uses of community action.

The public sector was not given *carte blanche,* however. Americans expected the government to do a great deal, but they also feared excessive intrusion into their daily lives. To some observers the expansion of the welfare state sustained "the central hope for a democratic politics of change that ultimately will become socialistic" (Clecak, 1977: 55). Yet the specter of a boundlessly powerful, centralized State terrified most Americans. The prospect of Big Brother impersonally making vital decisions about intimate aspects of their lives was threatening. Thus, Great Society legislation was laced with restrictive clauses, and new programs initially received limited funds. Officials did not want their new measures to fail, but they did fear the possibility of unleashing forces that would undermine the socioeconomic processes that had guaranteed national prosperity. Attempts to measure the legitimacy and efficacy of governmental actions, especially at the federal level, moreover, lacked universally acceptable criteria. People made judgments using incompatible yardsticks. On the one hand, those whose expectations had been raised when the federal government engaged in unprecedented activities developed ever more grandiose standards for judging the magnanimity of the Great Society. They expressed disappointment and frustration when their heightened expectations were not satisfied. On the other hand, those who hewed to the belief that the federal government should be the instrument of the last resort bemoaned every new action. The perennial confrontation between liberal and conservative in America thus took on new meanings. Significantly, few challenged the goals of the New Deal: these had become generally acceptable. Instead, the potentially divisive questions dealt with whether and when the federal government's "collective action" in the public interest was to become the equivalent of government control over the common interest. We can trace the ways this issue was handled in two areas: equity versus adequacy and self-reliance versus dependence.

Equity / Adequacy

Relatively speaking, the designers of the Great Society were more successful than were New Dealers in institutionalizing a concern for "adequacy" in public programs. Architects of Social Security had met such overwhelming opposition to their plan to establish "minimum standards of decency and health" at the national level that they had abandoned the proposal lest the entire package be rejected. By 1964, however, policymakers were able to talk in terms of a "poverty line." The term referred to the number of dollars per year a family needed to eke out a minimal existence; the amount depended on family size, location, and the age of the household head. Although there were serious technical flaws in the instrument (to be discussed in Chapter 5), the very fact that the federal government was attempting to make anti-poverty programs "adequate" represents a significant new focus in values orientation.

And yet, matters of equity were hardly forgotten. While the decision to eliminate poverty was genuine, this expansion of public services for the less fortunate appeared financially possible because of the booming economy. In other words, there was no direct confrontation between "adequacy" and "equity." There was no tough, potentially unpopular choice to be made, since it seemed economically feasible for the government to be concerned about poor people's conditions without unduly penalizing those who did not have to rely on public assistance. The issue of equity, therefore, was not dismissed. Even the most fervid Great Society architect knew that issues of equity remained dear to middle-class Americans, if only because the assurance of receiving a fair return on one's effort fostered the perception and bolstered an individual's ability to preserve his or her self-reliance.

Self-Reliance / Dependence

Leaders in federal government did not expect, and the American public certainly did not want, anti-poverty measures to create a permanently dependent population. Special (if not wholly successful) efforts were made to increase the economic opportunities available to impoverished Americans and to foster their abilities to maintain themselves (Anderson, 1979). The main thrust of the Great Society, according to its supporters, was to enhance people's incentives and their opportunities to participate fully in society, as measures grappled with the chronic and obdurate features of dependency. The goal was not to make the poor helpless or reliant on handouts.

Most observers acknowledged the fallacy of claiming or pretending that the deleterious effect of persistent racial and ethnic discrimination could be eliminated overnight. Some Americans would remain "dependent" despite federal interventions. Those who had been physically, emotionally, and financially broken by the weight of poverty could not be expected, coerced, or induced to change their life-styles or outlooks all at once. But manipulating the poor in order to keep them down was not an avowed policy goal. Elements of social control, to be sure, were inherent in the Great Society policy objectives and program guidelines (Piven and Cloward, 1971; Parenti, 1977). Nevertheless, the war on poverty was not a calculated attempt to create a two-class society in which only those who aspired to or had achieved a measure of self-reliance were able to enjoy the benefits of American life. One of the central purposes of the Civil Rights Acts of 1964 and 1965, after all, was to ensure that basic freedoms guaranteed under the law were accessible to every citizen. Privileges were not to be withheld on the basis of a person's "dependency." Policy experts even hoped that those who could not reasonably expect to escape poverty would not be stripped of their dignity in applying for benefits. But insofar as self-reliance was still viewed as preferable to dependency, welfare programs in general were intended to promote self-reliance, not to make dependency a perpetual or enjoyable way of life.

In its main lines, therefore, it appears that the Great Society truly aspired to the best of all possible worlds. Policymakers, when unveiling provisions, talked about ensuring the adequacy of anti-poverty measures without making them appear inequitable. Officials believed that they could establish universal standards of "adequacy" at the precise point where a better trained, less destitute target population would opt for self-reliance and maintain the incentive to work rather than sink further into dependency. Such a felicitous balance, moreover, appeared in the policies designed for all age groups. The Older Americans Act spoke about ensuring adequate incomes and health services on the one hand, and promoting independence and creative leisure on the other, without intimating that such goals were incompatible or involved difficult trade-offs. At least policymakers did not think at the time that these aims were impossible to attain simultaneously through the same set of measures. Yet, if we limit our focus solely to provisions for the elderly, we quickly see that the actual situation is quite complicated. The value system as it affected the aged was fraught with explicit contradictions and ill-considered dilemmas.

Work / Leisure

Given the work incentives included in most anti-poverty measures, job-training programs and employment-opportunity provisions might have been made part of the old-age policies. They were not. The Social Security system, in fact, weakened the aged's work incentives in at least three ways. An amendment to the 1960 earnings test, for instance, reduced monthly Social Security benefits by $1 for $2 of earnings from $1,201 to $1,500, and $1 for each $1 of earned income over $1,500. Amendments in 1961, 1965, and 1967 raised the ceiling slightly, but by 1972 the amount of income permitted without reduction in benefits was still less than $2,100 (*Social Security Bulletin Supplement,* 1976: 26). The cumulative effect of the test was obvious. Those who wanted to work full-time past the age of sixty-five had to be willing to forgo 50 percent of their earned Social Security benefits. Part-time work had to be limited so that earnings would not exceed the prescribed maximum. Second, the extension of the system's coverage encouraged organizations in the private sector to design retirement programs and establish payment schedules that were carefully integrated with Social Security's current eligibility rules. Very often corporations introduced mandatory retirement provisions, which forced older employees to quit work at a prescribed age. Unions began to press for retirement benefits based on years of service rather than chronological age. They did so in order to create more seniority for younger workers and to sweeten the financial package for workers who had toiled long and hard for decades. Thus even though fixing a universal mandatory retirement age had been eschewed by Social Security experts from the beginning, such an arrangement became prevalent. In 1956, female workers between the ages of sixty-two and sixty-four who were insured by the program became eligible for retirement benefits reduced by 5/9 percent per month under age sixty-five. A 1961 amendment permitted actuarially reduced benefits to men who retired at age sixty-two. These measures surely had the effect of stimulating interest in early retirement schemes. Third, the rising dollar amount of Social Security benefits made retirement attractive for many blue-collar and white-collar workers, particularly when they were combined with payments provided by former employers. Increasingly, the combination of retirement funds, tax laws, and the elimination of any job-related expenses provided the money needed to maintain a family's preretirement standard of living. In some instances, the financial package made it more advantageous to retire than to work. Such measures, in short, underscored the prevailing notion that working was not the preferred choice for (or of) the elderly population. This stance seemed all the more reasonable, since it was compatible with the rising preference for leisure.

Yet the trends toward mandatory retirement at age sixty-five and the growing interest in early retirement options among employers and employees alike began to alarm many economists and critics. There was a growing awareness in the 1960s that encouraging or enforcing leisure for the aged might be deleterious to society in general and to the elderly in particular. Officials were accused of inducing the old to retire or, worse, of reclassifying older unemployed workers as retired in order to allieve current unemployment problems. By confusing retirement policy with unemployment policy, argued Duke University economist Juanita M. Kreps, Americans were ensuring the creation of a large class of aged poor in the future, men and women who would have to survive on meager private resources and insufficient benefits based on their decision to take early retirement (Kreps, in McKinney and deVyver, 1966: 136–56; see also Clark and Anderson, 1967: 18; Pechman et al., 1968: 120–24). Indeed, some feared that enforced leisure brought psychosocial as well as economic woes to the aged. Not only did most older Americans lack the economic wherewithal to enjoy a life of leisurely consumption, but they were rendered incapable of seeking personally and socially meaningful roles to replace their careers. Those who deplored the growing support for shorter and shorter working careers sometimes pointed to actuarial estimates based on Social Security statistics. These data seemed to indicate that those who retired early had lower life expectancies than those who stayed on the job until the "normal" retirement age. This interpretation, however, ignored the fact that those who had been forced to quit work early might have had a disability or illness that was likely to shorten their lives anyway.[3]

---

[3] It is worth noting that even though there appears to have been an obvious difference between the value stance implicit in these criticisms of the retirement phenomenon and the choices increasingly made by older workers themselves, few commented on this disparity at the time. The case against retirement was not yet seriously discussed in policymaking circles.

Thus in a society in which having both money and a good job enhanced one's sense of worth, the aged were doubly damned. That the federal government was sensitive to the difficulties older workers had finding jobs is illustrated by passage of the Age Discrimination in Employment Act in 1967. Ironically, this measure specifically excluded workers over sixty-five, an anomaly not altered until the late 1970s. Hence, at the same moment that the federal government endorsed the right of older Americans to "adequate income" and the "pursuit of meaningful activity," it passed a measure that justified discriminating against the aged! No single instance better illustrates the public sector's contradictory posture on this issue. In fact, the situation was exacerbated by the fact that the economic and normative trade-offs between work and leisure were clearly identified, yet the federal government chose to ignore even obvious difficulties in its position.

Family / Individual

Washington's inconsistent posture regarding work and leisure was paralleled by its ambiguous position concerning the most desirable household structure for the elderly. On the one hand, the laws were rightly concerned about the welfare of an aged adult as an individual. They were meant to give a person a free choice about how and where to live. On the other hand, government officials, armed with a welter of survey data stressing the psychological and social benefits older persons derived from having a supportive family network, did not wish to impede the vitality or integrity of that unit. What was needed, under the circumstances, was a coherent program that simultaneously took the needs of an elderly person as an individual and as a family member into consideration. Such a policy, unhappily, did not evolve. Instead, the basic value tension between policies with the individual as the object of concern and those with the family unit as the target population was magnified by a new wave of legislation that further complicated the situation (Riley et al., 1968: 168; Carter and Glick, 1970: 155; Glick, 1975: 24; Chevan and Korson, 1972: 45–53). Social Security benefits typically were higher for elderly unmarried adults than for newly married couples. (This probably accounts in large part for the dramatic upsurge in the number of older persons who shared quarters with an unrelated elderly member of the opposite sex.) Restrictions in other legislation forced an older person to calculate the relative advantages of living alone compared to residing with kin. The rising availability of public funds to pay for the cost of providing care for the sick and needy generated, in turn, a variety of conflicting feelings about what the older and younger generations expected of each other.

Needless to say, the federal government was not unique in its mixed attitude toward the best way to view the elderly's familial position. State laws concerning whether adult children were required to support their elders varied greatly in rigor and methods of application. Fourteen states, in fact, required filial contributions. They adjusted public assistance even if support was *not* furnished (Schorr, 1968; 107; Morgan et al., 1962: 275–79). In addition, public opinion was divided on what children owed their parents. Most people, including the elderly themselves, did not want aged relatives living with them. However, they also felt that private individuals, rather than the government, were primarily responsible for maintaining well-being in late life. In this fluid context, the federal government did little to resolve ambiguities or eliminate confusion. If anything, it exacerbated the dilemma.

Entitlement / Expectation

The passage of the Older Americans Act dramatically underscored the belief that the elderly were entitled at last to national recognition of their collective plight. Yet, having made a commitment of public support, Washington seemed uncertain about what to do next. Annual budgetary authorizations under the act were miniscule. In the first year (1966), only $7.5 million was allocated. Five years later, the figure was $33.6 million, still a relatively paltry figure to cover the cost of administering the Act and encouraging research, training, and social services for the elderly (Benedict, 1978). Advocacy had been mandated as one of the federal government's chief roles in support of the elderly, but even the Administration on Aging did little in this area before 1972. Consequently, the elderly were entitled to unprecedented public support and federal promises, but it was not yet clear how much these entitlements were really worth in federal budget discussions, on Capitol Hill, and in any other segment of American life.

Older people plainly would have to fight along with and sometimes against other special-interest groups, if present commitments were to be honored and future gains secured. The politics of incremental liberalism, even in flush times, did not guarantee that current expectations would be readily or inexorably translated into rising entitlements. Hence the gray lobby became more important than ever before. Maintaining the illusion, if not necessarily the reality, of age-specific demands was essential at election time. Such tactics were most successful in lobbying for the demands of white, middle-class senior citizens. The special needs of minority groups and women, however, were generally slighted. Tragically, these were the very sub-groups within the aged population whose needs were most acute. And, as we shall see, it was the plight of the ignored and underrepresented older Americans that was least often the focus of intensive concern in either the private or the public sector.

Novelty / Tradition

Obviously, the Great Society represents a significant moment in the history of old age in twentieth-century America. The Older Americans Act and Medicare constituted important pieces of social legislation. They made the elderly an even more visible object of concern. They ensured greater governmental involvement, particularly at the federal level, in ensuring the well-being of older Americans. In conformity with the war-on-poverty objectives, the social adequacy dimensions of old-age welfare programs received intense consideration; new categorical rights were protected under the civil rights umbrella. These were novel developments indeed.

Nevertheless, on balance, the Great Society's normative impact on the elderly was mixed at best and regrettable at worst. Often the needs and desires of old people were explicitly or unwittingly segregated from the needs of those who were not yet sixty-five. Policy choices accentuated the significance of age-graded categories in popular thought and societal patterns. Existing tensions in American values and national policies were not resolved. Public officials in the 1960s set goals for federal activities that demonstrably went beyond the New Deal aspirations, but they did not articulate a new rationale for social intervention. Prevailing convictions about the meanings and experiences of being old—premises that had become increasingly obsolete—remained in force. Policy designers also failed to chart an internally consistent pattern in social programs that successfully welded traditional attitudes and innovative ideas. Indeed, the lack of consistency in the realm of values was more manifest in the 1960s than it had ever been before.

Ominous economic, social and political developments increasingly jeopardized the goals and accomplishments of the Great Society during the late 1960s and 1970s. Americans of all ages protested public policies that threatened their entitlements and way of life: young people burned draft cards; these senior citizens burned means-test cards. [Courtesy of The National Council on the Aging, Inc.]

Chapter

5

Drifting Along and Coming Apart

We have just seen that the goals enunciated in the war-on-poverty programs did not signal a fundamental turning point in the evolution of American social values during the last half-century. Perhaps we ask too much: can we really evaluate the accomplishments and deficiencies of a social agenda exclusively in terms of the cogency and internal consistency of its vision? After all, the New Deal constituted a watershed in the twentieth-century history of old age in the United States, yet the normative framework girding the legislation passed during the 1930s was riddled with value tensions, ambiguities, and contradictions. What, then, is the difference between the New Deal and the Great Society? What makes the former but not the latter a pivotal moment in American social welfare history?

Part of the answer lies in the dissimilarity in the political and social atmospheres that charged the two periods. Different historical settings prompted different responses to the steps taken during the 1930s and 1960s, and caused the responses to have divergent effects on the advanced industrial society that created them. In the depths of the Great Depression, preserving the democratic order, reviving the economy, and providing financial relief to Americans in dire straits were this nation's foremost goals. Translating social thought into constructive action definitely was complicated by a variety of administrative, political, and economic difficulties, but there was little doubt about what ultimately was at stake. In contrast, efforts to build a Great Society faltered. Some well-intentioned programs never really got off the ground in the 1960s because the architects' blueprints and cost estimates proved inadequate from the start. By the end of the 1970s, a devastating combination of domestic imbroglios and international crises had broken the social scaffolding so boldly erected in the Johnson years for the reconstruction of American society and culture. Indeed, it has now become fashionable for commentators at all points on the political spectrum to seize upon the "failures" emanating from policy initiatives of the 1960s. There has been mounting criticism of the Great Society programs to benefit aged Americans. Among others, gerontologist Carroll Estes deplores the politics of pluralism and excoriates "the aging enterprise" for "failing to ameliorate the disadvantaged condition of the elderly in the United States" since the passage of the Older Americans Act (1979: ix). To ex-liberals and neo-conservatives who shape opinions in the marketplace of ideas and who have powerful connections in Washington, universities, labor, business, and the media, the major tasks of the 1980s are ridding Government of the excesses associated with the Johnson years and instituting a fresh set of priorities. Even moderates and mainstream Democrats, with few exceptions, are unwilling to fight for bold measures and policy objectives that only a decade or so ago they claimed were necessary and just.

The Great Society cannot be dismissed, however, as an unmitigated failure. Nor can one argue that the major pieces of social legislation enacted were a sham, designed to camouflage rather than solve deeply rooted problems (Levitan and Taggart, 1976). Older Americans clearly benefited from programs inaugurated in the 1960s. Since then, the gray lobby has consolidated and capitalized on gains during both Republican and Democratic administrations. To be sure, past policy mistakes and unanticipated consequences cannot be discounted. Some federal programs did not work or proved far more expensive than originally estimated. The record is replete with unintended and unwanted side effects. Trends that went unnoticed and others that once seemed unimportant or transient now command attention. They require action, not just by the federal, state, and local governments, but also by the private sector.

Hence, basic issues surrounding the Great Society, particularly as it affected the relationship among old age, American values, and federal initiatives, must be recast into a larger historical perspective. The challenges and opportunities of the 1980s do not constitute a radical break with a past that no longer has any relevance for present policy options or future choices. In large measure, the calls for reform and the social programs being proposed today are in response to and reaction against the course of events during the past three decades. As such, they must be viewed as manifestations of the most recent phase of modernization in the United States.

The Ironies of Modernization

Even under ideal circumstances, war-on-poverty programs probably could not have accomplished as much as their proponents claimed they would. Government officials failed to comprehend the true dimensions of the issues they were attempting to address. They exaggerated their ability to solve problems quickly through concerted efforts and massive infusions of federal funds. Public officials' statements sometimes served symbolic functions. By assuring their audiences that much was being accomplished, they hoped to ease pangs of guilt among the middle class and reduce political volatility among the poor (Edelman, 1967 and 1977). There were serious shortcomings, moreover, with the basic instrument used to define and measure the extent of poverty in America. The "poverty line" employed in policy discussions was better suited for heuristic modeling than for designing large-scale policies to assist real people. Thus, despite their inspiring imagery and sophisticated survey tools, officials could not indisputably specify who really was poor in the United States.

Yet the sources of misperception concerning poverty in the 1960s went deeper than semantic distinctions and statistical artifacts. Contrary to the rhetoric and official assumptions of the 1960s, it now appears that policymakers were mistaken when they talked in terms of a ubiquitous "culture of poverty," in which poverty bred poverty in a cruel cycle of near inevitability. At most, there seem to have been (and still are) *pockets* of poverty. The social characteristics and attitudes of the poor even within a given geographic area varied, and continue to differ considerably (Miller and Roby, 1968; Valentine, 1968). Furthermore, only a subset of the impoverished remain "poor" from one year to the next. According to longitudinal evidence collected by University of Michigan researchers in the late 1960s and early 1970s on five thousand families, fewer than one out of ten American families were in the bottom fifth of the income/needs distributions every one of the five years studied (Morgan et al., 1974: 21–30, 292; Thernstrom, 1973: 92–93).

Thus, broad-scale programs premised on assumptions about a "culture of poverty" did not directly address the particular needs of many individuals who desperately needed help. Societal benefits, by necessity, can only be marginal unless funding is very generous. As commentators at the time claimed, the group of poor people targeted for benefits constituted only a fairly small—and relatively fluid—proportion of the total American population (Rossi, 1969: 219–20). Tragically, however, this line of reasoning elucidates the persistence of a certain cultural myopia concerning the condition of black America.

For the "culture of poverty" orientation did more than just obfuscate policymakers' understanding of the nature and extent of poverty in America. It also confounded approaches to the refractive racial feature of the nation's "poverty problem." It was well understood within and outside of government circles that many blacks lived in poverty. But the extent to which the war on poverty should—and realistically could—be tailored to address the plight of blacks in the rural south and in the northern ghettos was never firmly established. There appear, in retrospect, to have been several reasons for equivocation on this fundamental policy issue (Moynihan, 1968: 14; Duncan, 1968; Heilbroner, 1975: 68; A. H. Miller, 1974: 957). Social workers, academics, and policy officials at all levels acknowledged that a larger proportion of all blacks than of all whites were impoverished. They also noted that blacks represented only a minority of the total number of Americans who were living in poverty. Black poverty, in other words, was not viewed as *the* poverty problem. Consequently, while it seemed legitimate for the federal government to demonstrate its commitment to *protecting* blacks' political and social rights by passing and enforcing the Civil Rights Laws of 1964 and 1965, there was an extraordinary degree of angry debate and covert conflict concerning the government's obligation to *aid and abet* blacks' efforts to advance themselves. Some urged caution in a not too thinly veiled attempt to perpetuate systematic racism as long as possible. In other circles (and even here sentiments were alternately shrewd and cynical), a policy of "benign neglect" was recommended. Still others called for a broad range of programs whose primary but unstated purpose was to aid blacks.

No consensus on racial issues, in short, emerged during the 1960s. Officials who were genuinely prepared to help blacks help themselves to the fullest extent possible often were not sure how to proceed. They could not decide whether the "Negro problem" was the legacy of poverty, the inheritance of race, or both. Those opposed to expanding civil rights activities attempted to block and delay new initiatives at every turn. The fear of white backlash remained an ominous threat, because a significant segment of the population believed that remedial measures might have been enacted too quickly (Institute of Gerontology, 1979: 75–77).

Given this milieu, the urban violence of the sixties takes on profound significance. There were over one hundred major riots between 1964 and 1967. At least 130 persons were killed. The cost of property damage alone exceeded $714 million. The black riots shocked the nation, brutally forcing people of all political persuasions to reconsider their positions. Riots during the summer of 1967 prompted Lyndon Johnson to appoint a National Advisory Commission on Civil Disorders co-chaired by Otto Kerner, the governor of Illinois, and John Lindsay, the mayor of New York. The final report asserted that black resentment of white institutional racism had triggered the fiery outbursts. It called for a massive commitment to bolster the welfare services and to improve housing, education, and employment opportunities for blacks (Heath, 1975: 251–56). The Commission's analyses and recommendations were duly received, and then virtually ignored. Even if Congress and the President had been moved by the Kerner Report and had been willing to attack the underlying causes of urban unrest through a "domestic Marshall Plan," federal officials probably would not have allocated the money necessary to wage such a campaign. For another crisis, one with international repercussions, was dominating national attention.

This crisis was the Vietnam war. Throughout the early 1960s, most citizens believed that American involvement in Southeast Asia was a moral obligation, vital to the national interest. When General William C. Westmoreland ordered U.S. bombers in June 1966 to make fifteen hundred raids per week over enemy-held territory and requested that troop levels rise to 542,000 so that he could secure complete victory within eighteen months, the President granted his request and lauded his efforts. During the next eighteen months, however, the war did not wind down to an honorable end. The fighting dragged on. Casualties mounted: 14,589 Americans were killed and 46,797 were wounded in 1968 alone. Because Johnson refused to raise taxes to pay for the war effort, the national debt soared from $239.1 billion to $301.1 billion during the 1960s. The cost of living lunged upwards in a viciously inflationary wage-price spiral. In dollars alone, the Vietnam war cost more than $140 billion, rising from a mere $103 *million* in 1965 to a peak of over $28 *billion* four years later (Dollar et al., 1979: 1061–65). Thus while the government squandered billions in Vietnam, it offered comparatively small change for the administration's campaign to foster economic opportunity and social amelioration for the poor. Vast sums of money and precious human resources were diverted from domestic needs at a critical moment.

Of course, the true cost of Vietnam tragically went far beyond body counts and dollars. The war, or more precisely the anti-war movement, polarized Americans. Many began to doubt whether their leaders were capable of telling the truth, much less admitting mistakes. Others, confusing nationalism for patriotism, taunted those who dared to question this country's sense of mission. Some bitterly denounced the United States for having committed such a terrible wrong and, presuming it incapable of ever doing anything right, either left the country or simply "dropped out" of sight. By the late sixties, "Vietnam" had come to symbolize all that appeared wrong with "modern" America. It fostered a nationwide identity crisis by forcing Americans to question a whole galaxy of cherished beliefs about the essence of the American experience. It fueled the rhetoric of failure in a nation long conditioned to think that its actions at home and abroad were manifestly destined to succeed.

The sense of malaise and frustration accentuated by Vietnam was not unprecedented in twentieth-century American history. Long before napalm and Saigon became household words, after all, Kenneth Keniston had perceptively diagnosed, in *The Uncommitted,* that "alienation, once seen as imposed *on* man by an unjust economic system, is increasingly chosen *by* men as their basic stance toward society" (1960: 1). But the spreading protest against the war was hardly an isolated phenomenon. The tumultuous political events of the 1960s—the assassinations of John and Robert Kennedy, Malcolm X, and Martin Luther King, riots, flaming ghettos, draft-card burnings, campus demonstrations, and pervasive disregard for the law—were frightening. "There was a sense everywhere, in 1968, that things were giving. That man had not merely lost control of his history, but might never regain it. That palliatives would not serve, and nothing but palliatives could be found. That we had slipped gears somewhere, and a train of mismeshings was chewing the machinery up" (Wills, 1969: 34). The political and social center, bruised and battered as never before, seemed to be coming apart.

America's youth, especially college students who had participated in or were inspired by the civil rights struggle of the late 1950s and early 1960s, provided much of the energy behind the anti-war movement. They also waged a broad assault on middle-class conventions and mainstream politics. It is no mere coincidence that protest against American involvement in Vietnam began to escalate as student leaders at the nation's largest and most distinguished centers of higher education conducted teach-ins on campuses, staged rallies in major cities, and mobilized a series of marches to the Capitol between 1967 and 1971. By the end of the sixties, many colleges and universities were besieged by the very turmoil wracking society at large. The youth rebellion was not confined to campuses. Radicals and other instigators fanned anger and sporadic violence against academic, military, governmental, and corporate bureaucracies. Fighting against "the system" that seemed to dominate lives and dictate options frequently pitted the young against civil authorities in bloody conflicts (O'Neill, 1971; Patterson, 1976: 462–72; Broder, 1980: 473–90). Increasingly, social commentators talked in terms of a "generation gap." Some saw a revolution in the making as the sons and daughters of America's affluent population embraced the music, dress, paraphernalia, idiosyncratic behavior, and attitudes of self-proclaimed "hippies" and counterculture types. Yale law professor Charles A. Reich (1970) predicted that a new world order of freedom, creativity, honor, love, and community would be created by the "Consciousness III" generation. *The Greening of America* has yet to occur. Nevertheless, few in any age group were unaffected by the search for alternate life-styles, which youth hoped would offer more self-expression and meaning than they saw in their parents' lives.

Other segments of the population added to the confusion and turmoil of the times by demanding redress for their grievances against "the Establishment." Hispanic leaders organized strikes and boycotts to dramatize the plight of migrant workers in California and Texas. A series of ugly confrontations on Indian reservations underscored the centuries of dishonor and injustice in red-white relations. Calls for reparations, assertions of "black pride," and visions of a new cultural nationalism spread through ghettos and middle-class black neighborhoods. Proponents of "Chicano" power, "red" power, and "black" power captured headlines and attracted widespread media attention, but they also met with resistance from those whom they tried to win over. As a result, radical leaders proved more successful in provoking debate among and beyond their following and in heightening tensions than in gaining major concessions or affecting long-range and broad-scale alterations in the status quo.

Feminists organized the potentially most important protest movement. In several crucial respects, the course of the women's rights movement resembled the history of other liberation groups in the late 1960s and early 1970s. Women's experiences in the civil rights struggle and anti-war movements offered them models of and training in grass-roots mobilization. It also reinforced their awareness that sexist attitudes and chauvinistic behavior were rampant even among their presumably "liberal" co-workers. Just as black officials in the NAACP, SCLC, and CORE were doing, leaders of the National Organization of Women (founded in 1966) recalled a sorry history of discrimination and emphasized current inequities as they pressed for a voice, participation, and power equal to men's in all spheres of American society. They also tried to raise consciousness levels by exposing the ubiquitous and pernicious effects of "the feminine mystique" and by nurturing group solidarity (Friedan, 1963; Evans, 1979).

Like other "power" advocates, feminists sought recourse through the legal system. Effective use was made of existing legislation, such as Title VII of the 1964 Civil Rights Act, which prohibited discrimination on the basis of gender as well as race. Hoping to correct pervasive discrimination in the marketplace, they organized campaigns, which culminated in the passage of the Equal Employment Act (1972) and the Equal Credit Opportunity Act (1974). Women's right to choose how they wished to live their lives was underscored by the Supreme Court's controversial ruling on *Jane Roe* v. *Henry Wade* (1973), which overruled state laws prohibiting or restricting abortions. This landmark decision made the fight for an Equal Rights Amendment to the U.S. Constitution seem all the more important. By legally banning discrimination on the basis of gender, women and men who supported the amendment hoped to increase the pace and degree to which implicitly guaranteed rights were actually being realized by women regardless of race, income, marital status, education, or employment prospects.

Finally, as had been the case with other groups, internal disagreements over ideological issues and tactics led to deep rifts in the women's movement, even as the first fruits of the struggle were being enjoyed. Various factions made the fight for publicly funded abortions, against rape, for lesbianism, and against pornography the chief item on their agendas, and the movement lost momentum and needed support. Sexual politics often diverted attention from the basis issues of equal rights. It threatened or excluded women who still wished to define their roles in terms of their spouses, children, and home, and, ironically, fostered under the banner of "feminism" a new set of sexist assumptions about the physical and psychic nature of the sexes (Degler, 1980; Friedan, 1981).

In at least two ways, however, the feminist movement differed from other protest drives. On the one hand, women were not a minority group. Females constituted 51 percent of the total population and differed enormously from one another on every crucial criterion. On the other hand, the status of women had been changing dramatically since World War II. The young women of the baby boom were more likely than their mothers to have sexual intercourse without regard to marital prospects or commitments, to end an unsatisfying marriage in its early years, and to limit the number of their children by using the Pill or getting an abortion. More significantly, there was a remarkable increase in the number of females in the labor force. Women filled roughly two-thirds of the new jobs in the 1960s. (Because most of the openings were in relatively low-paying clerical, sales, and service positions, working women typically earned far less than men: median salaries for women were 59.4 percent of men's in 1970, compared to 63.9 percent in 1955.) Having children under school age or a husband with a good job was less likely than ever before to deter a woman from seeking regular employment. Over 43 percent of all female adults were in the labor force in the 1970s; the figure exceeded 50 percent by the end of the decade (Leuchtenberg, 1979: 194; Duskin, 1974: 532–34). Thus the central aims of women's liberation simultaneously reflected and accelerated long-term demographic and socioeconomic trends. For this reason, even when the feminist movement faltered, the issues it posed about the choices women had to make concerning work and home, as well as marital responsibilities and individual identity, remained salient within all segments of society.

The course of the women's movement since the early 1960s, therefore, affords us two important insights about the interrelationships among public policies, economic developments, political action, social trends, and cultural values. First, the struggle for equal rights under the law obviously predates the "Great Society." Sexual discrimination had long existed, and leaders of the movement built on the lessons of the past as well as previous successes (and failures) in order to achieve their current objectives. Yet social legislation could not eliminate inequities overnight. In and of themselves, laws did not require people to change their private beliefs. Assessments of the feminists' victories and defeats in the 1960s and 1970s, accordingly, should be viewed in the comparative context of a richly textured pattern of historical development. Second, the continuing process of modernization evolved in ironic and unexpected ways. It is quite clear that the women's movement was greatly affected, for better and for worse, by changes in the political economy and social structure, which altered the ideas and status of all groups. Hence, the link between feminism and anti-war protest, while not immediately self-evident, becomes a critical factor in explicating why certain spokespersons perceived the world and acted the way they did. These two insights have a direct bearing on the way we are to understand the actual impact of new social programs on the aged.

The Legacy of Social Reform for the Elderly

Programs to alleviate the problems of aging established during the last two decades must be evaluated not only in the context of the long-term evolution of old-age policies but also in light of recent developments in American society and culture. Our analysis thus far indicates why such a broad perspective is essential. Significant federal initiatives on behalf of older Americans began in the 1930s. As the original Social Security program matured, coverage was extended and eligibility requirements were liberalized. These changes manifestly affected the status of older Americans and influenced their choices about living and working arrangements. The cumulative impact of election-year politics—the attempt by the legislature and executive branches to stimulate the economy and influence the behavior of certain elements of the electorate in the voting booth—altered the benefits that older Americans derived from the system over time and changed the public's image of the elderly. New programs transformed the political-economic equation and the sociocultural calculus.

The elderly "fit" into the Great Society mold. The "problem" of old age was perceived as a legitimate "welfare" issue. The aged's needs could be reduced by increasing categorical allocations and inaugurating new social services. By presenting their case in politically astute terms, the elderly were able to capitalize on the politics of interest-group liberalism. They became entitled to more and more. The cost of aging programs rapidly became a major item in annual federal budgets. As a result, the position of older Americans in contemporary society paradoxically became both more sensitive to and more insulated from broader changes transforming American life.

Older Americans' Expanding Entitlements

The historical pattern of ever broadening categorical assistance for the elderly is most apparent in the evolution of federal income-support policies. The first major increase in Social Security benefits took effect in September 1950, when Congress passed and President Truman signed a 77 percent increase in the benefit levels established by the 1939 amendments to the original legislation. Subsequent increases in benefits were authorized in September 1952 (12.5 percent), September 1954 (13 percent), January 1959 (7 percent), January 1965 (7 percent), February 1968 (13 percent), January 1970 (15 percent), January 1971 (10 percent), September 1972 (20 percent), March–May 1974 (7 percent), and June 1974 (4 percent). It is not altogether coincidental, claims Edward Tufte (1978: 29–36), that these amendments increased the disposable income provided by the monthly Social Security checks sent to older Americans shortly before they went to the polls. Even after enthusiasm for Johnson's war on poverty waned, a coalition of liberals and moderates in Congress was able to secure ever more generous benefits for the aged. Automatic adjustments of monthly benefits for inflation, enacted in 1972, began in 1975. Indexing of earnings was legislated in 1977. While benefits rose, compulsory coverage increased. Between 1950 and 1967, various groups of employees not yet covered by Social Security—such as military personnel, the self-employed, and domestic workers—were brought into the program; the federal railroad retirement program was integrated into the system in 1974. Social Security now approaches universal coverage: nearly 95 percent of all Americans reaching sixty-five are eligible for benefits.

Perhaps the most significant change, one which clearly is consonant with major features of the war on poverty, was the adoption in 1972 of a Supplemental Security Income (SSI) program. Effective January 1, 1974, the federal government combined and nationalized all public assistance for the adult poor, aged, blind, and/or disabled who were unable to work. SSI thus replaced the method of old-age assistance established in 1935 under Title I of the Social Security Act. In so doing, it presaged a new era in American welfare history by providing a crucial precedent for a universal income-maintenance program. The cumulative effect of all these developments was the increase in old age security income benefits and other expenditures from roughly $25 billion in 1969 to $93 billion in 1979 (*Social Security Bulletin,* July, 1982: 29).

Legislative initiatives at the federal level certainly were not limited to the area of income security. Many policies were designed to increase the elderly's range of options and to improve the quality of later life. Like other "poor" people whose needs were earmarked for federal intervention, the aged benefited from wide-ranging categorical assistance initiatives. Under the umbrella of the civil rights movement, older Americans' "rights" were duly considered by officials. For instance, the enactment of the Age Discrimination Act of 1975 barred discrimination on the basis of age in any federally supported program if that program was not specifically designated for a particular age group (Neugarten, 1981). Bills amending the 1967 Age Discrimination in Employment Act received overwhelming support in Congress in the late 1970s. The current law bans mandatory retirement before age seventy for all workers in local, state, and private employment, except executives or persons in "high policy making positions" who are entitled to employer-financed private pensions exceeding $27,000 per annum. The upper age limit was eliminated for practically all federal workers (Graebner, 1980: 245–46). Furthermore, amendments to the 1965 Older Americans Act (OAA) have paid increasing attention to the aged's long-term medical needs and have been intended to help the elderly maintain their independence in the community. Representative of this commitment is the nationwide nutrition program that provides at least one well-balanced meal for five days a week in a variety of settings. In addition, Title III of the Older Americans Act and Titles XIII, XIX, and XX of the Social Security Act have attempted to correct some of the serious deficiencies and gaps in Medicare and Medicaid guidelines. They have enabled administrators to coordinate existing health-care programs in a more comprehensive, accessible, and equitable manner. Other federal initiatives have addressed the elderly's housing, legal, educational, and recreational needs. Advocates of the aged in Congress have succeeded in amending a variety of general-purpose programs so that they now allocate funds and services specifically to the elderly (Oriol, 1981: 39).

With the enactment, expansion, and extension of federal laws affecting older Americans has come a dramatic proliferation of public agencies. (We shall discuss the disturbing consequences of this phenomenon later in the chapter; for the moment, it will suffice to sketch its dimensions.) At the national level, at least eighty different bureaus and commissions offer more than 135 programs designed to aid the elderly in one way or another (Estes, 1979; Binstock, 1978).[1] Four deserve brief mention. The Administration of Aging (AoA), established in 1965, is the central agency charged with supervising existing programs and initiating new activities under the Older Americans Act. The National Institute on Aging (NIA) was created in 1974 to set research priorities essential to a graying society. NIA conducts basic investigations into senescence at the Gerontology Research Center in Baltimore and sponsors research in the biomedical and social sciences at aging centers, research institutes, and universities across the country. The Senate Special Committee on Aging, formed in 1961 and reorganized in 1977 as a permanent, nonlegislative body, monitors developments at the national level and makes recommendations for future action in its annual report. A House Select Committee on Aging performs a similar function.

Prior to 1972, many major programs (including key aspects of Social Security, Medicare, and Federal Housing) bypassed state- and local-level administration. Indeed, efforts to grapple with the needs of elderly persons at lower levels of government rarely matched those at the federal level. Governors periodically called conferences and sponsored forums on aging, but most state agencies were minimally staffed and maintained a relatively low profile in the bureaucracy. County welfare departments typically dealt with clients as part of their regular caseload. The 1973 Comprehensive Services Amendments to the Older Americans Act, however, changed the prevailing balance of power. The measure gave state agencies on aging considerable control over budgetary matters. It delegated to these offices some responsibility for planning and coordination. Furthermore, in order to receive federal funds for their programs, states were required to establish a network of area agencies on aging to act as brokers overseeing activities at the local level (Atchley, 1980: 306). Besides increasing the range of social services available to senior citizens throughout the United States, the horizontal growth and vertical elaboration of this bureaucratic arrangement in recent

---

[1] We shall be discussing the impact of Reaganomics on such social service and income-transfer programs in Chapter 6. Here, let me simply note that the scope of federal services for the aged probably will be reduced in the years ahead, if Reagan's policymakers have their way.

years have created an extensive old-age advocacy network at all levels of government.

Much of the impetus for this flurry of activity in the public sector on behalf of older Americans stemmed from the growing political sophistication of the gray lobby, which had formed at the grass-roots level during the 1920s and had begun to exert influence in Washington as a result of New Deal developments. More than a dozen groups built vital coalitions within and around service, labor, professional, fraternal, and community-action interest groups during the 1960s and 1970s (Binstock, 1974; Pratt, 1976; Binstock and Levin, 1976; Hendricks and Hendricks, 1981: 379–82).[2] Leaders of the gray lobby espoused intellectual positions that paralleled the logic and rhetoric of other interest groups. They borrowed strategies and tactics that had proven successful in the civil rights cause and the feminist movement. Working independently and sometimes in collaboration on ad hoc issues, organizations representing the aged expended considerable time, energy, and money to ameliorate the status of the elderly in America.

A New Shade of Gray?

Without question, the congeries of federal laws, public programs, bureaucratic networks, private organizations, and interest groups, as well as the individual efforts of senior citizens, have altered the experiences and meanings of being old in important ways. Rather than attempt to itemize every accomplishment and trace all

[2] Three organizations dominate the arena. The National Retired Teachers Association/American Association of Retired Persons (NRTA/AARP), founded in 1947 by Ethel Andrus, a retired California teacher, now claims a membership exceeding nine million people over the age of fifty-five. The National Council on Aging established with Ford Foundation support in 1950, currently represents more than 1,900 autonomous health-care, social-work, and social service agencies. Since 1980, NCOA has housed a National Aging Policy Center on Education, Leisure, and Continuing Participation. The National Council of Senior Citizens (NCSC), organized by some participants of the 1961 White House Conference on Aging, has more than 3,000 club affiliates—many with long-standing connections to labor unions. Several other bodies claim smaller memberships than the "Big Three," but command considerable influence. The American Association of Homes for the Aged (AAHA), the American Nursing Home Association (ANHA), and the National Association of State Units on Aging (NASUA) advance the views of people who provide or oversee the delivery of specialized services to the aged. The Gerontological Society of America and newer regional groups, such as the Western and Southern Gerontological Societies, have broadened links among academic specialists, policy experts, and social practitioners. Still other associations represent and fight for specific segments of the elderly population. The National Caucus on the Black Aged (organized in 1970), the Gray Panthers (formed by Maggie Kuhn in 1972), and the Asociacion Nacional Por Personas Mayores (founded in 1975) wield more political clout than their numbers and budgets might otherwise suggest. The National Association of Retired Federal Employees (NARFE) has existed for more than sixty years but did not vociferously lobby for its constituency until the 1970s.

positive developments that have occurred since the mid-1960s, let me illustrate this point by describing two key elements of the total picture in which there has been notable progress.

Gains have been dramatic in the area of economic security. Older Americans' aggregate financial condition has improved during the past two decades as a direct result of rising Social Security benefits, SSI, tax breaks, in-kind income (such as the food stamps program), and because of the growth of private pension systems and individual retirement arrangements. To be sure, incomes among the old vary greatly by age, race, marital status, current and past employment status, and the number of pensions and types of resources available to a particular individual or household. Nevertheless, more than ever before, Social Security is the economic mainstay of older Americans. It accounts for more than half of the income for 70 percent of all single beneficiaries and 50 percent of the elderly married beneficiaries. According to official estimates, 60 percent of the elderly population would live in poverty without the Social Security program (U.S. Senate, Special Committee on Aging, 1979: viii; 1981: vii). Furthermore, the extent of poverty in old age, as measured by government indices and verified through a host of independent studies, has been greatly reduced. The percentage of Americans over sixty-five with low incomes fell from 35.2 percent to 24.6 percent between 1959 and 1970. Despite the economic instability caused by unemployment and persistent inflation during recent years, the poverty rate for persons over sixty-five had dropped to about 14 percent by the late 1970s. This suggests that various cost-of-living measures built into public pension programs have compensated somewhat for the decreasing value of the elderly's private pensions and other financial assets. Concurrently, the depth of economic deprivation among minority groups and unmarried women far exceeded the mean for the aged as a whole. The poverty rate appeared to be rising among some older groups of people. As deplorable as the situation remains in the 1980s, considerable progress nonetheless had been made in reducing poverty among vulnerable subsets of the elderly population. For instance, 61 percent of all nonwhite older Americans were poor in 1965; the figure fell to 47 percent in 1968 and 35 percent in 1977. The poverty rates for aged persons in families with a female head fell from 49 percent to 24 percent in the same period (Achenbaum, 1978b: 150–51; Schulz, 1980: 38–39, 46–47).

These alterations in the types and levels of financial support available to older Americans have paralleled (and ofttimes contributed to) constructive shifts in attitudes toward aging and images of the aged. It would overstate the impact of public policies to claim that ideas about old age have changed simply because of federal involvement in the field of aging. Obviously, the causal connections are quite complex. But governmental involvement and heightened professional interest, as well as the increasing accessibility of research funds and social services and a greater media coverage of the aged's situation, did catalyze and accelerate attitudinal changes in a variety of areas. For instance, "pathological" models of aging (which characterize the process of growing older as one of inevitable, progressive deterioration, disengagement, and hardship) no longer serve as the ruling paradigm in gerontological research. Few scholars claim that chronological age per se homogenizes the elderly's physical, psychological, or socioeconomic conditions. Instead, they emphasize the great variability that exists among the aged. Such an orientation has made academic experts and policymakers more aware of the extent and virulence of *ageism* in contemporary America. "Ageism can be seen as a systematic stereotyping of and discrimination against people because they are old," asserts Dr. Robert N. Butler, the first director of the National Institute on Aging, who coined the term in 1968, "just as racism and sexism accomplish this with skin color and gender" (1975: 12; see also Thomas, 1981; Palmore, 1981). Accordingly, the aging network has made a concerted effort to debunk prevailing myths about aging and correct erroneous assumptions about the elderly that are fostered in the media and perpetuated in everyday situations. Such efforts, particularly as they reinforce and interact with new scientific information, popular insights about the dynamics of aging, and the elderly's own behavior and observations, have contributed to a redefinition of what it means to grow older.

New perspectives are becoming discernible among key elements of the population. Systematic analyses of children's and youth's perceptions of the elderly during the past two decades have documented a decline in negative attitudes, as well as a greater understanding of the problems and opportunities which are encountered in later years (Ansello, 1977; Seltzer and Atchley, 1971). Special training sessions in gerontology for health-care professionals and social workers, and workshops on aging in high schools and other adult education centers are demonstrably effective in remedying false notions about the aged. Among other things, they encourage service providers and family members to seek the elderly's advice about the type of help they really want and need. Data for large national surveys, moreover, repeatedly show statistically significant age-related increases in satisfaction with housing, community life, and work. Indeed, when asked to evaluate their sense of well-being in all domains of their lives, older people responded neutrally or positively (Harris et al., 1975; Cutler, 1979; Herzog and Rodgers, 1981). Although poor health and low family income do lower the aged's overall satisfaction, more positive opinions about old age are being disseminated and taking hold.

Clearly, then, a case can be made for genuine accomplishments of the Great Society toward improving the actual and perceived position of the elderly in the United States. Yet even in the two areas that we have discussed, much remains to be done. The number of elderly men and women living with minimal resources continues to be staggering. In 1977, the median income for aged families was about $9,000, nearly $7,000 lower than the figure for all American families. Roughly a quarter of the elderly lack an income sufficient to support "a minimum adequate permanent diet" (Binstock, 1978: 1839; Schulz, 1980: 46). There are acute pockets of poverty within the elderly population. The financial condition of a large proportion of older Americans is quite vulnerable and, in all likelihood, will remain so. Similarly, the emergence of new images of age and aging is encouraging. This development, however, does not signal the elimination of ageist sentiments in any segment of American society, much less indicate a well-informed sense of how to make further gains in this area (Harris and Feinberg, 1977). A Louis Harris poll, released shortly before the 1981 White House Conference on Aging, indicated that stereotypic images of what it means to grow old(er) continue to be widely held by all age groups.

Indeed, even the most sanguine, partisan supporter of Great Society initiatives must acknowledge the extent to which these efforts have not alleviated problems of aging that the federal government officially committed itself to remedying. Much of the criticism about current aging policies focuses on ironies in social-welfare reform efforts initiated since the 1960s. Ironies certainly do abound in the ways we plan, administer, and evaluate old-age programs. Nevertheless, their full ramifications can be grasped only in the context of central paradoxes that characterize their impact on the people they were designed to help. The elderly did quite well insofar as their presumed needs meshed with the reform impulse of the decade and their "problems" seemed remediable by Great Society "solutions." Yet while this approach was fruitful, it proved counterproductive insofar as the conditions of the aged did not "fit" into the welfare paradigm or the elderly's needs themselves changed. To illustrate this point, it is worth examining the gains and shortcomings of federal health-care programs.

Medicare and Medicaid as a Test Case

Medicare coverage now reaches nearly the entire elderly population. In 1972, benefits were also extended to the disabled and people suffering from chronic kidney disease. Though Medicare payment schedules for various services are subject to certain deductibles and co-payment provisions, the range of diagnostic and physical therapy has increased over time (*Social Security Bulletin,* 1976: 20; Gold et al., 1977: 13–16). Tracing the legislative history of Medicaid is more complicated. Washington reimburses the states for from 50 percent to 83 percent of the costs, depending on per capita income. Since the inauguration of the federal Supplemental Security Income (SSI) program in 1974, states have been required to cover everyone eligible for cash assistance, including families with dependent children. A 1976 amendment preserved the Medicaid eligibility of recipients who became ineligible for cash SSI benefits because of cost-of-living increases in Social Security benefits. The unanticipated growth in the cost of Medicaid provisions—program costs quadrupled between 1968 and 1976—has led to persistent attempts to trim expenditures by curbing the range of coverage for mandatory services and permitting states to drop certain options.

Considerable evidence indicates that Medicare and Medicaid have improved the nature and increased the amount of health-care services available to the elderly. There has been a remarkable rise in the hospital care received by the aged. The annual number of visits to doctors made by an average older person has increased. Survey data gathered by the National Center for Health Statistics reveal a marked decline among elderly Americans in the limitation of their activities because of chronic conditions. The number of restricted activity days has declined more than 15 percent (Davis and Schoen, 1978: 102–4, 118). Researchers also attribute to Medicaid most of the recent gains in health-care accessibility and reductions in morbidity and mortality rates among the nation's poor. Though the aged as a group derive fewer benefits from Medicaid than they do from Medicare, roughly 20 percent of all Medicaid beneficiaries are over the age of sixty-five; the elderly consume roughly 40 percent of that program's outlays. Indeed, Medicaid has contributed to—and subsidized—the expansion of institutional care for the elderly. The program can provide personal care, food, and shelter to the aged within nursing homes but not in private, independent residences. Hence, there is a clear incentive to consider institutionalization as a long-term health-care option. Since nursing home costs typically run between $10,000 and $12,000 annually, many older people rely on Medicaid and the matching federal grants to states to reduce the burden of medical expenditures to be borne by them, relatives, and friends. Not surprisingly, Medicaid currently pays 60 percent of this nation's nursing home bills; Medicare pays an additional 7 percent (Davis and Schoen, 1978: pp. 49–50; Gold et al., 1977: 15–16).

There are serious problems in existing programs, despite the extraordinary growth of federal expenditures for Medicare and Medicaid. Since 1965, the aged have found it more and more costly to stay healthy and get well. Access to services varies considerably by income, race, ethnicity, educational level, and geographic location (Levitan et al., 1975: 226–33; Davis and Schoen, 1978: 92–94). Sometimes potential beneficiaries are unable to avail themselves of services simply because they cannot travel to health-care centers. Getting plugged into the right network also poses difficulties. Current regulations and program restrictions occasionally put the aged into a "catch-22" situation. Medicare, for instance, does not cover such basic and expensive health-care costs as hearing aids, prescription drugs, eyeglasses, or dentures, but it will help defray the cost of cosmetic surgery. While the program covers most hospital costs, Medicare requires eligible patients to pay the deductibles before benefits begin. As a result, many decide to postpone necessary surgery because they do not think they can afford to pay the increased cost of deductibles. Delays and bureaucratic hassles in Medicaid reimbursements test the humanitarian spirit and liquidity of honest nursing home administrators. The welter of rules and number of vendors have enabled unscrupulous operators to bilk the system while they victimize the helpless and ill. The soaring cost of health care and hospitalization in America—often at a rate that exceeds inflation in other sectors of the economy—has placed a tremendous burden on all Americans. Those who need long-term treatment but cannot afford commercial insurance premiums are particularly vulnerable. Runaway costs and past failures to contain (much less control) price increases threaten the financial stability of the system as a whole.

Very often, disappointment over the "failure" of programs to achieve their original goals prompts analysts to underestimate their present value. According to Brandeis University political scientist Robert H. Binstock, who served as executive director of the White House Task Force under Lyndon Johnson, one of the major policy issues of the 1980s will be whether Americans can—and should—continue to support and expand costly measures that have failed thus far to improve significantly the physical well-being of an important and growing segment of the population:

> Federal expenditures for health care have done little to alleviate the health problems of the aging. The medicare and medicaid programs enacted in 1965 have helped to defray the costs of seeing doctors, staying in hospitals, and obtaining several additional specific health services and goods. But these programs have not had an impact on the health status of older persons, whether aggregated for all persons sixty-five and older or disaggregated for different groups within that population (Binstock, 1978: 1839).

Yet the truly significant shortcomings in health-care programs for the nation's elderly are not simply a function of distributional inequities, benefit gaps, and cash flow problems. Despite Binstock's gloomy evaluation, Medicare and Medicaid *have* improved the elderly's overall health status. The *real* crisis arises from a failure to analyze the aged's situation in terms other than those that neatly fit predetermined categories and policy strategies. By treating the elderly like every other "needy" group, policymakers have often ignored or missed the special needs that older Americans have. In retrospect, it becomes evident that Medicare and Medicaid have failed in at least three ways to focus on how a health-care program for the *aged* could—and should—differ from a program for the *aging,* that is, one for all age groups. These ways are as follows:

1. *The range of services now available to older people does not effectively meet their demonstrable health needs.* Existing health-care systems for the elderly reflect and result from the most recent stages of the "therapeutic revolution." Modern advances have transformed the ways that bio-medical scientists diagnose illnesses and prescribe treatments for infants, children, adolescents, youth, and the middle-aged. Programs intended for the aged also conform to a therapeutic model: Medicare and Medicaid are primarily designed to deal with acute illnesses and to enable physicians and other experts to take advantage of the latest advances in medical science when they treat their patients (Pellegrino, 1979: 254–56; Shanas and Maddox, 1976: 614). I do not mean to suggest that the intense search for pharmacotherapeutic cures, the preoccupation with ailments that can be "fixed" through corrective or radical surgery, and the liberal use of hospital services are pointless, needless, or frivolous. But one of the "lessons of the past" to be drawn from the history of geriatrics is that the therapeutic revolution has had little success in dealing with the degenerative and chronic illnesses of late life. Until a "cure" for old age is discovered, it may be more sensible to devote primary attention to the chronic illnesses and the physical and mental disabilities that afflict the aged. These are conditions that cannot always be relieved by "modern" therapeutic intervention, despite the usefulness of such intervention in improving the health status of younger people. Closer attention should be paid to how the elderly describe their health and adjust to their changing physical condition. Many old people have a resiliency and will to live that enables them to compensate for decrements that the young would consider "handicaps." Yet the American approach to dealing with the physical needs of late life too often filters out such evaluations.

2. *Because of current regulations, Americans do not utilize in-home care for the aged as a long-term care as much as they want or should.* Since the inauguration of Medicare and Medicaid, institutions have

played an increasingly significant role in delivering health services and providing care to the aged. The proportion of older Americans admitted to hospitals has risen steadily. The growth in the rate of short-stay admissions is especially striking. Nursing homes have become vital in-patient facilities, not only for the very old and disabled but also for healthy, aged men and women. Existing regulations, in fact, create situations in which a person would choose to be in an institution rather than at home. To qualify for Medicare reimbursement for home health care, for instance, a potential beneficiary must first have received treatment in a nursing home or hospital. Such uses of institutional resources have been deplored as wasteful, corrupt, and inefficient. There is considerable validity to these charges—as periodic nursing home scandals surely attest—but too often the critics seize on the wrong issue. While the need to reform nursing home practices and the conditions within that environment remains an important item on the policy agenda, the United States cannot afford to eliminate such institutions. They provide necessary services and an appropriate setting for a significant segment of the elderly population.

Furthermore, federal health-care programs are counterproductive because they ignore the fact that nursing homes and hospitals are not the major service providers to the aged. Though there is a 25 percent likelihood that a person over the age of sixty-five eventually will spend some time in a long-term care facility before he or she dies, only 5 percent of the aged population actually reside in nursing homes at any given moment. Historically, the family has been the primary caretaker for the aged sick. This remains the case today, in this country and abroad. There are more than twice as many older people bedfast and homebound than in institutions of any kind. Yet less than 3 percent of Medicare and roughly 1 percent of Medicaid reimburse home health care (Shanas et al., 1968; Shanas and Maddox, 1976: 608–10; Koff, 1982; statistics on reimbursement come from Wetle, 1980: 5). The increase in four-generation family networks, the rise of single households and the changes in women's working patterns and marital status, among other demographic trends, have placed new strains on the ability of family members to care for aged relatives. But it is doubtful that the family's role will diminish greatly in this area.

The health-care network established through Medicare and Medicaid, unfortunately, does not yet provide a "continuum" of care by relying on the comparative advantages of a "mix" of formal and informal institutions. Medicare and Medicaid fail to acknowledge the wide variety of living arrangements and health-care needs within the elderly population. Nursing homes and hospitals are one important resource, but so too are day-care centers that can offer temporary or respite care, programs that enable a person to stay at home by providing home-delivered meals and help with chores, and the wide range of familial networks and community services (E. Brody, 1979: 1828–33). Since Americans will continue to rely on institutions to provide necessary assistance to the aged, the definition of "institution" must be elastic enough to meet the needs of the elderly.

3. *Age-related and income-related programs do not form a coherent health-care policy for the aging.* Policymakers and social administrators have been understandably concerned with financial matters and logistical issues as they have sought to create an efficient system in which to deliver health services to the aged. In light of these concerns, the linking of Medicare to an age-related federal insurance program and the tying of Medicaid to an existing federal-state income-support system makes sense. However, a basic problem with this strategy is that the two-tiered system ignores several categories that are essential to any health-care policy. On the one hand, the system sidesteps the question of a patient's competency. The ability of a person to assess his or her overall well-being and to play a role in determining what is necessary to maintain and promote healthfulness does not depend on either age or income. If and when "competency" becomes an issue, therefore, it must be adjudicated by parties and bodies that are not necessarily expert in bio-medical or ethical affairs. As a result, since the 1960s the question of an elderly person's competency has been judged in an ad hoc, case-by-case manner (Tibbles, 1978: 127–51). On the other hand, neither an age-related or income-related health-care system has encouraged the development of new programs in preventive medicine. This is a regrettable consequence of current policies, since ample data confirm that men and women who eat and drink sensibly, refrain from tobacco, and exercise regularly throughout their lives increase their likelihood of enjoying good health in later years. From both an individual and a societal vantage point, preventing illness is less costly than trying to cure it. Thus, if health-care programs for the elderly are intended to be more cost-effective, encouraging the young and middle-aged to live in a more healthful manner should be an explicit policy goal.

The real problem, then, with Medicare and Medicaid is that they have failed to provide a coherent health-care program for the aged and the poor in an aging society. These programs were designed to accommodate new breakthroughs wrought by the so-called therapeutic revolution in bio-medical technology, but not to recognize the many features of human aging that elude such intervention. Existing legislation has failed to integrate public and private resources. Formal and informal institutions (such as the family and friends) are not linked into any health-care continuum. By continuing to institute reforms on an ad hoc, incremental basis, policymakers have shaped programs without serious consideration of whether radical reforms were needed to correct erroneous assumptions and ineffective policies.

And so, we arrive at a central paradox about the impact of Great Society legislation on the aged. On the one hand, older Americans greatly benefited from the politics of interest-group liberalism. Indeed, it would not be an exaggeration to argue that, by the mid-1970s, war-on-poverty initiatives had had a greater impact on the elderly than on any other segment of the population. Although old people were not the primary target of reformers during the Johnson years, the categorical programs designed for men and women over sixty-five survived the cutbacks and political controversies that vitiated legislative measures for youth, minorities, women, and other disadvantaged groups. Old-age programs actually continued to grow. They capitalized on well-established principles and expanded existing programs, which typically had a momentum of their own. On the other hand, the very success of this approach in dealing with older Americans' problems inhibited creative thinking about whether different strategies should be implemented. Too little consideration was paid to how all the various programs fit together. Possible changes to the status quo received scant attention because things, relatively speaking, were going well. Consequently, when reforms did become necessary, they were much harder to execute because they went against vested interests and sought to alter the political dynamics of inertia.

Concurrently, the prospects for reforming old-age programs were stymied by another ominous development. At the very moment that policy experts began to call for changes in the ways the elderly's problems were defined and dealt with, the federal government's capacity to reform and regulate its own programs diminished. There has been a pervasive breakdown in Washington's ability to manage its far-flung responsibilities and to anticipate new crises on the horizon. Paralleling the significant increase in activity and expenditures at the federal level has been a striking decline in governmental authority. Washington has been particularly unable to redress conflicts in the political economy and resolve tensions across various segments of society. Americans generally have become more skeptical about the ability and willingness of federal officials to do their jobs and attend to the public interest. As Figure 5.1 indicates, trust in government has dropped dramatically among all age groups since the

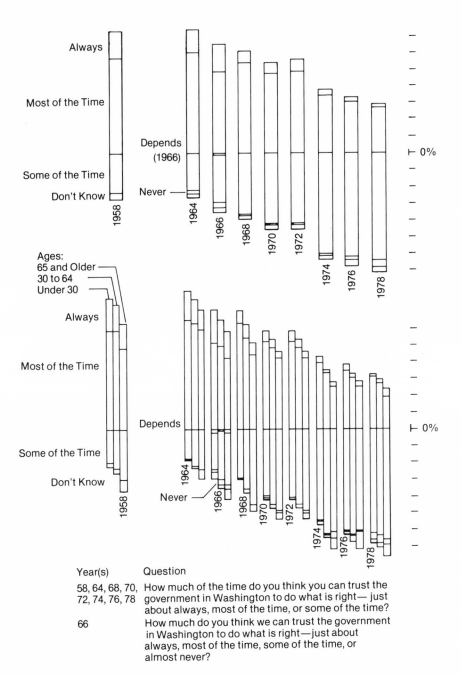

Figure 5-1. Trust in Government. [Source: Institute of Gerontology, *American Values and the Elderly* (Ann Arbor, 1979), p. S–64. Reprinted by permission.]

1960s. The decline is especially apparent among the elderly population.

Consequently, Americans have become increasingly disenchanted and disillusioned at the very moment that they have escalated their demands and begun to get progressively more generous benefits. Yesterday's expectations, ironically, have come to be viewed as today's entitlements. If dreams are not realized and initial goals not yet reached, discontent mounts, and indictments of the system seem all the more justifiable. To understand why this is so, it is instructive to look systematically at the crises that wracked the structure and dynamics of America's political economy, particularly since Lyndon Johnson left office on January 20, 1969.

The Shocking, Sobering Seventies

American society did not fall apart as a result of the anti-war protests, social violence, and social unrest of the late 1960s. Strains in the political economy nonetheless became more pronounced during the 1970s. The affairs of state preoccupying Johnson's successors illustrate the range of problems besetting the country at large. Presidents tried to impose order and inspire a sense of unity within the nation, but their actions served mainly to complicate matters by exacerbating mistrust and indifference among the electorate. Richard Nixon eventually managed to extricate American forces from Vietnam and scored dramatic diplomatic coups by promoting detente with the U.S.S.R. and visiting the People's Republic of China. He also sought to forge a new set of domestic policies (Moynihan, 1973; Burke and Burke, 1974). Nixon called for a "New Federalism" in order to reduce the scope and scale of federal involvement, which had been legitimized by the Warren Court and institutionalized through Great Society measures. The President succeeded in getting a measure of decontrol with a modest revenue-sharing program. Watergate, however, nullified his stunning victory in 1972 over liberal George McGovern and paralyzed the federal government. A golden opportunity to institutionalize a neo-conservative alternative to the Great Society had been squandered. Gerald Ford restored honor and decency to the Oval Office. He attempted to reduce the scope of Washington's activities by vetoing new bills for federal controls. Ford's inept handling of economic matters and seeming indifference to many persistent social problems, however, contributed to his defeat in 1976. Jimmy Carter correctly identified the central issues of the decade and proposed plausible ways to deal with the economy environment and international relations. Among other things, he pledged to reduce the number of federal programs. Yet Carter could not translate his vision of America into a viable program. He never really won support among congressional members of his own party. He failed to persuade the American people that his ideas would work.

Indeed, leaders in this country and other advanced industrial nations learned that three perennial economic issues—inflation, energy, and growth—posed new and largely unanticipated challenges that threatened their nations' very security and well-being. Inflation in the United States crept up from 2.2 percent in 1965 to 4.5 percent in 1968, rose to an annual rate of 5.9 percent by 1971, and then fluctuated between 5.5 percent and 11 percent during the mid-1970s. At the end of the decade, the inflation rate was still reaching double-digit figures and seemed virtually out of control. Steady rises in the wage-price spiral, presidential politics, inconsistencies and abrupt shifts in fiscal and monetary policies, and sudden alterations in international balances of trade and currency values all stoked the inflationary fires. Bad luck and poor timing also were contributing factors. Disappointing wheat and corn harvests here and abroad led to feverish and often shortsighted deals resulting in a 66 percent increase in American farm prices from 1971 to 1974. But the biggest shock to the economy was a series of decisions in 1973 and 1974 by the Organization of Petroleum Exporting Countries (OPEC), which tripled the price of oil and imposed embargos in order to demonstrate support for the Arab war against Israel. Americans, long accustomed to cheap and plentiful gas and oil, felt themselves vulnerable to the whims of sheiks and at the mercy of their own multinational oil companies. The impact of rampant inflation and rising energy costs, combined with the effects of a welter of new government regulations, rising interest rates, worker alienation, and an uncertain economic future, led in turn to a slowdown in the growth rate. Between 1948 and 1965, American productivity grew at 3.2 percent per annum. It declined to 2.3 percent during the next decade; then productivity fell to 1.1 percent from 1972 to 1978. At the same time, even though a greater percentage of Americans were in the labor force than ever before, unemployment rates rose to between 7 percent and 9 percent. The figures were much higher for young blacks and those without skills. The rate of idle capacity in the nation's factories and businesses soared. (Data in this paragraph come from Thurow, 1980: 43–46, 85, 191; and Wiebe, 1981: 922.)

Although the problems of inflation, energy, and growth were clearly interrelated, no quick panacea could ameliorate the situation. Keynesian macroeconomic remedies, which generally had worked in the past by lowering inflation at the expense of higher employment (or vice versa), no longer proved efficacious. It is not that the predicament defied solutions. Rather, the times demanded tough and politically unpopular choices about which segments of the American population would be forced to bear the costs of engineering a plan of recovery that would benefit all. "The problem with zero-sum games is that the essence of problem solving is loss allocation. But this is precisely what our political process is least capable of doing," observed Massachusetts Institute of Technology economist Lester C. Thurow. "When there are large economic losses to be allocated, our political process is paralyzed. And with political paralysis comes economic paralysis" (1980: 12). No group, including the aged, was prepared to jeopardize gains secured during the 1960s and 1970s to cope with the harsh new realities.

We now are in a better position to understand why the Great Society did not constitute a watershed in recent American history. Had the social turbulence triggered by the civil rights struggle, anti-war movement, and various protest groups been followed by a period of steady economic growth and societal tranquility, then it is quite possible that Americans would have returned to the tasks identified and challenges tackled in the war-on-poverty legislation. But the legacy and forecasts of boundless, endless affluence that originally inspired and justified the Great Society were dashed by stagflation. Americans' increasing misapprehension over the legitimacy and efficacy of their key societial institutions and their rising fears about the true "promise of American life," accentuated by ominous economic and ecological conditions at home and abroad, proved beyond the capacity of the political system. Optimistic game plans gave way to pessimistic dubiety. The modernization of twentieth-century America became vulnerable to the deleterious impact of the very demographic, economic, political, and social forces that had made its development the prototypical success story of all advanced industrial countries.

In this polarized and volatile context, the aged's current status and future prospects seemed more uncertain than they had for decades. A growing number of commentators argued that public policy measures adopted since 1965 to meet the needs and demands of an ever growing elderly population were "busting the U.S. budget." The aged, among the nation's most visible beneficiaries of federal concern and public intervention, were becoming the unwitting symbol for more widespread complaints about the course of recent federal initiatives. The passage of the Supplementary Security Income (SSI) program and the decision to implement automatic indexing of old-age retirement benefits, for example, surely justified the claim made by Social Security officials and by liberal and moderate commentators that 1972 was a red-letter date in the evolution of Social Security. In retrospect, however, there may be a less auspicious reason for hypothesizing that 1972 marked a critical turning point in the program's history. Congress made a serious technical error in the 1972 amendments to the Social Security Act, by adopting a double-indexed formula that overadjusted Title II benefits against the deleterious effect of inflation on retirement income (Kaplan, 1977). Although the formula for calculating benefits was subsequently corrected, this embarrassing—and expensive—error ushered in a new phase of criticism against the Social Security system itself, which persisted through the rest of the decade and continued into the 1980s. Since 1972, policymakers have debated and tinkered with various economic options for putting the system on a sounder financial basis. Yet, according to many media reports and critics of the program, Social Security continually seems to be on the brink of bankruptcy. As a result, public confidence in one of the nation's most successful social programs was shaken. Older Americans increasingly feared that a major source of their economic security would be curtailed. More and more young people believed that Social Security would not be as good a financial deal for them as it was for their grandparents and parents. Amid the bombast over the future of Social Security, stereotypic images of age were rampant. Concerns over Social Security colored attitudes about the elderly.

Analyses of government spending between 1969 and 1980, moreover, revealed that appropriations for income-security and health-care programs, as well as other direct benefits provided under the Older Americans Act, had risen from 20 percent to more than 40 percent of the total budget. Many appropriations for the elderly were regarded as "uncontrollable items" bound to become even more expensive (Samuelson, 1978: 256–60; Hudson, 1978: 428–40; U.S. Senate Special Committee on Aging, 1981: vii). Such estimates about the present and proximate price of maintaining old-age programs prompted closer scrutiny of cost-benefit ratios and undermined public sympathy for the elderly. Gerontologist Robert Binstock observed:

> The remarkably large proportion of federal spending that is devoted to programs for the elderly is becoming well known. . . . What has not been emphasized sufficiently, however, is the extent to which the current expenditure of $112 billion on programs for the aging represents an indictment of the American style of domestic public policy. One might expect that if the federal government allocates one-quarter of its budget to a particular target population of 23 million citizens, then that population's economic, health and social problems would be substantially alleviated. Yet, that is not the case (1978: 1838).

Some predicted that open generational warfare would ensue. They expected the gray lobby to be pitted against other special-interest groups in an increasingly factitious competition for smaller and smaller shares of the federal budget. Circumstances seemed propitious, at the very least, for a serious reassessment of the cultural values and political calculus that would influence policy choices in aging America during the years ahead. For this reason, the presidential campaign of 1980 may well be interpreted decades from now as a critical election. Returns on election night indicated that Americans were not altogether sure where they were headed, but they knew that they could not afford another four years of drifting from crisis to crisis. Hence, in overwhelming numbers, they had cast their ballots for a candidate who promised to turn things around.

Senator John Heinz (chairman of the U.S. Senate Special Committee on Aging), Representative Claude Pepper (chairman of the U.S. House of Representatives Select Committee on Aging), and Jack Ossofsky (executive director of The National Council on the Aging, Inc.) discuss the implications of "Reaganomics" for the elderly at a Joint Congressional Hearing. [Courtesy of The National Council on the Aging, Inc.]

Chapter
6

Toward the
Next Watershed in
the History of
Aging America

Reaganomics and the Future Direction
of Federal Activities

In their acceptance speeches, presidential nominees typically align their views on the contemporary political scene and visions of America's future with those expressed by luminaries from the past. Ronald Reagan was no exception. At the end of his acceptance speech to the delegates gathered in Detroit for the 1980 Republican convention, Reagan declared:

> The time is now to redeem promises once made to the American people by another candidate, in another time and another place. He said: " . . . We must consolidate subdivisions of government and, like the private citizen, give up luxuries which we can no longer afford . . . . I propose to you my friends, and through you, that government of all kinds, big and little, be made solvent and that the example be set by the President of the United States and his cabinet." That was (sic) Franklin Delano Roosevelt's words as he accepted the Democratic nomination for President in 1932 . . . Isn't it time that we, the people, carry out these unkept promises? That we pledge to each other and to all America on this July day 48 years later, that now we intend to do just that (*New York Times,* July 18, 1980: A8).

Invoking the name of Franklin Delano Roosevelt was a stroke of political genius. No president since Roosevelt has exercised so much influence on the course of twentieth-century American society and culture. Franklin Roosevelt's first one-hundred days set a standard by which journalists and politicians alike have measured every subsequent chief executive's initial style and performance. Legislation enacted and precedents established during the remainder of Roosevelt's tenure in office transformed dominant values and institutional structures in ways that continue to shape aging America. By reminding listeners of Franklin Roosevelt's legacy, the candidate was setting the stage for another revolution in the normative and social foundations of this nation's political economy, which he hoped his administration would effect. At the very least, Reagan was asserting that he had deviated from important political objectives far less than the Democratic party had during the last half-century. The Republican standard-bearer, after all, had begun as a New Deal Democrat. Reagan's neo-conservative philosophy of government—one which seemingly echoes Roosevelt's own outlook—was being celebrated as the basis for a new direction in public affairs. "The time is now to say that we shall seek new friendships and expand others and improve others, but we shall not do so by breaking our word or casting aside old friends and allies." By appealing to all factions, Reagan was attempting to carve out a centrist position—the place at which Roosevelt had shown all effective presidents must operate, particularly if they intend to change the nature and direction of American domestic policies.

After soundly beating Jimmy Carter and helping the Republicans to capture the Senate, Reagan accomplished enough during his first six months in office to indicate that the allusion to Franklin D. Roosevelt was no mere rhetorical ploy. The new President moved quickly. Contending that the economic crisis of the 1980s was as serious as the Great Depression itself, Reagan promised to act decisively in a variety of areas. His major initiatives were supported by "supply-side" economic theorists and conservative politicians. He slowed down the rate at which the federal government grew by reducing the scope of Washington's activities. He pressed for a simultaneous reduction in individual and corporate taxes in order to stimulate productivity. Like Roosevelt, Reagan tried to convince the American people that his actions were in the best interest of all segments of the population. Television cameras conveyed his warm personality and soothing words as effectively as the radio had transmitted presidential "fireside chats" decades earlier. Furthermore, even though he was the first governor since Franklin Roosevelt elected to the presidency, Ronald Reagan demonstrated that the experiences gained in governing a large, diversified, and densely populated state did prepare him for tackling the nation's biggest job. Besides mustering popular support, he skillfully used the perquisites of his office to win congressional approval of his legislative package. With few exceptions, he knew how to count votes. He consistently endeavored to appear above the fray, letting his lieutenants take the political heat.

Franklin Roosevelt's 1932 victory proved to be a critical election, because Democrats capitalized on volatile political realignments forming in the 1920s and then ushered into power a new liberal coalition, which sustained itself intellectually and institutionally for several decades. It is too early to tell whether Reagan's presidency will have a similar effect on the Republican party's fortunes. The 1980 victory may be short lived. The GOP clearly benefited from the rising tide of neo-conservative sentiments and the efforts of New Right political action committees, which have been gaining power in the American political arena since the early 1970s. Furthermore, national leaders, regardless of their political persuasions, must grapple with the skyrocketing national deficit and mounting number of "uncontrollable" items in the federal budget. Because reducing the federal deficit in the 1980s has become an essential feature of economic recovery and a condition for future growth, *any* administration would have made austerity and decentralization top priorities.

If neo-conservatism is indeed to become the reigning ideology and if the GOP is to regain its former dominance on the national and state level, then supporters of Reaganomics need to demonstrate that the 1980 election results were not a fluke. They must increase their majority in the Senate, dominate the House, and retain the White House. They must continue to hammer out a new set of programs and policy initiatives consistent with the party's political credo. Above all, Reagan's economic package must work.[1]

For this reason, it may prove in retrospect more accurate to draw parallels between Ronald Reagan and another Roosevelt, Franklin's second cousin, Theodore. On a superficial level, the two figures seem to be mirror images of each other. Upon taking office, Theodore Roosevelt was the youngest man ever to occupy the White House; Ronald Reagan was the oldest person ever to be inaugurated. Because of Teddy's reputation for brash, if not downright childish, behavior, even Republican party leaders feared what "that damned cowboy" might try to do when he assumed power after McKinley's assassination. Yet Roosevelt was probably the most effective chief executive since Abraham Lincoln because his comparative youth and boundless enthusiasm made for a vigorous presidency. Though

[1] Critics of the New Deal, of course, could note that it was World War II, not Roosevelt's remedies, that lifted the nation out of economic depression and kept the Democrats in power. Nevertheless, the legislation enacted during Roosevelt's first one-hundred days was not judged a failure by Wall Street and on Main Street even before it went into effect; the same cannot be said of Reagan's measures. By the fall of 1981, the United States had entered yet another deep recession. The President maintained his commitment to raise defense spending and cut social-welfare programs despite the gloomy economic forecasts and decreased revenues. As time went on, Reagan was forced to acknowledge that budget deficits would be far greater than he had anticipated. Many of his own advisors recommended a change in policies. Not surprisingly, the debate among top economic advisors, against the backdrop of soaring unemployment, high interest rates, and low productivity, fueled more and more doubts about the soundness of the Reagan program.

Reagan's age was never made a campaign issue, it surely was on voters' minds. The President's strong recovery from an assassination attempt as well as his dynamic style have underscored the contributions that can be made by older people blessed with sound health and an unwavering sense of purpose.

On a deeper level, historians may well conclude that both men were reformers who failed to re-form society as much as they desired because they were slighly ahead of their times. Theodore Roosevelt certainly reflected his era's prevailing attitudes, insofar as he passionately shared the soaring optimism and patriotic tide ushering in "the American century." But he disagreed with his contemporaries, who believed that America's success hinged on preserving the late-nineteenth-century political order. Roosevelt realized that the federal government had to take a more active role in regulating the political economy. Thus in the presidential campaign of 1912, he called for a "New Nationalism" in which Big Government would increasingly serve to counterbalance the growing power and influence of Big Business. Roosevelt lost the election and, with it, the chance to use the president's "bully pulpit" to achieve his objectives. But eventually his vision did become political reality. Woodrow Wilson had beaten Roosevelt by calling for a return to Jeffersonian and Jacksonian ideals. Once in office, however, Wilson adhered more closely to the principles of the New Nationalism than he did to his own party platform. The lines of continuity between Theodore Roosevelt's Progressivism and Franklin Roosevelt's orientation, moreover, have been well documented (Schlesinger, 1958; Blum, 1980; Steel, 1980). Ronald Reagan was in an analogous situation. He entered office when the American century seemed to be foundering. Though he disagreed with those who saw the United States entering an era of diminishing expectations, Reagan nonetheless seized on the rising dissatisfaction with Washington. He characterized the federal government as bloated, wasteful, and counterproductive. Reagan campaigned on the promise that he would reverse the historical tide of public affairs by revitalizing the private sector's role in managing the economy and restoring to lower levels of government prerogatives and responsibilities taken over by the federal establishment during the twentiety century. Reagan did not weaken the power of the presidency in setting national priorities, but he did seek a reduction in the range of bureaucratic activities in the Capital. He hoped to reorder institutional arrangements so as to conform to the growing belief that there were limits to what Washington could accomplish.

Even if Reagan fails to achieve his goals, it seems likely that his views on government and his basic principles would have to be utterly repudiated by an abysmal failure in actual practice for them not to have an impact on the way politicians and policymakers go about their business in the future. It appears doubtful at this point that any major national figure could advocate a return to the policy assumptions and programs of the Great Society. Both incumbents and aspirants to high office must come to grips, intellectually and politically, with the case against the Johnson years made by neo-conservatives and espoused by Reagan's advisors. The political dialogue has changed. Nixon, Ford, and Carter hoped to reduce waste and inefficiency in Washington. Through a succession of bloc grants and revenue-sharing schemes, they attempted to give state and local government more power. Despite their hopes, their reforms did not accomplish much. Reagan, in contrast, gave neo-conservatism a new respectability. He boldly set the stage for "the New Federalism" in less than a year. As a result, even aging liberals have had to modify their game plans and campaign promises. In that sense Ronald Reagan, like Theodore Roosevelt, may well help to usher in a new stage of political modernization without himself being at the epicenter of decisive change.

Of course, should Reaganomics prove to have disastrous consequences, and if the President's programs are vetoed at the polls, then any comparison between Theodore Roosevelt and Ronald Reagan would do the former a grave disservice. Reagan's "conservative counterrevolution" in macroeconomic policies has been praised by its theorists and supporters as a necessary antidote to the economic woes ushered in during the Vietnam era. Critics worry, however, that Reaganomics rests on untested hypotheses that might exacerbate the current crisis. Yale professor James Tobin, who won the 1981 Nobel Prize in Economics, observes:

> The "new federalism," as is only beginning to be realized, will have devastating effects on the finances of many state and local governments, and on the services they render, especially to the poor. Meanwhile the tax cuts will be widening the gulf between the living standards of the rich and those of the poor, without the promised compensation in the conquest of stagflation. . . . In the end, I think, a democratic polity will not tolerate in its government and central bank an economic strategy of indifference to the real state of the economy (1981: 14).

Should Tobin's gloomy forecast come true, it would be harsher but more historically accurate to suggest that Reagan, in spite of himself, had managed to combine the worst features of some of his predecessors. Journalists and political pundits will note that, like Calvin Coolidge and Herbert Hoover, Reagan hewed to obsolescent economic theories when nearly everyone else had become convinced that they were worsening the crisis. Like Johnson, he tried to increase defense spending without raising taxes and controlling inflation, and thus aggravated the situation. Like his immediate predecessors, the President proved unable to turn things around even though he assumed office with high public expectations that he would do just that!

While we certainly cannot judge yet whether Reagan is ahead of—or considerably behind—the times, there can be no doubt that he is attempting to change the status quo in fundamental ways. The new direction in federal activities is most evident in the area of welfare reform. Just as Theodore Roosevelt relied on Herbert Croly's *The Promise of American Life* (1909) to give intellectual cogency to his "progressive" proposals, Ronald Reagan initially turned to Martin Anderson as his chief advisor in reshaping the domestic agenda. Anderson had been helping Republican candidates and presidents to formulate national welfare policies since 1968. A senior fellow at Stanford University's Hoover Institution during the 1970s, he published a series of influential articles and books arguing that a strong President could reform America's welfare system by reordering its priorities and making programmatic changes to increase efficiency and popular support. The policy recommendations Anderson set forth in *Welfare* (1978) actually provided the conceptual framework for Reagan's welfare-reform proposals during his first year in office. The President's package rested on three premises:

1. *Future welfare initiatives should be targeted toward the truly "needy."*
   Reagan repeatedly embraced the New Deal principle that the federal government must bear responsibility for assisting those who cannot care for themselves. The administration intended to limit federal welfare programs, in fact, to those who were undeniably in need. To prevent a rise in the incidence of welfare, officials recommended enforcing incentives toward self-reliance. Anderson observed:

   > If a person is capable of taking care of himself, he is independent and should not qualify for any amount of welfare. . . . To the extent that a person is dependent—that is, to the extent that he cannot care for himself—to that extent he qualifies for welfare. If he can earn part of what he needs, then he has an obligation to work to that extent (1978: 162).

By equating "welfare" with absolute "need," Reagan and his advisors clearly eschewed the wide-ranging agenda established by architects of the Great Society, who had hoped to assuage "relative poverty" and eliminate deprivation. They also were less willing to allocate federal resources that might enable the disadvantaged to make rapid gains in enhancing their economic conditions and political status.

The Reagan administration's rejection of war-on-poverty

ideals and strategies did not mean that they considered the Great Society a "failure." On the contrary, one of Anderson's major theses is that the war on poverty has been won. The explosion in federal spending for new social services and income-transfer programs, coupled with the growth in jobs and income in the private sector, according to this interpretation, has virtually extirpated poverty in America. Citing evidence from Brookings Institution economists, experts at the Congressional Budget Office, and conservative analysts, Anderson claimed that official statistics overstate the extent of absolute deprivation in the United States. Less than 5 percent of the total population lacks basic goods and services, he argued, if one includes the cash value of in-kind benefits, adjusts for the underreporting of earnings among welfare beneficiaries, and considers all of the existing tax breaks and overlapping sources of support available to the poor.

Reagan and his advisors were appalled, however, by the costly side effects of the Great Society initiatives. They deplored (perhaps to the point of exaggerating) the amount of waste and corruption made possible by the proliferation of vast bureaucracies. They were alarmed by the soaring cost of entitlement programs, particularly at a time when they sought to contain and ultimately reduce government spending. They believed that these measures had created a new caste of "dependent Americans," whose basic wants were satisfied but who had become so comfortable on welfare that they preferred to remain wards of the state and live off the taxes of hard-working, middle-class Americans. Thus Reagan was committed to helping those who were truly "needy," but he did not want the system to provide services to cheats and free-loaders, or to do anything that might vitiate the work ethic.

2. *Radical welfare reform efforts should be opposed.* Although the President plainly intended to curtail the excesses of the Great Society, he had no panaceas in mind. Reagan's public statements were consistent with Anderson's opinion that "no radical welfare reform plan can be devised that will simultaneously yield minimum levels of welfare benefits, financial incentives to work, and an overall cost to the taxpayers that are politically acceptable" (Anderson, 1978: 132). In particular, the administration opposed the idea of providing a minimum income, except to those who truly could not fend for themselves. Thus Supplemental Security Income (SSI) was acceptable because it was targeted to the blind, disabled, and men and women over the age of sixty-five. In the administration's view, however, SSI should not become the basis for a more ambitious federal welfare program.

Guaranteed-income schemes, accordingly, were to be

avoided on ideological, economic, and political grounds. To Reagan, such schemes are ideologically suspect because they have been proposed by those who subscribe to "liberal" policies designed to redistribute income and ensure greater equality of result.[2] Guaranteed-income measures make no sense economically, because in theory and in some limited experimentation they can be shown to reduce people's incentives to work. Insofar as such schemes have failed to capture the popular imagination or win the endorsement of Republican leaders, they stand little chance of approval during the current administration.

3. *The trend toward a centralized, welfare bureaucracy must be reversed.* Rather than scrap the status quo, Reagan and his advisors proposed to reform the system by redefining the extent of coverage provided at the federal level. They also reevaluated the cost-benefit ratio of various programs in accordance with their overarching philosophical principles. This entailed a twofold strategy that was based on the President's prior experiences as governor of California and on Anderson's proposals in *Welfare.* On the one hand, it required streamlining federal activities in an effort to (a) eliminate fraud, (b) remove beneficiaries who did not deserve to be on the rolls, (c) improve the effectiveness and efficiency of federal operations, and (d) enforce rules requiring people to fulfill their moral and legal obligations to spouses and other relatives. On the other hand, it meant that the authority and responsibility for designing, administering, funding, and evaluating welfare programs would increasingly devolve to lower units of government and to the private sector. In order to implement a program that permits only the "needy" to gain benefits and insists that all others work to promote their own well-being, planners envisioned a more decentralized, people-oriented mode of welfare administration. Private foundations, churches, fraternal groups, and charitable organizations were expected to make up for lost federal revenues. Tax incentives were proposed to encourage individuals to give more generously to charity and to take care of their own.

President Reagan's proposed changes appealed to large segments of the population on both philosophical and political grounds. Emphasizing a needy-only approach to welfare sounded both reasonable and economical. It surely conformed to the perennial American

---

[2] The conservative economist and Nobel laureate Milton Friedman, who has advocated a negative income tax, at first glance seems an exception to this corollary. But Friedman, we are told by Anderson and other neo-conservative commentators, endorses some guaranteed-income measures because he thinks they would be more efficient and because he believes that they obviate the need for Social Security and other welfare programs. The Reaganites find that scenario dubious, fearing that it would be impossible to dismantle the entire social-welfare program. Social Security may be transformed, they believe, but it never can be dismantled.

celebration of the work ethic. Without reviving the nineteenth-century distinction between the "deserving" and "undeserving" poor, it nonetheless fed upon and was sustained by this nation's perennially negative attitude toward those who cannot achieve and/or maintain a middle-class standard of living (Patterson, 1981; Tropman, 1976, 1978). It enabled the Reagan administration to justify reducing the federal government's commitments in the welfare arena and to advance other priorities, such as defense buildups, all the while claiming that a "safety net" for the truly helpless remained intact. Efforts to eliminate waste and reduce abuse, moreover, are always judged commendable and fair. And insofar as Washington does better at setting guidelines and monitoring results than at administering programs, any reasonable proposal to reduce the distance (literally and figuratively) between welfare administrators and recipients was worth trying.

Reagan's proposals, however, made more sense on their own terms than they did in the context of recent American social-welfare history. The President and his experts may well have been correct in asserting that the war on poverty had been won. But that said, it must be quickly added that waging a "war" against poverty is an ongoing battle, particularly in a decade in which the economic outlook is uncertain and the employment prospects are bleak for the very people who will have to rely on welfare if they cannot find a job. Who is "needy" under such adverse circumstances? To what extent is that "need" compounded by prior discrimination, and thus not simply a function of hard times? Anderson's analysis studiously avoids a discussion of race. (It is noteworthy that "black," "Negro," and "race" do not appear in the index.) Yet surely the racial dimensions of poverty have loomed large for decades: can Americans really hope to reform the national welfare system without addressing this issue? Obviously not.

How do the aged fit into the New Federalism? President Reagan signed a three-year reauthorization of the Older Americans Act in December 1981, but left open the option of cutting back or eliminating current entitlements and social services. Do Reagan's reforms mesh with American values and current federal old-age programs, or do they interject a new shade of gray? Do they take account of recent changes in the meanings and experiences of being old in the United States? Do they treat the aged as a special group, or will the aged be categorized according to new criteria? Are the proposals premised on the assumption that new behavioral patterns among the aged and across the generations are desirable and/or imminent?

To address such questions, we should examine the points of divergence and convergence between Reagan's welfare program and the dynamics of recent American history. To what extent has Reagan attempted to alter the historical equilibrium across the seven value dimensions I have identified as inherent in any "modern" federal program for aging America? Has he ignored long-standing issues, by avoiding the implicit and explicit tensions within and among policy choices? Has he attempted to modify the status quo without really coming to grips with major normative dilemmas?

How Should the Federal Government Categorize the Elderly?

How should the federal government categorize who among the elderly get what, when, and why? The twentieth century's problem-oriented perspective that old age is a legitimate social-welfare category has proved beneficial. A nationwide institutional approach to the major health-related, financial, and social difficulties that threaten an older person's well-being has demonstrably improved older Americans' overall economic position. Vital social services and community programs are now provided across the country. Because of the availability of unprecedented amounts of research funds in the public and private sector, Americans presently have a better understanding of the personal, economic, biological, and social forces that may diminish the quality of late life than any preceding generation in American history.

Despite such laudable achievements, however, the prevailing method of defining and dealing with the aged's needs has come under tremendous fire. Policymakers increasingly acknowledge difficulties inherent in formulating, implementing, and assessing aging programs. They often make dubious policy assumptions and use inadequate social indicators because they are the most readily available. Officials bow to expediency in an effort to placate (or manipulate) constituencies, enemies, and special-interest groups—without determining how innovations and amendments interact with existing policies for the aged and how they affect different groups in society. Incumbents, critics, journalists, and other commentators use divergent criteria in designing and evaluating social programs: they typically claim success or concede failure according to standards that bear little relation to original objectives and initial goals.

Large-scale changes in cultural norms, societal expectations, and social processes in recent decades, moreover, have created a new set of policy-relevant circumstances. Programs for the aged too often are designed without a clear idea of whom they should assist and what impact changes in existing policies might have. Bureaucrats perpetrate policy assumptions that steadily have less and less basis in empirical reality. It is painfully clear that people over the age of sixty-five with similar needs are not invariably entitled to the same amount of assistance. Depending on the program, a household with a female head may get more assistance than one with an elderly male head, or vice versa. Because of the lack of integration among various anti-poverty programs, the elderly are sometimes hurt more than they are helped by reforms. The 20-percent increase in Social Security benefits in 1972, for instance, placed large numbers of older men and women over the poverty line, thus making them ineligible for Medicaid and food stamps. Ironically, more income actually worsened the situation of many elderly Americans.

Reagan's welfare reformers believe in categorizing older Americans primarily in terms of need. Those elderly men and women who are unable to care for themselves should receive assistance. They also should be eligible to receive benefits through existing programs of health care and social services. So far, so good: the Reagan philosophy seems consistent with prevailing views of categorical assistance. A major difficulty with this approach, however, is that it does not squarely confront the issue of whether chronological age per se should continue to serve as the basis for providing categorical assistance in a needy-only welfare system. Like the architects of the Great Society, the Reagan team seems to have ignored the extent to which programs for the aged do not mesh neatly with other "welfare" programs. They may be mistaken about the degree to which categorical policies for the *aging* will be too diffuse to meet the specific needs of the *aged,* and vice versa.

Can we create viable programs for older Americans that address their problems without, in the process, stereotyping old age and segregating the elderly from other segments of society? This question, of course, raises tough choices about some of the most important items on the domestic agenda today. At least two of the value dimensions we have discussed in this book bear directly on whom the federal government should assist. Regardless of what Reagan or his successors say they want to do, their programs must address and accommodate recent social and cultural trends that affect the way the elderly are categorized. As we shall see, the historical dimensions of the dependency/self-reliance and the entitlement/expectation issues have been transformed.

The Dependency / Self-Reliance Issue

Reagan's needy-only approach to old-age policies does not adequately deal with recent trends in the dependency/self-reliance issue. The continuing view of old age as a generic "social problem" has itself become problematic. Deliberately or unwittingly overestimating the extent of deprivation and dependency among the elderly often proved advantageous to those attempting to win new support for the gray lobby. It also enabled officials to maintain current benefit levels and press for more funds to assist the elderly. But this strategy had a stiff price. By focusing attention on the multitudinous woes of old age, lobbyists for the aged and commentators accentuated the pervasive image of the elderly as hapless, passive, pitiful "objects" different from the rest of the population. Those who read or heard the "facts" found their worst premonitions about growing older and deepest fears about becoming elderly confirmed. It typically was easier to seize on the dependency of older people than to acknowledge the aged's ability to maintain independence. Defining "old" as a social and political category for determining need tempted experts to discuss the problems of the aged as if they arose and persisted in a vacuum. Among other things, this attitude increased the probability that policymakers would ignore the elderly's ongoing links with other age groups.

And yet, if policymakers should no longer categorize all older people as "dependent," what labels are more appropriate? Unfortunately, Americans have been unable to come up with alternatives that do not interject their own set of regrettable ramifications. There has been a conscious attempt since at least the 1940s, for instance, to foster a more positive societal appreciation for the advantages of old age. As we have seen, this results in part from the search by middle-aged and older Americans for broader opportunities for intellectual growth, greater life satisfaction, and fuller participation in the mainstream of society. It reflects the findings of social researchers who have documented that the current generation of elderly persons actually *is* better able than previous cohorts to engage in voluntary service, gainful employment, and political activities—in short, to be self-reliant. It also stems from a calculated, albeit uncoordinated, effort by social workers, corporate executives, advertising consultants, labor officials, and other professionals motivated by a variety of self-interested and idealistic factors to enhance the image of old age in the marketplace, in the media, and in the public eye (Calhoun, 1978; Tibbitts, 1979).

Accentuating the self-reliance of old people surely is beneficial. Efforts to dispel negative stereotypes counterbalance excessively unflattering portraits of age in a culture deeply nurtured by ageist assumptions. The accomplishments of distinguished citizens such as Maggie Kuhn, Averill Harriman, Norman Vincent Peale, Armand Hammer, or Rep. Claude Pepper and artists such as Eugene Ormandy, Picasso, or Robert Penn Warren, not to mention the contributions of countless anonymous Americans over seventy, underscore the degree to which "modern" politics, diplomacy, religion, business, government, art, and culture have been enhanced by the creativity and achievements of people actively growing in late life. Yet because Pollyannaish perceptions of age and aging have been created by some image-makers, the disadvantages of extolling the virtues of growing older sometimes can outweigh the advantages. Though it serves no useful purpose for people to harbor exceedingly dour fears of aging or to vent their animus against age, pretending that the aches and pains of late life do not exist hardly represents a more balanced perspective on age. A candid and judicious assessment of both the strengths and weaknesses of the last stage of life seems no less essential today than it was in the past. Furthermore, if becoming old is really as "great" as many gerontological educators, advertisers, and well-intentioned commentators claim it is, then there seems to be little point for policymakers to continue to view old age as a high-priority social "problem." Being able to cite the sanguine perspectives on aging espoused by the "experts" might encourage leaders of some political circles, especially those now in power, to think that nothing more need be done to ameliorate the plight of old age. This would be an unfortunate position for any governmental body to take. There *are* subsets within the elderly population—such as the very old, widows with low incomes, and members of various minority groups—that still have major problems that need to be addressed.

Three other attempts of late to engineer redefinitions of senescence, which go beyond prevailing notions implicit in the dependency/self-reliance classification, appear promising. Each is bedeviled, however, by undesirable side effects. One approach seizes upon "new" problems within an "old" problem while acknowledging that old age itself is no longer a major social problem. It attempts to deal with demonstrable difficulties associated with the process of aging, which are painfully manifest among certain segments of the older population. The U.S. Administration on Aging, for instance, identified the "frail elderly" as a major target of concern during the Carter years. There was little doubt at the time that this subset had not been well served by programs and policies designed for the elderly as a group. Directing attention to the very old, whose needs had largely been invisible, was good politics, especially since the plight of handicapped Americans of all ages had been made one of the Carter administration's chief priorities. The strategy made sense economically: given the growing fiscal constraints at the federal level, budget-makers preferred to allocate limited resources to those who appeared to need help most. Above all, any effort to be precise about older Americans' specific needs, and to avoid generic problem statements, represented a clear advance. Regrettably, however, the emphasis on helping the frail elderly seemed like a fad: so quickly did officials make the vulnerabilities of men and women past the age of seventy a major research priority, so adamantly did they insist that this area receive major attention by social service deliverers in the aging network, that one had to wonder why the problem had been so long in surfacing. (And given the rapidity with which the Administration on Aging had changed its policy directives in the past, it was not altogether waggish to wonder how long the frail elderly would enjoy top billing!) Worse, the new policy thrust diverted attention from those who were not frail. The funding of novel programs was often at the expense of maintaining other initiatives or promoting preventive care. Dealing with the immediate needs of the most recently discovered "problem" group commanded the administration's attention far more than devising ways to reduce the likelihood that older people in the future would find themselves in a similar predicament.

A second contemporary approach builds on the fact that the elderly population is extraordinarily heterogeneous. It posits that older women, older blacks, older Hispanics, aging gays, and the rural aged, to mention just a few, have needs and concerns that often diverge from those of the elderly population as a whole. This statement is certainly correct, but it does not necessarily follow from this "fact" that diversity should serve as the sole or even major basis for (re)designing social programs for the aged. Such a strategy, however, might be consonant with the pluralistic nature of our value system and the dynamics of our political process at the national level.

And yet, pursuing this aged-are-diverse strategy confounds rather than clarifies the extent to which "age" is a more salient factor than gender, race, ethnicity, income, sexual preference, or geographic location in establishing social policies (Gelfand, 1982). It does not provide criteria by which we might rationally decide when age per se is the causal factor creating or exacerbating the problem at hand. The issue is central to any future reforms. What strategy best serves aged blacks and other minorities: dealing with the effects of ageism or tackling the problems of racism? Does the fact that most poor older Americans are female make the problem a women's issue or, alternatively, another special case of ageism? To paraphrase a major point raised in the debate unleashed by William Julius Wilson's *The Declining Significance of Race* (1978), the age-versus-class dichotomy does not help one determine the extent to which patterns of age discrimination in the past, particularly when compounded by racial prejudice or sexual exploitation, led inevitably to the present plight of many older men and women. It offers no guidelines by which to determine to what degree current age-graded barriers have been ensured permanent status by recent normative and structural changes in our advanced industrial political economy.

A third orientation compensates for the deficiency in the previous approach by stressing the need to study age-specific stages of development in the life course. The eminent gerontologist Bernice Neugarten, for instance, created quite a stir in a 1974 article in the *Annals of the American Academy of Political and Social Science,* in which she argued that old age consisted of two distinct phases. The "young-old," according to Neugarten, typically enjoy good health, adequate financial resources, and the comforts and reassurances derived from possessing strong links with kith and kin. In contrast, "the old-old" are more isolated and disengaged; they are likely to be afflicted by the difficulties and decrements associated with old age. The distinction Neugarten made between "young-old" and "old-old" quickly gained credibility. This two-stage model, along with her ideas concerning an age-integrated society, provided the intellectual framework upon which the initial plans for the 1981 White House Conference on Aging rested. But Neugarten's thesis was misused by those who read her ideas out of context. Rather than continue to build a set of programs for the population over sixty-five, some experts recommended instead that we have one cluster of programs designed for people between the ages of fifty-five and seventy-five, and another set for those over seventy-five. In a desire to abandon the possibly obsolete schema that used age sixty-five as an administrative baseline for categorical assistance, such commentators quickly reified new perspectives without sufficient scrutiny. Neugarten may be right in hypothesizing that there are two stages of old age in advanced industrial societies. Before redesigning programs to fit this hypothesis, however, officials should ascertain how much the young-old/old-old continuum resembles and diverges from premodern conceptions of the difference between a "green old age" and "decrepitude." They certainly should not add a new set of chronological parameters to our existing repertoire of age-graded societal norms and institutions unless it makes sense to do so.

No single image, or cluster of ideas, in short, sufficiently embraces our contemporary understanding of the meanings and experiences of growing older and being old. New efforts at redefinition are underway, but no particular one prevails. This work cannot predict which, if any, of these perceptions might take hold. But Reagan's needy-only approach clearly is too neat and sweeping to embrace the nuances in the old-age imagery and to resolve the conceptual difficulties in agreeing upon any age-specific categorization.

The Entitlement / Expectation Issue

How can policymakers recast the dependency/self-reliance issue? The reformulation of ways the federal government categorizes the elderly will hinge on how the current status and needs of older

Americans are sorted out. Officials should fuse changing perceptions of "age" with new developments in how Americans define and intend to deal with the problem of "need." This intellectual task, in turn, will be greatly affected by the posture taken by the gray lobby— whose views count as much as the opinions of those in public office. For this reason, the deficiency in Reagan's needy-only approach to welfare reform goes beyond the age-salient dimensions just discussed. Reagan's staff has also ignored the entitlements and expectations that Americans associated with federal old-age programs.

Politically, there are grave repercussions in failing to gauge the reaction to *any* proposed changes in federal programs for older Americans (and particularly Social Security) in the population at large. The pertinence of this observation surely was brought home in the first months of the Reagan administration. In May 1981, amidst the congressional debate over the President's proposed changes in the budget and tax laws, the White House recommended a series of alterations in the Social Security system in order to ensure the program's solvency during the next five years. Among other things, Reagan proposed reducing the benefit formula for those who retired at age sixty-two after December 1981 from the then current 80 percent level to 55 percent of "normal" retirement benefits. He also wanted to tighten disability rules. In making these specific recommendations, the White House seemed to be discounting the merits of other plausible ways to deal with the short-term and long-range financial predicaments besetting the federal government's program. (These included the proposal that money be borrowed from intra-agency trust funds to deal with the anticipated imminent short-fall in revenues. Some experts were convinced that raising the age at which one would become eligible for old-age insurance benefits was also a necessary step.)

The timing and specifics of Reagan's Social Security reform package caught nearly everybody by surprise. Senior-citizen groups uniformly denounced the package. The Senate swiftly rejected the proposals by a 96–0 vote. The haste with which the White House had presented its proposals and the clumsiness with which it defended itself seemed all the more jarring in light of the way the Reagan administration assiduously had sought congressional advice and support and shrewdly had enlisted key lobbyists in all quarters for its proposed changes in the federal budget, even before the legislative particulars had been unveiled. The rebuff not only embarrassed the Administration at a critical moment, but also reduced the probability that major reforms in Social Security would take place in the proximate future, unless the system itself seems on the verge of collapse or politicians can contrive a course of action that gains nearly unanimous bipartisan support.

This is an unfortunate situation. Even Social Security's most loyal advocates concede that changes are necessary in the calculation of benefits and the operation of the system. If something is not done soon, it will prove even more difficult to effect necessary reforms later, since the cost, both in human and fiscal terms, will have grown far greater. Reagan demonstrated true political courage in taking the lead in confronting problems with a program that most politicians view(ed) as a "sacred cow."[3] But by limiting the range of options to be discussed and by setting forth a set of recommendations that seemed deficient in major respects, his administration raised anxiety among all age groups. The President's proposals prompted questions about his ulterior motives: was he mainly interested in restoring public confidence in Social Security, or was he really trying to balance the federal budget? Senior-citizen groups found that they could justifiably rebuke the President by saying that they were "entitled" to their benefits. Reagan realized that he could hardly afford to disagree. Indeed, he claimed that his efforts represented a benign strategy designed to save the system. But what about the entitlements of future cohorts of older Americans? What were they entitled to receive? What could they expect? The same return on their contributions that their parents were likely to receive? Greater benefits? Different, perhaps more costly, benefits? This set of questions was lost in the politics and histrionics of the moment. Yet it is precisely the issue of balancing the potentially conflicting demands between present entitlements and future expectations that must be addressed.

There can be no doubt that the gray lobby resembles a host of other special-interest groups. It claims to represent a large and politically influential segment of the American population. It is well financed and quickly mobilized. It has won, or at least takes credit for winning, a dazzling array of benefits and social services during the past several decades. But the gray lobby differs from other interest groups in at least two important respects. On the one hand, there are important though hitherto muted and relatively unappreciated ideological and political schisms within and among the various organizations that represent and work for the elderly.[4] On the other

---

[3] A less charitable interpretation is possible, of course. The President may simply have revealed the extent to which he perceived Social Security as just another "welfare program" that needed to be cut in the face of new defense priorities and budgetary constraints (Greider, 1981).

[4] Insofar as the labor-union preferences of the National Council of Senior Citizens dovetail with the vested interests of the National Association of Retired Federal Employees, lobbyists engage in concerted action. However, there are issues, such as whether governmental employees should be required to contribute to the Social Security system, that frustrate efforts to build a coalition among old-age interest groups. When and where lobbyists disagree reveals important differences of opinion within the ranks. Such cleavages are not wholly unexpected, given the diversity of political orientations and vested interests among older Americans.

hand, the gray lobby is the only coalition to which every living American can reasonably hope to aspire. Thus the leaders of senior-citizen groups cannot afford to view policy choices in an ad hoc, short-term manner: they must weigh the future ramifications of current decisions. What may make sense in the short run might have disastrous implications for elderly men and women in the year 2001, and vice versa.

More than any other group, consequently, the gray lobby must balance the needs of their current constituency against the best interests of the commonweal. This does not mean that the aged's entitlements are any less valid than the benefits allocated to other sectors of society, nor does it mean that the elderly's expectations must be deferred in the face of larger issues. (The leaders of old-age coalitions would not stay in power long if they advocated shortchanging the current generation of aged Americans!) The issue of entitlements/expectations is fraught with touchy issues, ones that hinge on what we think the elderly should do to contribute to their own well-being. It is to this set of questions that we now turn.

What Can the Federal Government Expect the Elderly to Do for Themselves?

In deciding how to categorize the aged, policymakers will have to assess the elderly's ability to maintain or enhance their current standards of living. They will focus not so much on perceptions of the elderly's assets and liabilities, but rather on the depth and breadth of resources at older people's disposal. The Reagan administration probably will point out that most older Americans need less assistance from the federal government than is generally presumed. Officials will note the dramatic decrease during the past two decades in the proportion of men and women over the age of sixty-five who fall below the official poverty line. The numbers on the extent of absolute poverty in old age look even better when adjusted to include the impact of in-kind transfers (particularly the dollar value of medical care, food stamps, subsidized rents) and tax credits. To be sure, the most recently available data do suggest at least a temporary reversal in this downward trend: the total number of elderly members of minority groups counted as "poor" rose 10.4 percent between 1976 and 1977. According to U.S. Census Bureau estimates, there was a 10.9 percent increase in the number of Americans over sixty-five and below the poverty level (Oriol, 1981: 38). Nevertheless, persistent inflation adversely affects all age groups. And given the way public programs operate, the elderly may in fact be more insulated from the current economic crisis than are younger people. The aged's federally sponsored income is raised annually in line with the consumer price index—a measure, incidentally, which some economists believe presently overestimates the impact of inflation on their resources.

Furthermore, even if one doubts that Reaganomics will work, it does not necessarily follow from this prognosis that Washington must go beyond honoring past commitments in responding to the needs of older Americans. More likely, the Reagan administration will search for ways to reduce the current size and future magnitude of old-age dependency, if only to ensure that soaring welfare costs do not make budget deficits even greater. Domestic policymakers, consequently, will seek to determine what the federal government can expect the elderly to do for themselves. In this context, two more value dimensions discussed in this work will become especially relevant.

The Work / Leisure Issue

Encouraging older Americans to work is quite consistent with the overarching welfare principles of the Reagan administration. As we saw in the previous section, providing income and resources to people who can care for themselves is viewed as wasteful and unfair to middle-class Americans. But this stance does not simply constitute an article of neo-conservative philosophy. By containing the relative cost of retirement pensions, or at least reducing its real growth rate, Reagan's budget-makers hoped that they could limit the overall expense of maintaining the income base of a rapidly growing segment of the population. This "saving," in turn, would enable the administration to allocate limited resources to other areas.

Such a strategy also made sense for the private sector. Most corporate executives once thought that establishing mandatory retirement programs was a "progressive" policy in terms of both a firm's cost-benefit ratio and its utilization of human resources. Now, the pacesetters are begining to change their stance. They increasingly chafe at the "hidden" costs of early retirement (particularly if superannuated workers are to be replaced), because of the need to make periodic adjustments in benefit levels for former employees and, in most cases, their widow(er)s. According to a study by the pension consulting firm of Towers, Perrin, Forster and Crosby (1981), retirement benefits have risen from 12.3 percent to 17.7 percent of payroll costs since the early 1970s. Many companies, moreover, are finding real advantages in retaining and retraining employees past the age of sixty. Prejudices against the elderly worker are becoming harder to justify in the face of mounting evidence that older workers' skill, loyalty, and reliability typically outweigh the decrements of age. Indeed, making room for older people in the work force will become all the more necessary in the future. Currently, people between the ages of twenty and thirty-four constitute 45 percent of the work force; the percentage is expected to fall to 35 percent by the year 2000 (Sheppard, 1976). In an economy beset by energy shortages, the aged represent a natural resource that can no longer be squandered.

The current economic crisis also makes it in the elderly's best interest to work as long as possible. Persistent inflation has a devastating impact on the worth of one's retirement assets. At an annual inflation rate of 12 percent, a pension loses about two-thirds of its value in ten years; it is worth 90 percent less in twenty years. Only those who can depend on inherited wealth, exceptionally shrewd investments, and exceedingly generous compensation from prior employment can count on having funds that will last until a retired worker and his or her spouse die. Few older people are in such a fortunate position. By postponing retirement by one or two years, on the other hand, most workers can significantly increase the earnings base upon which pension benefits are determined, thereby ensuring a better hedge against inflation.

Thus it is not surprising that we see various efforts in both the public and private sector geared toward inducing older people in good health to continue working. Social Security subcommittees in the Senate and the House endorsed recommendations in 1981 that the age of eligibility for full benefits be gradually raised from sixty-five to sixty-eight. There is also growing support for raising the earnings ceiling for Social Security beneficiaries. Many legislators and special-interest groups propose eliminating it altogether. The Age Discrimination in Employment Act now protects workers between the ages of forty-five and seventy; some suggest that the next logical step is to replace all mandatory retirement provisions with competency-based criteria for retaining or retiring workers. New work arrangements, such as part-time employment, phased retirement, ad hoc executive consulting, and multiple-career training, are gaining acceptance among personnel managers and corporate planners (Jacobson, 1980). The Gray Panthers and other aged individuals offer countless examples of the continued value of older workers in the marketplace.

Despite these initiatives, however, there are countervailing forces that restrain the extension of most employees' working lives. Established hiring practices (including those not couched in stereotyped ideas about the aged's presumed health, vigor, productivity, and ambition), labor-union policies (especially those calculated to provide more jobs for younger workers and secure better and earlier retirement for those over fifty-five), and the current slow-growth economy (which reduces the employment prospects for both young and old) all reduce the likelihood that older workers can stay on the job or secure new employment (Work in America Institute, 1980).

Structural constraints are not the only inhibiting factor: personal choices count. When older workers choose to retire depends in large part on market calculations and prevailing policies. Many quit work when they feel that they can get the best deal on the money they have invested through Social Security and other means. (Some capitalize on their disabilities and take early retirement, but the extent of abuse has been exaggerated; the regulations actually are quite stringent.) Above all, Americans retire because they find working in later years an unsatisfying and unattractive option. This is why, over the past two decades, increasing numbers have chosen early retirement even at financial sacrifice: the labor force participation rate for men and women between the ages of sixty and sixty-four stood at 82.5 percent in 1957; by 1977, the percentage had dropped to 62.9 percent. So far, the percentage of white-collar and blue-collar workers deciding to stay on the job beyond the point at which they became eligible for full retirement benefits has been relatively small. Apparently, a sizable proportion of aging workers do not consider it a "privilege" to continue working past the age of "normal" retirement.

Recent retirement patterns indicate, therefore, that we need to rethink the relationship between work and leisure in late life. Except in a minority of cases, older people wish to be occupied and enjoy a satisfying personal life, but they do not want to continue working. Those who have to worry about surviving from an economic standpoint work as a matter of necessity, not preference. Those whose careers define(d) and provide(d) everything that really mattered to them want to work to maintain their sense of identity and self-worth. Yet most Americans have come to view a healthful and financially adequate retirement as a desired and desirable goal, a right they have earned. The form, range, and intensity of their leisure time vary enormously. Research indicates that age, health, gender, education, location, family and friendship network, occupational status, social class, disposable income, and prior leisure experiences all affect the types of activities that people pursue and the pleasure they derive from their participation (Gordon and Gaitz, 1976; Neulinger, 1981).

The inherent tension between work and leisure in making public policy and designing private programs remains, however, even if government officials and business executives conclude that Americans are entitled to enjoy meaningful leisure time in late life. For instance, do older workers have a "right" to early retirement?

Among other pertinent facts, it is important to recall that Social Security did not finance early retirement prior to the 1950s. Do we need to revise the replacement-income ratio now used to determine (early) retirement benefits to reflect recent changes in wage structures and current actuarial estimates of life expectancies of men and women past sixty? Similarly, is it a "right" to enjoy tax-free Social Security benefits? How far should earnings ceilings be raised in order to encourage a larger proportion of the older population to seek part-time employment? If we do this, should we then tax all income—earnings, savings, dividends, and Social Security benefits—in order to get more revenues to bolster existing retirement programs? Would this violate the elderly's "right" to retirement? Addressing such questions will require a firm grounding in logic, an understanding of the economics and social psychology of the marketplace, and familiarity with tax codes and interest-group politics.

The Family / Individual Issue

Given their enthusiastic endorsement of traditional values and their commitment to strengthening basic societal institutions, officials in the Reagan administration not surprisingly expected children to be an important source of financial and interpersonal support for older Americans. This was a sensible orientation. Policymakers cannot ignore the historical role and current familial bonds among the generations. Empirical evidence documents that family members do more for their aged relatives than media reports would suggest or most Americans believe. Despite the fact that older people do not come to live with their children as a matter of course, the younger generation does provide services to disabled elders. Most people in nursing homes are there not because their children have chosen to avoid taking responsibility for their well-being, but because there are no kin nearby or there is nothing more that nonprofessional personnel can do for the person in need. Nevertheless, at least three social trends do indicate that there are limits to how much we can count on the family to fill a void in the existing "safety net" should the government decide to reduce its commitments in this area.

First, the most important structural change in American family history in recent decades has been the continuing increase in the number of independent households. According to preliminary results released by the U.S. Bureau of Census, twenty-three percent of all households in 1980 consisted of one person living alone. Most of the increase was reported among those under the age of thirty-five who were divorced or never married. Women accounted for about 60 percent of the independent households; the number of men living alone rose 92 percent during the 1970s. Americans are marrying later, and more are getting divorced. The number of unmarried couples living together tripled. The ratio of divorced people to married people living with their spouses soared from 47 per 1,000 to roughly 100 per 1,000 (*The New York Times,* October 19, 1981: A20). This suggests, of course, that Americans value their privacy and that adults want to maintain their physical independence regardless of marital status. The aged are no exception. The proportion of aged parents residing with adult children has declined over time: in 1952, a third of all people over sixty-five lived with children; today, less than a sixth do so.

Second, changes in household structure, combined with the increasing availability of retirement income from public and private sources, have affected the economic arrangements across generational lines. Cash assistance from children to their parents, especially if they maintain independent residences, is not a pervasive pattern. Alvin Schorr (1980: 3) reports that 5 to 10 percent of the aged received contributions from their children. The liberalization of retirement income increasingly is viewed as a benefit not just to the old but also to the young and middle-aged. If anything, in fact, the exchange of money and services from the older generation to their children is more important than ever before, as middle-aged, middle-class prospective homeowners will surely admit, particularly if they have kids at home.

Third, several demographic trends indicate that in the future the family network may be even less able to provide for its elderly members. The four-generation family has not yet become the modal structure. Gains in life expectancy, however, will increase the probability that ninety-year-old parents will be cared for by "children" themselves beyond the age of sixty-five, *if* these trends persist. With the declining birth rate and the rise in "child-free" marriages, moreover, tomorrow's aged will have a much smaller pool of children and siblings upon which to depend if and when they need assistance.

Such changes have led some analysts to recommend the formation of family programs that are targeted not just to the elderly but to all age groups. The distinguished family historian Tamara Hareven contends:

> We must think . . . of the kind of policy which, on the one hand, would effectively utilize the very valuable role that family and kin could play in caring for the elderly in a way which agencies, institutions and asylums never could. On the other hand, in order to use the family creatively for the care of the elderly, we will have to come up with support mechanisms for the family itself which would enable the family to carry its burdens. . . . We need a policy which supports not only

family units when they are broken down, but a policy which supports family units as they go through life (1978: 12–13).

Hareven's recommendations gain special plausibility because of the contemporary roles she attributes to the family. She clearly has no single image of the family in mind, but envisions a family structure that varies from one household to the next at any given moment, and that undergoes fundamental changes over its own life course. Furthermore, Hareven is careful to note that this very range of family dynamics necessitates the formulation of a broad set of policy options. The choice is not just between targeting benefits to an aged individual or designating the household with an elderly member as a potential recipient. The family must be considered as an alternative to extra-familial institutional supports, but one which is not always available or even the best solution (Steiner, 1981).

Once again, then, admitting the complexity and fluidity of the situation represents a step forward, but it does not reduce the salience of the value dimension. "The independence of family patterns," Schorr (1980: 41) concludes, "is more impressive than the connections." Despite reports to the contrary, the American family has not become an endangered species. Intergenerational responsibilities have not been forgotten. But the variations in family exchanges across ethnic and racial lines and by age and marital status are wide. Hence, the perennial ambiguity in family ties and the potential for intergenerational conflict remain. The Reagan administration may succeed in altering some of the pivotal features of the connection between the individual and the family in aging America. Nevertheless, as is the case with retirement policy, there are real limits to how far public policies can change perceptions and behavior without a concurrent change in the historical actors themselves.

Why Would Washington Say No to the Elderly?

There will be mounting pressure for limits to be placed on the scope and ceilings put on the cost of federal social policies. And yet, precisely because there is no other institution in the United States that has such vast resources and personnel at its disposal or that can be held accountable by all elements in society, there will be boundaries on how much the federal government can be limited. The basic issue to be discussed, then, is *how* much more (and less!) Washington can be expected to do for older Americans. Two value pairs are germane here.

The Public / Private Issue

One of the major objectives of Reagan's welfare-reform package was to reverse the historical tide that has swelled Washington's involvement and expenditures in dealing with poverty. The New Federalism envisioned a return to earlier institutional arrangements for handling the needs of the poor. Officials made two assumptions to justify this policy goal. First, they deplored the inefficiency, waste, and vast impersonality of a welfare system operated and funded by a centralized bureaucracy. Accordingly, they wanted to let state and local officials direct and finance programs at the grass-roots level. Second, insofar as lower levels of government would not be able to raise revenues to make up for the anticipated loss of federal tax dollars, Reagan's policymakers expected private institutions to increase their involvement in social philanthropy. Indeed, they contended that the private sector would be more efficient and effective than the public sector in dealing with poor people, since governmental operations are inured from those very pressures of the marketplace that place a premium on maximizing cost-benefit ratios. Both assumptions, however, rested on historically questionable premises.

While there surely is ample justification for criticizing the ways that Washington goes about its business, it is imperative to bear in mind that a large, activist government did not grow like a hybrid leviathan, without any compelling reason or apparent aim. The need for a strong central government has been recognized since the earliest days of the republic. The Founding Fathers, fearful of lodging too much power in the hands of one person or governing unit, initially did set up a loosely federated system of government adhering to the Articles of Confederation. Under the Articles, the thirteen newly independent states retained their sovereignty except in those areas in which duties were specifically handed over to the central legislative body. But because the central government had no power to back up its responsibilities—it did not have the right to raise taxes, it lacked an executive to enforce interstate laws, and there was no supreme court to which grievances might be appealed—the new republic quickly found itself in a vulnerable position. A special session was convened in 1787 to remedy deficiencies in the Articles; as every schoolchild used to know, the delegates to that convention went beyond their mandate and created a new form of government. It was at this historical juncture that the framers of the Constitution debated the advantages and disadvantages of delegating to a central government the explicit and implicit right to expand powers as the need arose. The Founding Fathers were careful to establish a series of checks and balances at the federal level and to ensure that states' rights were not subverted. In order to get the Constitution ratified, they also had to endorse a Bill of Rights, which gave explicit guarantees to various civil and individual liberties. But the view of human nature set forth in James Madison's Federalist Paper No. 10 was compelling: just as the new nation had to be wary of vesting too much power in one body, its citizens had to be equally fearful of "factions." The essential interests of the commonweal could not be protected, Madison and his peers believed, if there was no way to get beyond petty, parochial concerns and the selfishly motivated desires of powerful people.

During the past two centuries, the expansion of federal responsibilities has been unsteady and uneven. With few exceptions, Washington took on new responsibilities when, and only when, it was clear that problems that were national in scope had arisen and that existing institutional arrangements could not cope with the situation. Hence, the Interstate Commerce Act of 1887 was passed only after it became painfully evident that states could not coordinate efforts to control the abuses arising from the growth of railroads. Even then, every branch of the federal government moved very deliberately, lest private and corporate interests be unduly impeded or states' rights threatened. The regulatory responsibilities assumed by Washington during the Progressive era conformed to this pattern of cautious, circumscribed intervention. The passage of the Social Security Act in 1935, similarly, represented a decisive change in methods of defining and dealing with old-age dependency. But Roosevelt's administration responded to the plight of older Americans only after reviewing the policy constraints that the executive, legislative, and judicial branches imposed upon any extension of federal responsibilities. The conservative features of the original measure, and the ways it was designed to fit into existing arrangements, are as impressive as its innovations.

The real choice posed by Reagan's call for a New Federalism, thus, is not really between a bloated, insensitive big government and a trim, personalized, localistic system. Rather, like the Founding Fathers, Americans must decide whether or not the operational and philosophical liabilities of a centralized government are more pernicious than the problems that probably would ensue in a polity in which power was fragmented and dissipated, and in which no single unit could really be held responsible for the public interest. The decision is not made any easier, alas, by extolling the virtues of the private sector. Waste and inefficiency certainly abound in Washington and in lower levels of government. Yet is this an inherent defect in public institutions or a flaw intrinsic to all "modern" organizations—private and public?[5]

Given the fuzziness of boundaries between the public and private sectors and the striking operational commonalities of all "modern" organizations, distinctions between the "public" and "private" realms in a classical nineteenth-century manner have become anachronistic. The real issue is one of accountability. And on those grounds, it is imperative to keep in mind that only the federal government has been accountable to "promote the general welfare" of the commonweal. The actions of those who wield power in Washington, whether for well-intentioned or misguided reasons, involve the common interest of men and women of all ages.

The Adequacy / Equity Issue

We have already seen that the definition of "adequacy" utilized in Reagan's welfare program opts for as limited and austere a set of social services and income-transfer programs as the President can get through Congress without alienating his electoral constituency. Officials consistently attempted to whittle away "entitlement" provisions so as to embrace only the "truly needy" who have no other option for survival but to depend on the government's "safety net." This strategy was not necessarily as heartless as it might initially appear. After all, in the process of evaluating existing programs and proposing new ceilings and eligibility criteria, the current administration may succeed in systematizing the welter of federal programs in a way that more liberal crusaders for welfare reform could never achieve. And because the current administration will have to defend in a politically hostile environment its definition of "minimal ben-

---

[5] There is abundant scholarly evidence suggesting that the nature and direction of growth in all large and complex bodies has a pattern that depends as much upon internal dynamics as on the most logical and feasible options at any given moment. Funds are mismanaged and irrationally allocated by private as well as public officials. Managers in both sectors, moreover, are interested in maintaining a measure of control and in anticipating possible risks (be they fiscal, political, ecological, demographic, or international) to the stability of their day-to-day operations (Galbraith, 1967; Lindblom, 1977). A short-term mentality pervades both sectors: what, after all, is the difference between worrying about one's reelection chances and manipulating the next quarter's bottom line? Critics of this line of reasoning might argue that the private sector differs from the public sphere because the former is profit-motivated. But does that distinction still make sense in "modern" America? Have not many traditionally "private" concerns become "public" issues, and vice versa? Consider the social-welfare arena. Since the mid-1960s, public funds have been used to finance private social-service operations. Contracts under Title XX of the Social Security Act have exceeded the billion-dollar mark. At the same time, there has been an influx of profit-making organizations into the private sector of social welfare, particularly in the aptly named "nursing home industry" (Gilbert, 1981). Where does one draw the line?

efits," it is conceivable that a constructive national debate will ensue concerning the lowest acceptable level of support this country can morally and socially tolerate. Establishing a legitimate and acceptable criterion for "adequacy" at the national level surely would be a positive contribution.

Ideally, of course, the potentially deleterious effect of stringent definitions of "adequacy" in neo-conservative welfare proposals will be counterbalanced by the Republicans' recovery program. According to the scenario for an *American Renaissance* (1980) drawn by Congressman Jack Kemp, one of Washington's most articulate and enthusiastic advocates of supply-side economics, expanding opportunities in all sectors of the economy will enable those who are un(der)employed or struggling on welfare to obtain steady jobs with good salaries, and be less dependent on public assistance. At that point, Kemp argues, Americans will have less desire to raise the adequacy level of social-welfare programs. Equity issues will be paramount. Hence, Reaganomics seems to be reverting to a pre–Great Society worldview in which the issue of "adequacy" is secondary to concerns over "equity." Policymakers assume that an expanding economic pie will guarantee that public programs will be adequate.

One of the advantages of this way of thinking is that it builds on the historically engrained distincion that politicians and policy experts draw between adequacy and equity. Paradoxically, however, one of the difficulties with this approach is that it does not let us decide *which* definitions of adequacy and equity we should use. The choice is critical, as the recent debate by economists over the adequacy/equity features of Social Security certainly underscores. There is general agreement, for instance, that the purchasing power of an initial benefit should be maintained over a recipient's lifetime. But by what standard should we measure the "social adequacy" of an initial benefit? Some suggest that benefits awarded now should be measured in terms of the prevailing standard of living. Others advocate establishing some universal and uniform replacement ratio. Still others advocate limiting future retirement benefits to the level of those enjoyed by current beneficiaries (Campbell, 1977; for other options, see Myers, 1975; Robertson, 1978). Similarly, there are at least three definitions of "equity" that could be used in determining benefits. A measure of individual equity, which bases benefits on an employee's prior contribution history, is plausible. Ensuring that persons in similar situations are treated equally also satisfies a definition of (horizontal) equity. Alternatively, allocating benefits among recipients with different levels of lifetime earnings according to a measure of (vertical) equity is reasonable (Munnell, 1977). The difficulty, of course, is that benefits would vary enormously depending on which pair(s) of definitions was used in calculating benefits. There is, at the moment, no consensus.

Ultimately, though, one must put the question of equity versus adequacy into a larger context. What if the supply-siders are wrong and economic recovery is not quickly achieved? Then, we shall be left with ever larger deficits and commitments to increased defense spending, which drain the civilian economy without promoting greater productivity. Under these circumstances, critics will have a field day. Indeed, they have already begun: Seymour Melman, a professor of industrial engineering at Columbia University, points out that the cost overrun, to 1981, on the Navy's FFG-7 frigates constitutes a figure ($5 billion) equal to "the minimum additional annual investment needed to prevent water pollution in the United States from exceeding present standards" (*New York Times,* July 26, 1981: E21). It is on such statistics that the public/private, equity/adequacy calculus will be sorely tested. In this context, the issues of adequacy and equity in dealing with the broader challenges and more diffuse problems of an aging society may well be lost in the shuffle. The President's program has not grappled with fundamental issues that affect the tension between equity and adequacy.

Is the Reagan Program a Viable Alternative?

As the preceding section suggests, I frankly am skeptical that the actions of the Reagan administration will result in a watershed in the evolution of the federal government's responsibilities for the aged that will be comparable in significance of the passage of the Social Security Act in 1935. Reagan's proposals have novel features. They are consistent with the rising neo-conservative political viewpoint. They are designed to reflect the limited posture for federal initiatives advocated by a new set of political advisors and seemingly necessitated by the current economic crisis. Indeed, the attempt to reduce the scope and to contain the costs of federal responsibilities for older Americans constitutes an attempt to reverse the course of historical developments since the New Deal. The effort to redefine "adequacy" to embrace only those who are "needy" establishes new criteria for planning and evaluating federal programs. For this reason, the Reagan administration can make a plausible case, arguing that its "novel" approach is designed to restore "traditional" ends: the approach is intended to correct an imbalance in priorities caused by previous administrations, notably those that embraced the ideals and sustained the programs of the Great Society.

Ironically, however, Reaganomics may prove so novel as to be unable to come to grips with "traditional" issues in twentieth-century American social-welfare history. Reagan's economic plans disrupt the historical equilibrium that has developed since the New Deal, apparently oblivious to the delicate balance that has long existed in policies for older Americans. Reagan's administration operates as if one must choose *between* equity and adequacy, the family and the individual, and the proper locus of public and private concerns, rather than recognizing that it is really faced with a both/and situation. By coming down so hard on one pole, Reagan's approach has simplistically seized upon anomalies and absurdities created by conflicting yet necessary policy objectives. It conveniently but shortsightedly ignores the real task of deciding *where* on the continuum to place his priorities in order to capitalize on the cybernetic benefits that emanate from such a creative tension in policy choices. Worse, Reagan's program seems to have been designed in a vacuum, with the campaign pledges firmly in mind, but with little sense of how to translate rhetoric into a coherent and consistent approach to policymaking. Little attempt has been made to come to grips with the profoundly important changes in the meanings and experiences of being old in the United States since World War II. Nothing has been said about fundamental alterations in the realms of work and leisure. The acute difficulties inherent in categorizing the elderly do not bother the President's welfare advisors and social planners. Little thought has been given to the potential differences between an old-age policy and an aging policy. This is a lamentable situation. For it is not enough to criticize the excesses of the Great Society and to bemoan the folly of big government. In order to devise an alternative, Reagan's advisors must come to grips with the tough issues that have been bedeviling thoughtful Americans concerned about the welfare and the well-being of older people amid changing circumstances. They have not really done so yet.

The difficulties in forging a coherent aging policy for the 1980s were underscored at the 1981 White House Conference on Aging. Because of persistent charges that the Reagan administration had changed program guidelines, delegate selection, and voting procedures in order to control proceedings, this gathering had a more partisan flavor than had characterized previous conferences. To their credit, officials and delegates took the unprecedented step of making the special concerns of older women a major item on the agenda. They strongly recommended the continuation of a high level of federal support for older people, the elimination of mandatory retirement, and no reduction in Social Security, Medicare, and Medicaid benefits.

But no consistent posture emerged from the deliberations. Consonant with the politics of liberal incrementalism, leaders of major old-age organizations and their supporters at the conference proposed the creation of costly new governmental services, including a national health insurance program that would include home health care for the aged. Their chief spokesperson was Representative Claude Pepper, age eighty-one, whose national political career began in the U.S. Senate during the New Deal. Ronald Reagan, age seventy, set forth an alternative course of action. His administration opposed national health insurance and wanted to put limits on social services for the aged and poor and make changes in Social Security. Consequently, the conference's final set of recommendations "includes some striking conflicts. For example, the report contains a call for 'general revenue funding of public retirement' and, in another section, the statement that the use of general revenue funds would 'jeopardize the fiscal integrity' of Social Security" (*New York Times,* December 4, 1981: A18).

It remains to be seen whether genuine compromises can be obtained. That the prime actors of the liberal and conservative camps are themselves "senior citizens" does not minimize the differences between them. At this point, unfortunately, it appears that the 1981 White House Conference on Aging will be remembered as the first such gathering that failed to chart new directions in social programs for the elderly.

Chapter

7

Conclusion

Contemporary American society has reached an important historical crossroads in its development. Many of the structural foundations and normative assumptions that gave coherence and vitality to the original provisions of the Social Security Act and to the politics of incrementalism during the last half-century have been eroded by fundamental changes in the political economy. Long-standing demographic trends, the emergence of new social patterns, and the rise of alternative sets of personal attitudes and mass beliefs have altered the shape and dynamics of the American experience in recent decades. The liberals' attempt to wage a "war on poverty" did not result in the creation of a Great Society. I suspect that the current reforms proposed by the neo-conservatives will also founder. Concurrently, Americans' complaints against "the system" have been mounting for years. Citizens are disturbed by the present state of affairs. Conditions are right, therefore, for a new direction in federal aging policies.

The future status of the elderly clearly hangs in the balance. This survey began with the assertion that the aged were among the last groups in the population to be affected by the long-term process of modernization. Now, the elderly have all the earmarks of a "modern" force in society. Before 1920 the elderly were unable to engage in collective action in order to deal with the social problems of growing old. A potent gray lobby now exists at the national level. The aged once engaged in traditional occupational pursuits, rarely at the cutting edge of change. The ways old people currently maintain their economic status have become a central issue in public-policy circles: the economics of aging is quite vulnerable to budgetary constraints and broad macroeconomic developments. Americans in the past described the elderly as a homogeneous group with common afflictions. Today, few deny that the "new old" are more diverse on every salient dimension than any other age group. The old used to be scorned for their old-fashioned mores. Nowadays, it seems that older Americans' ability to make more out of less and to come to grips with diminishing expectations as they grapple with the finitude of life actually may point the way to the future posture of everybody else in society. I am not prepared to claim that the elderly are at the vanguard of society, blazing the next frontier of America's evolution. But I am convinced that they will play a key role in that transformation.

If I have interpreted recent structural and cultural trends correctly, I think it likely that the *next* "shade of gray" coloring the relationships among old age, American values, and federal policies will somehow blend the bright idealism of the architects of the Great Society with the somber appreciation of the limits of federal action espoused by the neo-conservatives. It is reasonable to forecast that the meanings and experiences of growing older and being old will be significantly altered in the process. To say more than that would be inappropriate: historians, after all, gaze into the same cloudy crystal balls as everyone else! Still, in composing my thoughts for this conclusion, I have been mindful of the sentiments expressed by Saul Friedlander about the relationship of a historically sensitive critic trying to come to grips with the swirl of events affecting his life and that of his loved ones. Because "a living community follows paths that are often impossible to predict or map out in advance," he observes, ". . . at best the role of each individual remains to affirm certain principles that are essential to him, in an attempt to erect dikes along the shores, and guardrails along the edges of history" (1978: 170–71). Let me conclude, therefore, by proposing some "guardrails" consonant with the analysis presented here.

The time has come, I believe, for being more precise in talking about and distinguishing between images of aging and images of old age in "modern" America. Ideally, we should keep those historically conditioned perspectives on senescence that remain valid and discard the rest. This in turn requires devising and applying an explicit new set of criteria for public policy. On the one hand, we should acknowledge that all age groups have certain basic rights and responsibilities and face common problems. On the other hand, we have to recognize that the cumulative experiences of living dictate that people at different stages of life may have divergent priorities, desires, hopes, and needs.

At the same time, we must review current policies not simply in light of their past effectiveness and current utility, but also with critical regard for their ethical ramifications. We need to reconsider under what conditions chronological age should be a criterion for bestowing benefits upon and for discriminating against particular segments of the population. *And,* we must decide when it is an inappropriate factor. Changes in the status quo made in accordance with this principle, of course, would benefit the elderly in some respects and penalize them in other regards. I, for instance, would press for the elimination of all age-specific mandatory retirement programs because there is no empirical justification for using chronological age as an indicator of a worker's competence. However, I would oppose categorical allowances to defray the elderly's winter heating bills, unless it can be demonstrated that only the aged need such assistance or unless we are prepared to offer relief to anyone who cannot afford shelter from the cold. Programs that unduly favor or disfavor people because they happen to be "old," in short, should be reconsidered, and then either scrapped or reformulated.

Consistent with this view, I would favor the establishment of a double-decker social-welfare program for America's aging society. The first tier would include all income-maintenance, health-care, and social-service programs for which eligibility is determined on the basis of income, disability, or some other socially accepted criterion. The aged thus would be eligible for assistance because they satisfied specific program criteria, not because they had lived a certain number of years. Those legitimate, age-specific needs that were not met sufficiently by this first set of policies would then be covered in the second tier, which would consist of all programs allocating categorical assistance for specific age groups. This second set of programs would include categorical benefits for the elderly. It would also allocate special grants for school-aged children and others for whom a legitimate age-specific case of "need" can be made. Needless to say, all new initiatives proposed to promote the well-being of older Americans would have to be designed in light of this programmatic reorganization. Existing programs would also have to be reordered. For instance, under this scheme, it might make sense to revamp the administrative and funding mechanisms of the Social Security system. Since the Supplemental Security Income program (SSI) covers blind people and disabled persons, as well as the indigent aged, this function of Social Security should be viewed as an *aging* program and thus is better funded through general revenues. In contrast, since the retirement-pension component of OASDI (the original Title II) and Medicare are clearly targeted to "older" men and women, these categorical measures should be viewed as the cornerstone of the national *old-age* policy.[1]

---

[1] It is worth noting that this proposal receives support, on somewhat different historical and philosophical grounds, from J. Douglas Brown, who headed the first federal advisory council established for the Social Security Board in the late 1930s. See Brown (1977).

Ultimate control and responsibility for all programs under this two-tiered arrangement would rest with the federal government. Washington must guarantee, and be held accountable to provide, whatever the American people, through their elected officials, deem to be the least amount of support that a just and ethical society must furnish its citizens. The national government has to ensure that no one in America is denied his or her rights and that everyone has access to those goods and services thought to be essential to the "American" way of life. Officials, however, would surely exploit resources, ideas, and programs existing in state and local levels of government, as well as in the private sector, so that this revamped program could be run on an "adequate" yet cost-effective basis. It is important to note that under this scheme the elderly would not necessarily be entitled to receive more and more. The expansion of the scope of any given social program would require a reevaluation of specific benefits and existing needs in light of a changing world.

A double-decker system for the present welfare program would force us to rethink our respective old-age and aging policies in a more systematic manner than is currently possible. Nevertheless, adopting this structural change would neither resolve nor eliminate many thorny philosophical issues. It would not tell us, for example, how to define or implement "socially accepted criteria" in designing, administering, or evaluating social programs. It would not automatically reduce the likelihood of vertical, horizontal, or intergenerational inequities in any categorical assistance program. My proposal, in fact, guarantees more, not less, potential controversy over such issues at the federal level. It cannot be any other way.

It is worth emphasizing, however, that this restructuring of federal social programs for the aged and aging is consistent with the major motifs of the analysis presented in *Shades of Gray*. Executing these changes would not radically alter the basic dimensions of the political economy or social structure. The politics of aging, I anticipate, will evolve in much the same way that it has in the past—at all levels of government. The gray lobby will continue to be a special-interest group. Its successes and failures will hinge on how well its leadership and constituency can respond to ideational and structural changes in the political arena. The aged's power in the political arena will also depend on the degree to which members of the old-age coalition can coordinate their efforts in establishing national priorities for the years ahead.

Current assessments and future projections about older Americans' economic status probably will become even more intimately linked to the overall state of the economy and its prospects for growth. The elderly surely will benefit along with the rest of society if inflation is brought under control, and if significant technological advances in telecommunications, robotics, and the bio-medical and computer sciences are achieved. On the other hand, if stagflation persists, productivity rates in critical industrial and service areas languish, and this nation becomes more and more vulnerable to environmental constraints and international developments beyond its control, then it is highly unlikely that the body politic will tolerate policies that insulate the elderly from the adverse circumstances afflicting everybody else. Basic American beliefs will change, but not radically. Americans will continue to uphold their commitment to the country's liberal, democratic, capitalist, egalitarian traditions and Judeo-Christian ideals. Yet the centripetal and centrifugal forces that paradoxically have made this society simultaneously more homogeneous and more fragmented will remain prevalent. I doubt that intergenerational warfare will break out. Ageism, racism, parochialism, sexism, and nativism in all likelihood will continue to fester, however, despite efforts to extirpate their most visible and deleterious consequences.

The preceding observations and recommendations quite deliberately are designed to mesh with recent transvaluations in the nation's normative foundations, at least insofar as they have a bearing on the meanings and experiences of old age, and on the evolution of federal aging policies. Let us consider them in light of the value scheme used in this book:

• *Public / private.* I seriously doubt that the public sector can abandon its commitment to address the challenges and opportunities of an aging society. The elderly as a group will remain a legitimate target for categorical assistance. Nonetheless, I expect three changes to occur. First, the "planning" function so gingerly implemented by presidents since the Progressive era will become an increasingly major task in Washington. Officials and representatives of various special-interest groups will become even more intensely engaged at the federal level in setting priorities, in debating the pros and cons of various new initiatives, and in assessing the overall quality and effectiveness of existing programs. Second, state and especially local levels of government will assume more responsibility and accountability for administering, monitoring, and evaluating categorical programs on a day-to-day basis. This does not mean that Washington will maintain a hands-off posture in these areas: national officials cannot abdicate total responsibility, since federal monies will be used. Rather, federal officials will acknowledge their past difficulties in administering the complex mechanics of multitudinous and multifaceted programs from afar. Third, deliberate efforts will be made to coordinate public policies with private programs. Government officials will do all they can to nurture private initiatives. Greater emphasis will be placed on the role that charities, civic groups, businesses, families, and informal associations play in maintaining the well-being of older Americans. Bureaucrats cannot afford to assume, however, that the private sector has the resources or obligation to do everything.

- *Equity / adequacy.* Only the federal government has the political, economic and social power to maintain minimal standards of financial and social well-being for all segments of the population, including the elderly. It alone has the mandate and influence to ensure that essential civil liberties and rights are protected under the law. Consequently, Washington must be concerned with the issue of adequacy. Yet, while I believe that adequacy issues should be given greater priority in the designs of federal programs for the elderly than they have been accorded lately, the degree of "social adequacy" this society chooses to establish cannot be decided primarily on its own terms, or even exclusively on the merits of a particular proposal. Equity questions have always loomed large. They should continue to do so, because of our national sense of fairness and long-standing commitment to promoting equal rights under the law. The benefits that the aged might receive from changes in the status quo must be weighed in light of the costs and benefits of such amendments to the aging. In this context, the issues of entitlement/expectation and self-reliance/dependency become quite pertinent.

- *Entitlement / expectation.* Because I have already argued that the federal government cannot renege on past commitments, it follows that I think that Washington should take the question of entitlements very seriously. The absolute worth of benefits and current range of those social services mandated by public law cannot be cut back on the whims and desires of those in power. But rising expectations do not have to become automatic entitlements. Their acceptance at the federal level must be a function of prevailing economic and social conditions and the logical outcome of political maneuvering. It is not the responsibility of the public sector to claim that people are automatically entitled to additional perquisites: if Americans through their representatives are unwilling or unable to provide these benefits and services, then it will fall upon other institutions in society and individuals themselves to bear the costs.

- *Self-reliance / dependency.* As far as is practicable, federal programs should promote economic, physical, psychological, and social independence in late life. They should recognize the extraordinary resilience, creativity, and resourcefulness with which many older men and women can fend for themselves. Even those who do not enjoy excellent health or vast savings can achieve a level of self-reliance sufficient to maintain themselves. At the same time, it is the responsibility of the public sector to address the acute needs that cause hardships for pockets within the elderly population, particularly among the frail, the very old, women, and minorities. Those who design and evaluate public programs and private policies for the old must determine the extent to which the problems of these subsets are age-related and the degree to which they reflect and result from the cumulative impact of racial and gender discrimination, limited income and employment opportunities, and chronic disabilities. Depending on the best available evidence, policymakers will be able to decide whether it makes more sense to create new categorical programs for the aged or to amend current aging policies.

- *Work / leisure.* Federal policies should not intentionally express a preference for either work or leisure. Such impartiality, at least in the short run, is essential, given the conflicting retirement patterns and divergent views on the social merits of working expressed by various subsets of the aged population. An impartial posture, however, does not have to be neutral. Indeed, it is naive to pretend otherwise. Raising the requirement age for Social Security benefits or strictly enforcing the Age Discrimination in Employment Act, for instance, will be criticized because these efforts may force people to work longer than they might otherwise have done. Yet such policy decisions certainly could be justified in light of increases in life expectancy and more positive attitudes about the true worth of older workers. Even those who would prefer not to work past a certain age, moreover, may find they have no other choice, given gloomy economic conditions. Thus, public policies must accord those older people who want to work or who have to work the right to do so, and, simultaneously, it must devise macroeconomic policies that will be able to sustain a system in which retirement remains a "right" and in which older people have the wherewithal to pursue meaningful activities once they have quit their job through choice or disability.

- *Family / individual.* Similarly, the federal government should not try to establish a single family policy to embrace all of the needs and circumstances in which people in late life might find themselves. Household arrangements are diverse. Changes will continue to occur in intergenerational exchanges and intragenerational relations over the life courses of family members. It would be far better, in my opinion, to address the rights of elderly Americans as individuals, independent of their family situation. Taking *individual* rights seriously obviously is a central feature of our legal system; it is not implicitly an anti-family posture. Rather, such a stance is based on the assumption that individuals are not unmindful of familial duties or responsibilities, and that by and large they will continue to act as they think best or feel they should, regardless of what the law says. It makes more sense, then, to let the elderly choose the household and institutional arrangements that most appropriately meet their particular needs, as well as those of their relatives, and not to try to dictate generic options.

• *Tradition / novelty*. My recommendations are quite traditional, insofar as they are sensitive to historical trends in the value metastructure during at least the past half-century. They do not posit an either/or choice. On the contrary, they try to build on the creative tensions and ambiguity inherent in any both/and situation. Yet they are novel in at least two ways. On the one hand, they do try to synthesize the best features of Great Society initiatives with the stark realities of our current situation. On the other hand, even if they fail in this regard, they at least make explicit the reasoning behind the value positions I have taken. And this represents a constructive advance in policymaking deliberations.

The tensions and contradictions in prevailing values and social policies in aging America are not merely the product of our pervasive cultural pluralism and "modern" relativism. Our current attitudes and programs are manifestations of the richness and the contrarieties in the human condition—phenomena surely not exclusive to advanced industrial political economies. The philosophical underpinning and empirical impact of these programs are both amazingly resilient and molded by the interplay of historical forces and varying societal circumstances. The proper balance between American values and federal policies that affect the aged and the aging will remain shades of gray in the foreseeable future. We can attempt to change our values and reform our programs, but there are limits to our ability to create incentives or to manipulate ideas in ways that have no basis in historical traditions or in current reality.

It is for this reason that continually scrutinizing our assumptions about the nature and dynamics of growing old(er) is imperative in a society that continues to be at the cutting edge of worldwide modernization. Because the society in which we live is constantly changing, the normative foundations and socio-cultural political economy that sustain the realm of ideas and social policy are continually shifting. Thus if we truly hope to address people's real needs and help them satisfy their desires, we must forever be sensitive to the tension between tradition and novelty. We must be prepared to alter our conceptions and policies to conform more accurately to current circumstances.

Technical Appendix

Competing Models for Understanding Recent American History

Scholars need a way to analyze and synthesize all the information relevant to understanding the interconnections among old age, American values, and federal policies since 1920. Because the options seem limitless, making a good decision about what sort of conceptual framework to employ becomes formidable. Yet *some* choice is necessary: there is simply no construct available that preempts the field.

Researchers can pick and choose from a wide assortment of paradigms and models proffered by structuralists, functionalists, relativists, and pluralists. First-class models disavowing any theoretical predilections are available. Or, investigators can select a conceptual framework that rests on a literary device—such as an apt "metaphor," a central "irony," or a perennial "paradox"—rather than a full-blown theory or set of middle-range hypotheses. Even those whose works claim allegiance to (or revulsion against) a particular school of thought or style of presentation typically defy easy classification. The nuances individual authors interject into their research are too subtle and the distinctions too idiosyncratic to permit a critic to fit their contributions under the rubric of some rigid category.

Covert and overt ideological perspectives that color interpretations invariably affect their conceptual value for an analysis of older people's place in recent American history. Some scholars purposely or unintentionally endorse liberal, capitalist, democratic principles in their studies. A few do so in veiled attacks against the New Left, the

New Right, or both. Marxists and non-Marxists are always fighting with one another. Neo-Marxists generally find the ideas of both camps simplistic.

Researchers must also reckon with the units and levels of analysis set forth in somebody else's study. It matters greatly whether a model deals with one nation or one segment of society, whether it attempts cross-national comparisons and broad, synthetic generalizations, and whether its time frame consists of a year, decade, century, or epoch. Some authors write as if society were the sum of its institutions, studiously avoiding allusions to human actors. To others, recounting the foibles and accomplishments of individuals is far more important than comprehending the society in which they live(d). Ideas count for nothing in some works. Elsewhere, they constitute everything worth knowing. Some investigators are interested in the centripetal forces that amalgamate various groups in society. Others are preoccupied with the centrifugal forces that cause groups to clash. Micro-studies seize on different issues than do macro-analyses.

One way to begin getting a grip on the range of theoretical issues and conceptual choices is to review the literature in an orderly if arbitrary and selective manner. Various perspectives can be organized by identifying the prime causal agent set forth in any given model, which deals with values and structures that alter(ed) the meanings and experiences of old age. What factor above all else causes the change affecting the ongoing evolution of public programs for the aged? What acts as a major catalyst within "modern" society? In my opinion, the "motor" that investigators have argued typically moves society, and which has a decisive impact on older people, appears to be either economic, political, or sociological in character. This motor, of course, rarely operates in a vacuum—it influences and is affected by the other components of society mentioned in the particular analysis. But ultimately, this single force in one way or another seems central, and remains so throughout the time frame under consideration. Let me now amplify what I mean with a few examples. Needless to say, the survey presented here is intended to be illustrative, not definitive.

There is a considerable body of literature that argues that the "modern welfare state"—of which programs for the elderly are plainly an important feature—is the result of economic growth. "The logic of industrialism," in this view, has shaped and continues to move society. Welfare programs and institutions are the natural consequence of changing technological imperatives, rising standards of living, and shifting modes of industrial production, capital formation, and human consumption. With the increase in urbanization, industrialization and bureaucratization, an unprecedented degree of prosperity, economic growth, institutional differentiation, and societal complexity has arisen. At the same time, however, these forces have unleashed a new set of unpleasant side effects, including a form of poverty and dependency quite unlike that found in predominantly agrarian or preindustrial settings (Wilensky and Lebeaux, 1958; Kerr et al., 1964; Pryor, 1968). Variations abound on this basic theme. For instance, Harold L. Wilensky suggests in a recent study that "economic level is the root cause of welfare-state development, but its effects are felt chiefly through demographic changes of the past century and the momentum of the programs themselves, once established" (1975: 47). Hence, in Wilensky's opinion, the economic motor affects demographic changes and influences policy choices, independent of a society's ideological commitments and political system.

Most classical Marxists also assume that the social relations of production determine the nature and dynamics of societal change. The welfare state in such interpretations is usually portrayed as an inevitable effect of a capitalist state impelled by its overriding need, albeit manifested often in curious and contradictory ways, to protect, sustain, and advance capitalist economic structures. Thus, in their attempt to legitimize and effect their particular mode of accumulating capital, bourgeois societies created welfare programs, not primarily to benefit the needy, but to ensure "the continuous expansion of social investment and social consumption projects that in part or in whole indirectly increase productivity from the standpoint of monopoly capital" (O'Connor, 1973: 24; see also Myles, 1981: 4–11). The specific needs of the aged and the categorical benefits they derive may well vary from place to place and historical moment to historical moment. In the final analysis, however, such variations are less salient than the inexorable similarities in strategies and objectives shared by all capitalist societies.

Rather than seizing on economic issues, a second set of interpretations argues that political forces led to the creation of social services and public income-maintenance programs for less fortunate members of society, including the elderly. American scholars used to contend that government's increasing concern for the rights and needs of people at lower levels of the socioeconomic order was both a reflection and the result of its extending the franchise and increasing participation by those previously excluded from the democratic polity (Boorstin, 1953; Hofstadter, 1955). Alternative formulations of this theme remain popular. To some, the civil rights movement and war-on-poverty initiatives are a logical extension of commitments made to advance the Enlightened ideals that had inspired the American and French revolutions. The political fortunes of working-class movements and the ebb and flow of socialism in western nations are of considerable interest to those who believe that efforts to promote equality have been percolating up from the grassroots level as the balance of power has shifted downward (Lipset, 1960; Lenski, 1966; Hewitt, 1977). Another variation on this thesis seeks to explain the rise of "interest-group liberalism" as an ongoing struggle by increasingly more sophisticated coalitions to gain more entitlements and perquisites from governmental bodies. Underscoring the "pluralist" nature of contemporary democracies, theorists such as David Truman (1951) and Theodore Lowi (1968) describe particular governmental decisions about the welfare state as being the outcome of demands and constraints imposed by the need to reconcile conflicting organized-group interests. This interpretation has appealed to many students of the politics of aging, especially in the United States, since it offers a plausible explanation for the timing of the enactment of Social Security and developments during and after the passage of Great Society legislation (Pratt, 1976; Hudson and Binstock, 1976).

Neo-Marxists recently have offered subtle though divergent interpretations about the ways capitalists have controlled state activities through their monopoly of economic power. Nearly all neo-Marxists argue that the "modern" welfare state is an effect of class struggles, but they emphasize different points within this broad framework. Thus, some debunk the pluralist interpretation by claiming that the power elite sanctioned welfare initiatives in a (desperate) attempt to save the state and rationalize the system. To varying degrees, scholars espousing this view attribute shrewd and farsighted qualities to those in power. Or, they claim that policymakers were basically formulating an instrumental solution to a malfunction in the system (Weinstein, 1968; Miliband, 1969; Domhoff, 1971; Radosh, 1972). Critics of these "corporate liberal" models propose instead that welfare reforms were not simply a way to protect the vested interests of the ruling class. Reforms were also a way of placating the competing interests of various potent forces and reducing the forces of insurgency manifest in the lower classes (Poulantzas, 1973). In attempting to explain the limited degree to which the United States has embarked upon a "full employment welfare state pattern of economic policy," Martin (1973) places great emphasis on the fact that American business elites are rarely challenged in the democratic process. In other highly industrialized, pluralist countries (such as Sweden), on the other hand, labor elites have been dominant in policymaking circles. These are promising lines of inquiry. Yet as Theda Skocpol recently noted, "No self-declared neo-Marxist theory of the capitalist state has arrived at the point of taking state structures and party organizations *seriously enough*" (1980: 199–200). Indeed, in order to appreciate the independent role that bureaucracies have played in shaping the aged's welfare programs, it is necessary to read the intellectual successors of Max Weber, not Karl Marx.

Political sociologists have offered invaluable evidence indicating that bureaucracies develop a momentum of their own. They also have demonstrated the surprisingly narrow range of options available to policymakers in charge of any particular program (Heclo, 1974; Wildavsky, 1979). Here too, of course, one detects unmistakable differences in ideological predilections. Hence, Claus Offe claims that "the margin of 'feasible' policy alternatives is too small to allow for principled choice . . . no government can afford to expand welfare services beyond a certain limit without being punished by inflation, unemployment, or both. The margin of decision thus becomes so slight in a capitalist society as to be barely visible" (1972: 484–85). In her prize-winning study *Policy-making in Social Security* (1979), Martha Derthick offers a contrasting view of the scope and function of government. She claims that until the mid-1970s Social Security was actually insulated from tough political choices, because it had become a "sacred cow." The system had grown very much as its original creators had intended, thanks to the nation's long-term growth—and, more importantly, because a cadre of experts who shuttled from government posts to academic and consulting positions made certain that the program evolved in a politically feasible and manageable way. To understand the "politics of aging," in this view, one needs to make an intensive analysis of the mind set and activities of a fairly small number of "elite" actors (Pechman et al., 1968; Skidmore, 1981).

Others who opt for sociological interpretations of the rise of the welfare state insist on studying the interplay among a much larger population. For instance, interpretations of Social Security that describe the legislation as a genuine act of "social welfare" tend to emphasize the extent to which public officials built on steadily more liberal precedents and responded to the needs of the aged poor and unemployed in moments of acute distress (Schlesinger, 1958; Altmeyer, 1966; Lubove, 1968). From a social control perspective, however, the original enactment of Social Security was a shrewd but relatively stingy attempt to defuse political clamor and, in particular, the social unrest fomented by Townsendites and other radicals (Piven and Cloward, 1971; for a critique of this work, see Achenbaum, 1980). Note that these sociological arguments dovetail with political interpretations. What sets them apart is their focus on the forces that bind and divide American society across ethnic, racial, and class lines, rather than an emphasis on party coalitions or voting patterns.

Though a wide range of interpretations are available, none of the theories sketched above is completely satisfactory. A major problem with each is that the central interpretive "motor" is too deterministic: under fluid historical circumstances, there is little indication that the truly salient forces might converge and diverge in different configurations. The models are so neat that it is hard to discern where an investigator would put an anomalous case or how one would handle evidence that simply does not fit the framework. With few exceptions, none of these theories takes "ideas" seriously. One must assume that ideas count for little, or discount their potential significance at the outset.

For these reasons, I have used a modernization model in formulating my interpretation rather than relying on one of the monocausal theories surveyed in this section. I have done so despite all the charges about its inadequacies as an analytic device. In my opinion, the case against "modernization" is not devastating. A well-designed modernization model remains useful to describe and explain disparate but manifestly significant socio-cultural phenomena over time. Indeed, such a model has a temporal perspective that is either missing, understated, or too mechanistically imposed in the other theories.

The model set forth in *Shades of Gray* should enable historians and gerontologists to talk to one another intelligently about the interconnections among "modern" values, public policies for the aged, and the fundamental changes that have occurred in the evolution of America's political economy and social structure. It serves as a heuristic tool, which enables us to formulate questions that may not have been initially apparent. It permits us to engage in purposive, systemic analysis (Janowitz, 1978). And since our ultimate task here is to trace the evolution of social programs for the aged and aging in the context of continuities and changes across a variety of dimensions, this sensitivity to the unevenness and messiness of the historical process becomes a major conceptual advantage. For our present purposes, in fact, a reformulated modernization model sharpens our focus—as long as we profit from past mistakes and are explicit about how we intend to use the model.

The Case for Using a Modernization Model

The intellectual foundations supporting the concept of "modernization" were laid by Adam Smith, Condorcet, and Malthus roughly two centuries ago. The main lines of modernization theory, however, were formulated in earnest after World War II by economists, political scientists, anthropologists, and sociologists concerned with developing nations outside the western community (Levy,

1966). Some students of aging were in the vanguard of theorists. For instance, Leo Simmons's *The Role of the Aged in Primitive Societies* (1945), which argued that an older person's status in a given society was inversely related to the level of technological development and occupational structure, remains one of the most influential applications of modernization theory to gerontology. Simmons's hypotheses have been refined by international teams of scholars engaged in cross-national, comparative research (Cowgill and Holmes, 1972; Maddox and Wiley, 1976; Hendricks, 1982).

Historians, philosophers, and other humanists began to write critiques of "modernization theory" only during the past fifteen years. Few have studied how the process of modernization has affected the aged and the aging across geo-political boundaries and over time. Nevertheless, most of the currently available histories of old age build on insights derived from an understanding of how the processes of democratization, industrialization, urbanization, immigration, secularization, and bureaucratization have affected the broader contours of society in general, and attitudes toward age and the elderly's status in particular (Achenbaum, 1982). Thus despite their belated interest in old age and modernization when compared to other social scientists, historians have helped to identify various problems with existing modernization theories and to propose refined models (see, for example, Grew, 1977 and 1980; Stearns, 1980a).

That said, it must be quickly added that familiarity really can breed contempt. During the 1960s and early 1970s, it was fashionable to cite the works of Daniel Lerner, S. N. Eisenstadt, Cyril Black, and Alex Inkeles, and to claim that one's research confirmed or elaborated upon a major insight set forth by these seminal thinkers. It is now the style to criticize "modernization." Familiarity with the major tenets of modernization theory, moreover, has led to a certain looseness of usage. Gerontologists have invoked the concept largely to contrast the circumstances of past times to current conditions. Historians have used it as an analytic construct—or straw man—to interpret nineteenth-century developments. They rarely have applied it to investigate trends during the last half-century. Fundamental limitations in the schema's applicability, consequently, seem so apparent that the objections to modernization have become ritualized, possibly even trivialized.

Many of the reservations are quite legitimate. At least four criticisms of modernization must be squarely addressed. Indeed, this volume self-consciously attempts to move beyond the problems found in other modernization models in these specific areas:

1. We must acknowledge that many experts have confused "mod-

ernization" and "development" in recommending that western technology, social philosophy, and political economics be adopted by newly independent nations of the Third World (Tipps, 1973). Equating the history of western civilization with the dynamics of modernization is fallacious. The danger in assuming that all "progressive" societies have evolved and will continue to advance in roughly the same way has been painfully demonstrated in the international arena since World War II. This book, in fact, suggests that the relationships among dominant values, political policies, social and economic structures, and various segments of the population have depended greatly on the distinctive nature and dynamics of recent American history itself. Needless to say, such a pattern of development is not easily replicated.

2. Similarly, we must guard against the implicit teleological assumption that whatever path of evolution conforms to "the American way" *ipso facto* is "good"—or, depending on your politics, "misguided" or "bad." As I have attempted to demonstrate in *Shades of Gray,* the course of American history has never been ever upward or steadily downward. The making of recent American society has been irregular and uneven. Older people's successes and failures in adapting to new developments have not always dovetailed precisely with the experiences of other age groups.

3. Keeping these first two points in mind will help us avoid another fundamental problem with many analyses that use "modernization" as an organizing device. Two-stage models, in which the process of modernization serves as both the description of and explanation for all that changed, are too neat. Typically they use chronological boundaries as arbitrary markers for encapsulating an array of familiar if contrapuntal forces—such as the growth of individual freedom and the rise of bureaucratization, or the impact of secularization and the celebration of civic religion—that are said to converge decisively in a given time frame.

Certainly, it is not too difficult to remedy some of the obvious deficiencies in such a mode of presentation. Because rates of change during an historical era are rarely continuous and because overall rates seldom are the same as component rates, two-stage models must give way to temporal constructs that differentiate eras from periods and that permit one to trace epicycles and discontinuities within a historical context. This requires, in turn, careful delineation of the forces of modernization. It is imperative to acknowledge that concomitant demographic, economic, social, political, normative, psychological, and attitudinal processes do not interact according to prescribed formulas. They affect various segments of the population in distinctive ways, often at different

times (Stearns, 1980b). Thus there must be room in a modernization framework for variations and anomalies.

4. Finally, the predictive value of modernization theory is debatable,
    because fundamental changes in society generally have occurred
    in unexpected ways. We have little reason to expect that they will
    become any more regular in the future. It would be quite useful,
    for instance, if modernization theory could resolve the debate
    over whether we are in the midst of entering yet another stage of
    development. Daniel Bell (1973) contends that recent trends in
    the United States signal "the coming of post-industrial society";
    Amitai Etzioni (1968) argues that the "post-modern" era began in
    1945 with the explosion of new technologies of knowledge; Alvin
    Toffler celebrates the freedom and progress to be achieved once
    existing technologies usher in "the Third Wave" (1980). But after
    nearly a decade of debate in scholarly journals and the popular
    press, terms such as "post-industrial" still lack precise meaning. It
    is hard to imagine how a "post-modern" world will really differ all
    that much from our own. Yet, by definition, any general theory is
    suspect if it fails to generate testable hypotheses that can be
    rejected with empirical evidence. Others concerned with the
    future of "modernization" present their scenarios of "the brave
    new world" as bald statements of fact. They leave little room in
    their analyses for competing visions and alternative arrangements.
    Knowing something about the process of modernization, in short,
    does not afford us irrefutable insights into the long-term sig-
    nificance of contemporary developments.

    Nevertheless, the primary reason for using a modernization
model here is not to forecast future developments. Instead, this
analysis uses the device to make sense of our recent past: it helps
us extend the mode of analysis already effectively utilized to
describe and explain crucial developments in eighteenth- and
nineteenth-century American society and culture. It is modernization's retrodictive power rather than its predictive function that
makes the model so applicable here.

    Indeed, the modernization model presented in *Shades of Gray*
differs from other versions in at least two ways. To the best of my
knowledge, it constitutes the first time that a historian has used such
a heuristic construct specifically to analyze the history of older Americans in the twentieth century. More importantly, it takes "values"
seriously. The normative dimensions of modernization, particularly
as they have influenced the evolution of federal old-age policies, are
a major concern here.

The Modernization of American Values

The interaction of values in the process of modernization is as important to comprehend as the cumulative effects of bureaucratization, urbanization, industrialization, secularization, professionalization, and immigration on western civilization in general and aging America in particular. "Problems of values," claims the distinguished Cornell University sociologist Robin Williams (1968: 286), "appear in all fields of the social sciences, and value elements are potentially important as variables to be analyzed in all majors areas of investigation." The causal connection among the structural, material, and ideational components of modernization has preoccupied countless Marxists, non-Marxists, structuralists, relativists, and specialists of most humanistic and social science disciplines. Studies of "national character," which endeavored to trace continuities and changes in individual and collective aspirations, were in vogue among American scholars during the 1950s and 1960s. Thus Berger, Berger, and Kellner are not alone in hypothesizing that "technological production and bureaucracy constitute primary carriers of modern consciousness" (1974: 110), or that "social mobility has its correlate in cognitive and normative mobility" (184).

This is not to suggest that "modern" values have been treated by all investigators as a function or a by-product of social patterns and economic structures that emerged during the past two centuries. Classical social theorists, to be sure, long have emphasized points of *convergence* between culture and social structure in any given country. Because Marxists believe that modes of production shape all other dimensions of society, they tend to treat the development of value systems as a substructure without any autonomy of its own. Many non-Marxists, similarly, presume that people's feelings and beliefs, patterns of behavior, and ways of structuring their community are highly integrated in all major features of bourgeois life (Bell, 1976). Nevertheless, scholars have hardly ignored the nature and degree of *divergence* between the normative and structural components of modern life. Successive generations of social scientists, elaborating insights formulated by Weber, Durkheim, and Sorokin, have hypothesized that the disjunction between social structure and culture is one of the major sources of tension and contradiction characterizing individual and societal values since the Industrial Revolution.

Historians, moreover, have been very interested in tracing the value implications of American culture, as it has been transforming from a relatively youthful, industrial base to a demographically older and service-oriented political economy. Intellectual and cultural historians have documented the remarkable resiliency of dominant beliefs and prevailing attitudes from one generation to the next.

Premodern attitudes flourished in various regions of the country and among certain ethnic groups well into the twentieth century (Berkhofer, 1978; Wyatt-Brown, 1982; Yans-McLaughlin, 1977). Antimodernist strands of thought were being nurtured by the very sociocultural forces and politico-economic trends that ushered in the Progressive era (Jaher, 1964; Lears, 1981). Hence, students interested in the modernization of American values must perform two complementary tasks. On the one hand, they must devise an analytic construct that enables them to dissect the fluid structure of value clusters. On the other hand, they must attempt to trace the relationship of ideas, values, and beliefs to other societal developments. To study "the modernization of American values," in short, an analyst must view some values as a source of continuity altering changes occurring in different areas and treat other values as changing factors themselves.

There are many ways to conceptualize America's value systems. The schematics designed by deTocqueville (1835), Riesman et al. (1950), Lipset (1963), Myrdal (1944), Erikson (1963), Free and Cantril (1967), and Potter (1954) are among the best known and remain instructive. In *Shades of Gray,* I prefer to use a modified version of the model built for the "American Values and the Elderly" project at the Institute of Gerontology in The University of Michigan. As a member of an interdisciplinary research team (including professors and graduates students of sociology, social work, political science, philosophy, English, economics, public welfare, art, statistics, and American culture), I helped to identify a set of seven enduring, discrete, and complementary dilemmas that appeared again and again in quite a variety of old-age programs. The seven were (1) self-reliance/dependency, (2) struggle/achievement, (3) work/leisure, (4) individual/family, (5) equity/adequacy, (6) private/public, and (7) religious/secular.[1] These values generally have had an impact on national policies in sets of multiples. Hence, building on insights gained from my participation in the Michigan study, I have sought in this book to determine how all seven pairs, each qualifying and enhancing the meaning or import of some of the others, might affect the shape of any specific policy outcome. Such interlocking of values implies ambiguity and conflict, but it does not necessarily signify mutual exclusivity. Indeed, as noted in Chapter

---

[1] My revision of the Michigan model differs mainly in nomenclature. In my opinion, the policy tension described by the Ann Arbor research report as religion/secular is better conveyed by describing the inherent conflict between the forces of tradition and novelty. Similarly, I think that the original intent of the values conflict between "struggle" and "achievement" is more effectively discussed by highlighting the tensions between expectations and entitlements. For a fuller accounting, see Institute of Gerontology, 1979. Tropman (1976) presents the original rationale for the set of values studied in the Michigan project.

One and illustrated throughout this book, policy outcomes affecting the aged and the aging reflect and result from the choices and constraints intrinsic to a dynamic, dualistic, and pluralistic system of values.

Likely objections to the scheme used here to comprehend the modernization of American values must be faced. My hope is that they can be countered with a sufficient degree of clarity and conviction. Some critics might contend that a set of fourteen values is too small to analyze. There are, however, intuitive, empirical, and theoretical grounds for believing that a relatively small set of values guides an individual's behavior or viewpoint (Rokeach, 1976). I am inferring that similar grounds pertain at the national level. Perhaps one example will suffice. If we were to study all possible interrelationships among these fourteen values, they could be arranged in order of importance in fourteen factorial ways, which would result in roughly 6.71 *billion* combinations! Surely this is a universe far too vast for anyone to contemplate. It is also greater than needs to be considered. By looking at combinations with a sense of history and an understanding of human nature and social organizations, one can eliminate many possible scenarios.

But even if a set of fourteen values is plausible, how do we know that these are the right ones? After all, certain obvious alternatives—capitalism, equality, democracy—are conspicuously missing from the list. Such values actually were considered, but in the end members of the "American Values and the Elderly" project decided not to include them because such concepts evoked multiple connotations at any given moment, and meant different things to different groups of people at different points in time. Consider "equality." What does that word mean in the American experience? According to Pole (1978), throughout our history the term has simultaneously referred to equality of condition, equality of opportunity, and equality of result; at other times, the word has taken on other meanings. Such diverse connotations speak to the essential, even necessary, ambiguity of highly important cultural values. Ironically, however, a high level of abstraction limits the real significance of such pivotal beliefs on nittygritty decisions of policymaking. The policy elite appeal to abstractions; in reality, however, the men and women who make policy have more operational definitions in mind. It is from this level, therefore, that the value dualisms used here are derived.

Shades of Gray neither discounts nor dismisses the significance of broad concepts such as "democracy" or "equality." Rather, I attempted to reduce the "bigger" values into smaller, more manageable components. This was accomplished by seizing on the terms policymakers used in the course of their deliberations over time. To compile a list of policy-relevant values, members of the "American

Values and the Elderly" project read widely and argued vociferously. We also did extensive analyses of the language of old-age programs and got reactions to our schema from bureaucrats, as well as from academic experts in the policy-science fields and values areas. While some of the meanings of the fourteen values changed during the last half-century, the operationalization of such transvaluations did not prove to be an insurmountable task. This research strategy, needless to say, does not preclude a certain arbitrariness in criteria. I suspect, however, that no meta-structure can convincingly dispel that charge.

At this point, skeptics probably would shift their criticisms from a theoretical plane to a more pragmatic level. They might rightly ask whether policy influentials really care about how modern values affect the elderly in aging America. There is, frankly, little evidence to suggest that specialists in the field *do* care. Experts invariably express the need to understand values, but the systematic analysis of values toward the aging and the aged remains a relatively low priority on most research agendas. Nevertheless, there is a growing sense in policy circles and the public at large that the prevailing methods of defining and dealing with the challenges and opportunities of growing older need to be reviewed and revamped. As various segments of the professional aging network prepared for the 1981 White House Conference on Aging, several leaders in the field echoed a former Senate Special Committee on Aging staff director's opinion that the Michigan project's value system "could help intensify societal self-appraisal" (Oriol, 1981: 42; see also National Council on the Aging, 1981; National Interfaith Coalition on Aging, 1981). Thus even though precise links between this particular value meta-structure and the policy arena remain ill defined and untested, the schema seems to have attracted enough attention to merit further reflection. Ideally, *Shades of Gray* will advance our thinking even more.

References

Achenbaum, W. A. Fall 1974. The Obsolescence of Old Age in America, 1865–1914. *J. Soc. Hist.,* **8,** 45–64.

Achenbaum, W. A. 1978a. From Womb through Bloom to Tomb. *Rev. in Am. Hist.,* **6,** 178–184.

Achenbaum, W. A. 1978b. *Old Age in the New Land: The American Experience since 1790.* Baltimore: The Johns Hopkins University Press.

Achenbaum, W. A. December 1980. Did Social Security Attempt to Regulate the Poor? *Res. on Aging.* **2,** 270–288.

Achenbaum, W. A. Summer 1982. Further Perspectives on Modernization and Aging. *Soc. Sci. Hist.,* **6,** 347–368.

Achenbaum, W. A. Forthcoming. Societal Perceptions of Old Age and Aging. In R. H. Binstock and E. Shanas (eds.), *Handbook of Aging and the Social Sciences,* 2nd ed. New York: Van Nostrand Reinhold.

Achenbaum, W. A., and Stearns, P. N. June 1978. Old Age and Modernization. *The Gerontologist,* **18,** 307–313.

Ahlstrom, S. E. 1972. *A Religious History of the American People.* New Haven: Yale University Press.

Albrecht, R. 1951. Social Roles in the Prevention of Senility. *J. of Gerontology,* **6,** 380–386.

Altmeyer, A. J. November 1942. The Desirability of Expanding the Social Insurance Program Now. *Social Security Bull.,* **5,** 3–8.

Altmeyer, A. J. 1966. *The Formative Years of Social Security.* Madison: Univ. of Wisconsin Press.

Anderson, J. E. 1979. *Public Policy-Making.* 2nd ed. New York: Holt, Rinehart and Winston.

Anderson, M. 1978. *Welfare.* Stanford: Stanford University, Hoover Institution.

Ansello, E. 1977. Age and Ageism in Children's First Literature. *Ed. Gerontology,* **2,** 255–274.

Ariès, P. 1962. *Centuries of Childhood,* trans. R. Bardick. New York: Knopf.

Atchley, R. C. 1980. *The Social Forces in Late Life,* 3rd ed. Belmont, CA: Wadsworth Publishing Co.

Bailyn, B., Davis, D. B., Donald, D. H., Thomas, J. L., Wiebe, R. H., and Wood, G. 1981. *The Great Republic,* 2nd ed. Lexington, MA: D. C. Heath.

Baldwin, S. 1968, *Poverty and Politics.* Chapel Hill: University of North Carolina Press.

Bane, F. December 1939. The Social Security Act Expands. *Social Service Review,* 13, 608–609.

Barron, M. L. 1953. Minority Characteristics of the Aged in American Society. *J. of Gerontology,* 8, 477–482.

Beard, B. B. 1949. Are the Aged Ex-Family? *Social Forces,* 27, 274–279.

Becker, E. 1973. *The Denial of Death.* New York: Free Press.

Belasco, W. 1979. *Americans on the Road.* Cambridge, MA: MIT Press.

Bell, D. 1960. *The End of Ideology.* Glencoe, IL: The Free Press.

Bell, D. 1973. *The Coming of Post-Industrial Society.* New York: Basic Books.

Bell, D. 1976. *The Cultural Contradictions of Capitalism.* New York: Basic Books.

Benedict, R. C. 1978. Trends in the Development of Services for the Aging under the Older Americans Act. In B. R. Herzog (ed.), *Aging and Income.* New York: Human Sciences Press.

Berg, G., and Gadow, S. 1978. Toward More Human Meanings of Aging: Ideals and Images from Philosophy and Art. In S. F. Spicker, K. M. Woodward, and D. D. Van Tassel (eds.), *Aging and the Elderly,* pp. 83–92. Atlantic Highlands, NJ: Humanities Press.

Berger, P. L., Berger, B., and Kellner, H. 1974. *The Homeless Mind.* New York: Random House.

Berkhofer, R. F., Jr. 1978. *The White Man's Indian.* New York: Knopf.

Berkowitz, E., and McQuaid, K. 1980. *Creating the Welfare State.* New York: Praeger.

Binstock, R. H. August 1974. Aging and the Future of American Politics. *Annals Am. Acad. of Pol. and Soc. Sci.,* 201–212.

Binstock, R. H. November 11, 1978. Federal Policy Toward the Aging—Its Inadequacies and Its Politics. *National Journal,* 1838–1844.

Binstock, R. H., and Levin, M. A. 1976. The Political Dilemmas of Intervention Policies. In R. H. Binstock and E. Shanas (eds.), *Handbook of Aging and the Social Sciences,* pp. 511–536. New York: Van Nostrand Reinhold.

Binstock, R. H., and Shanas, E., eds. 1976. *Handbook of Aging and the Social Sciences.* New York: Van Nostrand Reinhold.

Blum, J. M. 1980. *The Progressive Presidents.* New York: W. W. Norton Co.

Blum, J. M., Morgan, E. S., Rose, W. L., Schlesinger, A. M., Jr., Stampp, K. M., and Woodward C. V. 1981. *The National Experience,* 5th ed. New York: Harcourt, Brace, Jovanovich.

Bogue, D. J. 1959. *The Population of the United States.* Glencoe, IL: The Free Press.

Boorstin, D. 1953. *The Genius of American Politics.* Chicago: The University of Chicago Press.

Braeman, J., Bremner, R. H., and Brody, D., eds. 1975. *The New Deal: The National Level.* Columbus: Ohio State University Press.

Brandes, S. 1975. *American Welfare Capitalism.* Chicago: The University of Chicago Press.

Broder, D. S. 1980. *The Changing of the Guard.* New York: Simon & Schuster.

Brody, E. October 27, 1979. Women's Changing Roles, the Aging Family and Long-Term Care for Old People. *National Journal,* 1828–1833.

Brown, J. D. 1972. *An American Philosophy of Social Security.* Princeton: Princeton University Press.

Brown, J. D. 1977. *Essays on Social Security.* Princeton: Princeton University Press.

Brown, R. D. 1976. *Modernization: The Transformation of American Life, 1600–1865.* New York: Hill and Wang.

Buchanan, A. R. 1977. *Black Americans in World War II.* Santa Barbara: ABC-Clio Press.

Burgess, E. W. 1957. The Older Generation and the Family. In W. Donahue and C. Tibbitts (eds.), *The New Frontiers of Aging,* pp. 158–171. Ann Arbor: The University of Michigan Press.

Burke, V. J., and Burke, V. 1974. *Nixon's Good Deed.* New York: Columbia University Press.

Butler, R. N. 1975. *Why Survive? Being Old in America.* New York: Harper & Row.

Calhoun, R. B. 1978. *In Search of the New Old: Redefining Old Age in America, 1945–1970.* New York: Elsevier.

Campbell, A., Converse, P. E., Miller, W. E., and Stokes, D. 1960. *The American Voter.* New York: Wiley.

Campbell, A., Converse, P. E., and Rodgers, W. L. 1976. *The Quality of American Life.* New York: Russell Sage Foundation.

Campbell, J. C., and Strate, J. December 1981. Are Old People Conservative? *Gerontologist.* **21,** 580–591.

Campbell, R. R. 1977. *Social Security; Promise and Reality.* Stanford, Calif: Hoover Institute Press.

Carter, H., and Glick, P. C. 1970. *Marriage and Divorce.* Cambridge, MA: Harvard University Press.

Cetina, J. G. 1977. A History of Veterans' Homes in the United States, 1811–1930. Unpublished Ph.D. dissertation Case Western Reserve University.

Chandler, A. D., Jr. 1977. *The Visible Hand.* Cambridge, MA: Harvard University Press.

Chevan, A., and Korson, J. H. 1972. The Widowed Who Live Alone. *Social Forces.* **57,** 45–53.

Clark, M., and Anderson, B. G. 1967. *Culture and Aging.* Springfield, IL: Charles C Thomas.

Clecak, P. 1977. *Crooked Paths.* New York: Harper & Row.

Cohen, W. J. 1952. Income Maintenance for the Aged. *Annals Am. Acad. of Pol. and Soc. Sci.,* **279,** 153–160.

Cohen, W. J. 1957. *Retirement Policies under Social Security.* Berkeley: University of California Press.

Conant, L., Jr. *A Critical Analysis of Industrial Pension Systems.* New York: Macmillan Co.

Conkin, P. K. 1967. *The New Deal.* New York: Thomas Y. Crowell Co.

Converse, P. 1964. The Nature of Belief Systems in Mass Politics. In D. E. Apter (ed.), *Ideology and Discontent.* New York: Free Press.

Cottrell, F. 1960. Governmental Functions and the Politics of Age. In C. Tibbitts (ed.), *Handbook of Social Gerontology,* pp. 624–665. Chicago: The University of Chicago Press.

Cowgill, D., and Holmes, L. 1972. *Aging and Modernization*. New York: Appelton-Century-Crofts.

Cox, A. November 1966. Foreword: The Supreme Court. *Harvard Law Review*. **80**, 1–125.

Croly, H. 1909. *The Promise of American Life*. Indianapolis: Bobbs-Merrill Co.

Cumming, E., and Henry, W. 1961. *Growing Old*. New York: Basic Books.

Cunliffe, M. 1968. American Watersheds. In H. Cohen (ed.), *The American Experience*. pp. 366–380. Boston: Houghton Mifflin.

Cutler, N. E. 1979. Age Variations in the Dimensionality of Life Satisfaction. *J. of Gerontology*. **34**, 573–578.

Dahlin, M. 1980. Perspectives on the Family Life of the Elderly in 1900. *The Gerontologist*, **20**, 99–107.

Davis, K., and Schoen, C. 1978. *Health and the War on Poverty*. Washington, DC: Brookings Institution.

de Beauvoir, S. 1972. *The Coming of Age*. New York: G. P. Putnam's Sons.

Degler, C. N. 1975. *Affluence and Anxiety*, 2nd ed. Glencoe, IL: Scott, Foresman and Co.

Degler, C. N. 1980. *At Odds*. New York: Oxford University Press.

Demos, J. 1978. Old Age in Colonial New England. In M. Gordon (ed.), *The Family in Social-Historical Perspective*, 2nd ed., pp. 220–257. New York: St. Martin's Press.

Demos, J., and Boocock, S. S., eds. 1978. *Turning Points*. Chicago: The University of Chicago Press.

Derthick, M. 1979. *Policy-making in Social Security*. Washington, DC: Brookings Institution.

de Tocqueville, A. 1835. *Democracy in America*, 2 vols. New York: Vintage Books.

Dickstein, M. 1977. *The Gates of Eden*. New York: Basic Books.

Dinkel, R. M. August 1944. Attitudes of Children toward Supporting Aged Parents. *Am. Soc. Rev.*, **9**, 375–389.

Dollar, C. M., Holland, R. A., Gunderson, J., Satz, R. N., Nelson, H. V., Jr., and Reichard, G. W. 1979. *America: Changing Times*. New York: John Wiley & Sons.

Domhoff, G. W. 1971. *The Higher Circles*. New York: Vintage.

Donahue, W., Orbach, H. L., and Pollack, O. 1960. Retirement: The Emerging Social Pattern. In C. Tibbitts (ed.), *Handbook of Social Gerontology*, pp. 330–406. Chicago: The University of Chicago Press.

Donovan, J. C. 1973. *The Politics of Poverty*, 2nd ed. Indianapolis: Bobbs-Merrill Co.

Dos Passos, J. 1944. *State of the Nation*. Boston: Houghton Mifflin Co.

Douglas, M., and Wildavsky, A. 1982. *Risk and Culture*. Berkeley: University of California Press.

Douglas, P. H. 1936. *Social Security in the United States*. New York: McGraw-Hill.

Drucker, P. F. 1976. *The Unseen Revolution*. New York: Harper & Row.

Dubofsky, M. 1975. *Industrialism and the American Worker*. New York: Thomas Y. Crowell.

Duncan, O. D. 1968. Inheritance of Poverty or Inheritance of Race. In D. P. Moynihan (ed.), *On Understanding Poverty*. New York: Basic Books.

Dushkin Publishing Group. 1974. *The Study of American History*, 2 vols. Guilford, CT: Dushkin Publishing Co.

Edelman, M. 1967. *The Symbolic Uses of Politics*. Urbana: University of Illinois Press.

Edelman, M. 1977. *Words That Succeed, Policies That Fail.* New York: Academic Press.

Eisenstadt, S. N. 1956. *From Generation to Generation.* New York: The Free Press.

Ekirch A. A. 1969. *Ideologies and Utopias.* Chicago: Quadrangle Books.

Elder, G. 1974. *Children of the Great Depression.* Chicago: The University of Chicago Press.

Erikson, E. 1963. *Childhood and Society,* 2nd ed. New York: W. W. Norton.

Estes, C. L. 1979. *The Aging Enterprise.* San Francisco: Jossey-Bass.

Etzioni, A. 1968. *The Active Society.* New York: Free Press.

Evans, S. 1979. *Personal Politics.* New York: Vintage.

Fass, P. 1978. *The Damned and the Beautiful.* New York: Oxford University Press.

Federalist Papers. Essays prepared by Hamilton, Madison, and Jay. 1787–1788. New York: Mentor, 1961.

Ferris, E. 1933. *Who Says Old?* New York: Harper Bros.

Fischer, D. H. 1977. *Growing Old in America.* New York: Oxford University Press.

Fischer, D. H. 1978. *Growing Old in America,* expanded ed. New York: Oxford University Press.

Fishman, L. 1966. *Poverty amid Affluence.* New Haven: Yale University Press.

Fogelson, R. M. 1981. The Morass: An Essay on the Public Employee Pension Program. In D. J. Rothman and S. Wheeler (eds.), *Social History and Social Policy,* 145–173. New York: Academic Press.

Frank, L. 1946. Gerontology. *J. of Gerontology,* 1, 1–12.

Free, L. A., and Cantril, H. 1967. *Political Beliefs of Americans.* New Brunswick: Rutgers University Press.

Freeman, J. T. 1979. *Aging: Its History and Literature.* New York: Human Sciences Press.

Friedan, B. 1963. *The Feminine Mystique.* New York: Dell.

Friedan, B. 1981. *The Second Stage.* New York: Simon & Schuster.

Friedländer, S. 1978. *When Memory Comes.* New York: Avon.

Friedmann, E., and Havighurst, R. J. 1954. *The Meaning of Work and Retirement.* Chicago: The University of Chicago Press.

Galbraith, J. K. 1958. *The Affluent Society.* Boston: Houghton Mifflin Co.

Galbraith, J. K. 1967. *The New Industrial State.* Boston: Houghton Mifflin Co.

Garraty, J. A. 1978. *Unemployment in History.* New York: Harper & Row.

Garraty, J. A. 1979. *The American Nation,* 4th ed. New York: Harper & Row.

Gelfand, D. E. 1982. *Aging: The Ethnic Factor.* Boston: Little Brown.

Gilbert, J. 1981. *Another Chance: Postwar America, 1945–1968.* Philadelphia: Temple University Press.

Gilbert, N. September/October 1981. The Future of Welfare Capitalism. *Society,* 18, 28–37.

Gillis, J. R. 1974. *Youth and History.* New York: Academic Press.

Glasson, W. H. 1918. *Federal Military Pensions in the United States.* New York: Oxford University Press.

Glick, P. C. February 1975. A Demographer Looks at American Families. *J. of Marriage and the Family,* 37, 15–26.

Gold, B., Kutza, E., and Marmor, T. R. 1977. United States Social Policy on Old Age: Present Patterns and Predictions. In B. L. Neugarten and R. J. Havighurst (eds.), *Social Policy, Social Ethics and Aging Society,* pp. 9–21. Washington, DC: Government Printing Office.

Gordon, C., and Gaitz, C. M. 1976. Leisure and Lives: Personal Expressivity Across the Life Span. In R. H. Binstock and E. Shanas (eds.), *Handbook of Aging and the Social Sciences,* pp. 310–341. New York: Van Nostrand Reinhold.

Gordon, M. S. 1960. Aging and Income Security. In C. Tibbitts (ed.), *Handbook of Social Gerontology,* pp. 208–261. Chicago: The University of Chicago Press.

Gordon, M. 1978. *The American Family in Social-Historical Perspective,* 2nd ed. New York: St. Martin's Press.

Gordon, M. 1979. *The American Family.* New York: Random House.

Grabill, W. H., Kiser, C. V., and Whelpton, P. K. 1958. *The Fertility of American Women.* New York: John Wiley and Sons, Inc.

Graebner, W. 1980. *A History of Retirement: The Meanings and Function of an American Institution, 1885–1978.* New Haven: Yale University Press.

Graham, O. L., Jr., 1976. *Toward a Planned Society.* New York: Oxford University Press.

Greider, W. December 1981. The Education of David Stockman. *The Atlantic,* **248,** 27–54.

Grew, R. November-December 1977. Modernization and Its Discontents. *American Behavioral Scientist,* **12,** 289–312.

Grew, R. Winter 1980. More on Modernization. *J. Soc. Hist.,* **14,** 179–189.

Gruman, G. J. 1978. Cultural Origins of Present-day "Age-ism": The Modernization of the Life Cycle. In S. F. Spicker, K. M. Woodward, and D. D. Van Tassel (eds.), *Aging and the Elderly,* pp. 359–387. Atlantic Highlands, NJ: Humanities Press.

Haber, C. 1979. Mandatory Retirement in 19th Century America. *J. Soc. Hist.,* **12,** 77–97.

Hall, G. S. 1922. *Senescence.* New York: D. Appleton & Co.

Hareven, T. May 24, 1978. Historical Changes in the Life Course and the Family: Policy Implications for the Aged. Testimony in Joint Hearing before the Select Committee on Population, U.S. House of Representatives and the Select Committee on Aging, 95th Congress, vol. 1, no. 9. Washington, DC: Government Printing Office.

Harrington, M. 1963. *The Other America.* Baltimore: Penguin Books.

Harris, A., and Feinberg, J. F. 1977. Television and Aging. *Gerontologist,* **17,** 464–469.

Harris L., and Associates. 1975. *The Myth and Reality of Aging in America.* Washington, DC: National Council on the Aging, Inc.

Hart, E. J. March 1941. The Responsibility of Relatives under State Old Age Assistance Laws. *Social Service Review,* **15,** 24–54.

Havighurst, R. J. 1952. Social and Psychological Needs of the Aging. *Annals Am. Acad. of Pol. and Soc. Sci.,* **279,** 11–17.

Havighurst, R. J. 1954. Flexibility and the Social Roles of the Aged. *Am. J. of Soc.,* **59,** 309–311.

Havighurst, R. J., and Albrecht, R. 1953. *Older People.* New York: Longmans, Green & Co.

Heath, J. F. 1975. *Decade of Disillusionment.* Bloomington: University of Indiana Press.

Heclo, H. 1974. *Modern Social Politics in Britain and Sweden.* New Haven: Yale University Press.

Heidenheimer, A., Heclo, H., and Adams, C. T. 1975. *Comparative Public Policy.* New York: St. Martin's Press.

Heilbroner, R. L. 1975. Benign Neglect in the United States. In H. I. Safa and G. Levitas (eds.), *Social Problems in Corporate America*. New York: Harper & Row.

Helton, R. October 1939. Old People: A Rising National Problem. *Harper's Monthly*, 179, 449–459.

Hendricks, J. Summer 1982. The Elderly in Society: Beyond Modernization Theory. *Soc. Sci. Hist.*, 6, 321–345.

Hendricks, J., and Hendricks, C. D. 1981. *Aging in Mass Society*, 2nd ed. Cambridge, MA: Winthrop Publishing.

Herberg, W. 1956. *Protestant, Catholic and Jew*. Garden City: Anchor Books.

Herzog, A. R., and Rodgers, W. L. July 1981. The Structure of Subjective Well-Being in Different Age Groups. *J. of Gerontology*, 36, 472–480.

Hewitt, C. June 1977. The Effect of Political Democracy and Social Democracy on Equality in Industrial Societies. *Am. Soc. Rev.*, 42, 450–464.

Higham, J., and Conkin, P. K. 1979. *New Directions in American Intellectual History*. Baltimore: The Johns Hopkins University Press.

Hirschfield, D. S. 1970. *The Lost Reform*. Cambridge, MA: Harvard University Press.

Hofstadter, R. 1955. *The Age of Reform*. New York: Vintage Books.

Hofstadter, R., and Wallace, M. 1970. *American Violence*. New York: Vintage Books.

Hohaus, R. 1938. Equity, Adequacy and Related Factors in Social Security. In W. Haber and W. J. Cohen (eds.), *Readings in Social Security*. Englewood Cliffs, NJ: Prentice-Hall.

Holtzman, A. 1954. An Analysis of Old Age Politics in the United States. *J. of Gerontology*. 9, 56–66.

Hudson, R. B. October 1978. The "Graying" of the Federal Budget and Its Consequences for Old-Age Policy. *The Gerontologist*, 18, 428–440.

Hudson, R. B., and Binstock, R. H. 1976. Political Systems and Aging. In R. H. Binstock and E. Shanas (eds.), *Handbook of Aging and the Social Sciences*, pp. 369–401. New York: Van Nostrand Reinhold.

Huntington, S. P. Fall 1975. The Democratic Distemper. *The Public Interest*, 41, 9–38.

Independent. August 28, 1913. Independent Opinions, 75, 504.

Institute of Gerontology. 1979. *American Values and the Elderly*. Final Project Report. Ann Arbor: Institute of Gerontology.

Jacobson, B. 1980. *Young Programs for Older Workers*. New York: Van Nostrand Reinhold.

Jaher, F. C. 1964. *Doubters and Dissenters*. Urbana: University of Illinois Press.

Janowitz, M. 1978. *The Last Half-Century*. Chicago: The University of Chicago Press.

Jensen, R. J. 1978. *Illinois*. New York: W. W. Norton & Co.

Kaplan, R. S. 1977. *Indexing Social Security*. Washington, DC: American Enterprise Institute.

Karl, B. 1963. *Executive Reorganization and Reform in the New Deal*. Cambridge, MA: Harvard University Press.

Kasson, J. F. 1978. *Amusing the Million*. New York: Hill & Wang.

Kastenbaum, R. 1979. Exit and Existence: Society's Unwritten Script for Old Age and Death. In D. D. Van Tassel (ed.), *Aging, Death and the Completion of Being*, pp. 69–94. Philadelphia: University of Pennsylvania Press.

Keith, J. 1982. *Old People as People: Social and Cultural Influences on Aging and Old Age.* Boston: Little, Brown and Company.

Keller, M. 1977. *Affairs of State.* Cambridge, MA: Harvard University Press.

Kelso, R. W. 1929. *Poverty.* New York: Longmans, Green & Co.

Kemp, J. 1980. *American Renaissance.* New York: Harper & Row.

Keniston, K. 1960. *The Uncommitted.* New York: Harcourt, Brace & World.

Kerr, C., Dunlop, J. T., Harbison, F., and Myers, C. 1964. *Industrialism and Industrial Man,* rev. ed. New York: Oxford University Press.

Kett, J. 1977. *Rites of Passage: Adolescence in America, 1790 to the Present.* New York: Basic Books.

Klein, P., et al. 1938. *A Social Study of Pittsburgh.* New York: Columbia University Press.

Koff, T. H. 1982. *Long-Term Care.* Boston: Little, Brown and Company.

Kreps, J. M. 1966. Employment Policy and Income Maintenance for the Aged. In J. C. McKinney and F. de Vyver (eds.), *Aging and Social Policy.* New York: Appleton-Century-Crofts.

Lampman, R. J. 1971. *Ends and Means of Reducing Income Poverty.* Chicago: Markham Publishing Co.

Lampman, R. J. 1974. What Does It Do for the Poor? In E. Ginzburg and R. M. Solow (eds.), *The Great Society,* pp. 66–82. New York: Basic Books.

Lane, R. E. December 1965. The Politics of Consensus in an Age of Affluence. *American Pol. Sci. Rev.,* **59,** 874–895.

Lasch, C. 1977. *Haven in a Heartless World.* New York: Basic Books.

Lasch, C. 1979. *The Culture of Narcissism.* New York: W. W. Norton Co.

Laslett, P. 1977. Societal Development and Aging. In R. H. Binstock and E. Shanas (eds.), *Handbook of Aging and the Social Sciences,* pp. 87–116. New York: Van Nostrand Reinhold.

Lears, T. J. J. 1981. *No Place of Grace.* New York: Pantheon Books.

LeFevre, C., and LeFevre, P. 1981. *Aging and the Human Spirit.* Chicago: Exploration Press.

Lenski, G. 1966. *Power and Privilege.* New York: McGraw-Hill.

Leotta, L. Summer 1975. Abraham Epstein and the Movement for Old Age Security. *Labor History,* **16,** 364–382.

LeRoy Ladurie, E. 1979. *Montaillou.* New York: Vintage Press.

Leuchtenberg, W. E. 1963. *Franklin D. Roosevelt and the New Deal.* New York: Harper Torchbooks.

Leuchtenberg, W. E. 1979. *A Troubled Feast,* rev. ed. Boston: Little, Brown.

Levitan, S. A. 1968. *The Great Society's Poor Law.* Baltimore: The Johns Hopkins University Press.

Levitan, S. A. 1976. *Programs in Aid of the Poor,* 3rd ed. Baltimore: The Johns Hopkins University Press.

Levitan, S. A., Johnston, W. B., and Taggart, R. A. 1975. *Still a Dream.* Cambridge, MA: Harvard University Press.

Levitan, S. A., and Taggart, R. A. 1976. *The Promise of Greatness.* Cambridge, MA: Harvard University Press.

Levy, M. 1966. *Modernization and the Structure of Society.* Princeton: Princeton University Press.

Lilienthal, D. 1944. *TVA: Democracy on the March.* New York: Harper and Bros.

Lindblom, C. E. 1977. *Politics and Markets.* New York: Basic Books.

Lipset, S. M. 1960. *Political Man.* Garden City, NY: Doubleday.

Lipset, S. M. 1963. *The First New Nation.* New York: Basic Books.

Lipset, S. M., ed. 1979. *The Third Century: America as a Post-Industrial Society.* Stanford: Stanford University, Hoover Institution.

Lowi, T. 1968. *The End of Liberalism.* New York: W. W. Norton.

Lubove, R. 1968. *The Struggle for Social Security.* Cambridge, MA: Harvard University Press.

Lynd, R. S. 1939. *Knowledge for What?* Princeton: Princeton University Press.

Lynd, R. S., and Lynd, H. M. 1929. *Middletown.* New York: Harcourt, Brace & World.

Lynd, R. S., and Lynd, H. M. 1937. *Middletown in Transition.* New York: Harcourt, Brace.

Maddox, G. L. 1968. Retirement as a Social Event in the United States. In B. L. Neugarten (ed.), *Middle Age and Aging,* pp. 357–365. Chicago: The University of Chicago Press.

Maddox, G. L., and Wiley, J. 1976. Scope, Concepts and Methods in the Study of Aging. In R. H. Binstock and E. Shanas (eds.), *Handbook of Aging and the Social Sciences,* pp. 3–34. New York: Van Nostrand Reinhold.

Mandelbaum, S. Winter 1977. The Past in Service to the Future. *J. Soc. Hist.,* 11, 193–205.

Mark, J. A. December 1957. Comparative Job Performance by Age. *Monthly Labor Review,* 80, 1467–1471.

Marmor, T., ed. 1971. *Poverty Policy.* Chicago: Aldine-Atherton.

Marmor, T. 1973. *The Politics of Medicare.* Chicago: Aldine-Atherton.

Martin, A. 1973. The Politics of Economic Policy in the United States: A Tentative View from a Comparative Perspective. In H. Eckstein et al. (eds.), *Sage Professional Papers in Comparative Politics,* vol. 4. Beverly Hills: Sage Publications.

McKinney, J. C., and DeVyver, F. T., eds. 1966. *Aging & Social Policy.* New York: Appleton-Century-Crofts.

Maves, P. B. 1960. Aging, Religion and the Church. In C. Tibbitts (ed.), *Handbook of Social Gerontology.* Chicago: The University of Chicago Press.

Michelon, L. C. January 1954. The New Leisure Class. *Am. J. Soc.,* 59, 371–378.

Miliband, R. 1969. *The State in Capitalist Society.* New York: Basic Books.

Miller, A. H. September 1974. Political Issues and Trust in Government. *Am. Pol. Sci. Rev.,* 68, 951–972.

Miller, D. T., and Nowak, M. 1977. *The Fifties.* Garden City, NY: Doubleday.

Miller, S. M., and Roby, P. 1968. Poverty: Changing Social Stratification. In D. P. Moynihan (ed.), *On Understanding Poverty.* New York: Basic Books.

Mills, C. W. 1951. *The Power Elite.* New York: Oxford University Press.

Moberg, D. O. June 1965. Religiosity in Old Age. *The Gerontologist,* 5, 78–87.

Modell, J., Furstenberg, F. F., and Hershberg, T. September 1976. Social Change in Historical Perspective. *J. Family Hist.,* 1, 7–31.

Moody, H. R. 1979. Portrait of the Artist as an Old Man: The Late Self Portraits of Rembrandt. Unpublished paper prepared for the 1979 Gerontological Society meeting, Washington, D.C.

Moore, R. L. April 1982. Insiders and Outsiders in American Historical Narrative and American History. *The Am. Hist. Rev.,* 87, 390–412.

Moore, W. E. 1951. The Aged in Industrial Societies. In W. E. Moore (ed.), *Industrial Relations and the Social Order,* rev. ed. New York: Macmillan Co.

Morgan, J. N., David, M. H., Cohen, W. J., and Brazer, H. E. 1962. *Income and Wealth in the United States.* New York: McGraw-Hill.

Morgan, J. N., et al. 1974. *Five Thousand Families,* 8 vols. thus far. Ann Arbor: Institute of Social Research.

Moynihan, D. P. 1968. *On Understanding Poverty.* New York: Basic Books.

Moynihan, D. P. 1973. *The Politics of a Guaranteed Income.* New York: Random House.

Munnell, A. 1977. *The Future of Social Security.* Washington, DC: Brookings Institution.

Myers, R. J. 1975. *Social Security.* Homewood, IL: Richard D. Irwin.

Myles, J. F. November 1981. Comparative Public Policies for the Elderly: Frameworks and Resources for Analysis. Unpublished paper prepared for the 1981 annual meetings of the Gerontological Society of America and the Canadian Association on Gerontology in Toronto.

Myrdal, G. 1944. *An American Dilemma,* 2 vols. New York: Harper & Bros.

National Council on the Aging. 1981. *The Arts, The Humanities and Older Americans.* Washington, DC: National Council on the Aging.

National Interfaith Coalition on Aging. 1981. *Spiritual and Ethical Values and National Policy on Aging.* Athens, GA: National Interfaith Coalition on Aging.

Nelson, D. H. 1969. *Unemployment Insurance.* Madison: University of Wisconsin Press.

Nelson, D. H. 1975. *Managers and Workers.* Madison: University of Wisconsin Press.

Neuberger, R. L., and Loe, K. 1936. *An Army of the Aged.* Caldwell, ID: Caxton Printers.

Neugarten, B. L. September 1974. Age Groups in American Society and the Rise of the Young-Old. *Annals Am. Acad. of Pol. and Soc. Sci., 320,* 187–198.

Neugarten, B. L. 1981. Age Distinctions and Their Social Functions. *Chicago Kent Law Review, 57,* 809–825.

Neugarten, B. L., and Hagestad, G. O. 1976. Age and the Life Course. In R. H. Binstock and E. Shanas (eds.), *Handbook of Aging and the Social Sciences,* pp. 35–57. New York: Van Nostrand Reinhold.

Neugarten, B. L., and Havighurst, R. H., eds. 1977. *Social Ethics, Social Policy and the Aging Society.* Washington, DC: U.S. Government Printing Office.

Neulinger, J. 1981. *To Leisure: An Introduction.* Boston: Allyn and Bacon.

The New York Times. July 18, 1980. Text of Ronald Reagan's Acceptance Speech at the Republican National Convention, A8.

The New York Times. July 26, 1981. Looting the Means of Production, by Seymour Melman, E21.

The New York Times. October 19, 1981. U.S. Census Bureau Says Divorces and Unmarried Couples Increased in 70s, A20.

The New York Times. December 4, 1981. White House Aging Parley Adopts Agenda for Decade, A18.

Nie, N. H., Verba, S., and Petrocik, J. 1976. *The Changing American Voter.* Cambridge, MA: Harvard University Press.

O'Connor, J. 1973. *The Fiscal Crisis of the State.* New York: St. Martin's Press.

Offe, C. Summer 1972. Advanced Capitalism and the Welfare State. *Politics and Society, 2,* 479–488.

O'Neill, W. L. 1971. *Coming Apart.* New York: Quadrangle Press.

Oriol, W. E. February 1981. "Modern" Age and Public Policy. *The Gerontologist,* 21, 35–46.

Orshansky, M. January 1965. Counting the Poor: Another Look at the Poverty Profile. *Social Security Bull.,* 28, 3–25.

Owen, H., and Schultze, C. L., eds. 1976. *Setting National Priorities: The Next Ten Years.* Washington, DC: Brookings Institution.

Palmore, E. 1981. Social Values and Attitudes toward Aging and the Aged: Stereotypes. Unpublished position paper prepared for the National Institute on Aging, National Research Plan on Aging.

Parenti, M. 1977. *Democracy for the Few.* New York: St. Martin's Press.

Parsons, T. 1954. Age and Sex in the Social Structure of the United States. In T. Parsons, *Essays in Sociological Theory,* rev. ed., pp. 89–103. Glencoe, IL: The Free Press.

Parsons, T. 1970. *Social Structure and Personality.* New York: The Free Press.

Paschal, E., and Koellner, E. October 1942. Wages in Place of Benefits. *Social Security Bull.,* 5, 1–12.

Patterson, J. T. 1976. *America in the Twentieth Century.* New York: Harcourt, Brace, Jovanovich.

Patterson, J. T. 1981. *America's Struggle Against Poverty, 1900–1980.* Cambridge, MA: Harvard University Press.

Pechman, J., Aaron, H. J., and Taussig, M. K. 1968. *Social Security: Perspectives for Reform.* Washington, DC: Brookings Institution.

Pellegrino, E. D. 1979. The Socio-Cultural Impact of Twentieth-Century Therapeutics. In M. Vogel and C. E. Rosenberg (eds.), *The Therapeutic Revolution.* Philadelphia: University of Pennsylvania Press.

Perrett, G. 1973. *Days of Sadness, Years of Triumph.* Baltimore: Penguin Books.

Philibert, M. 1968. *L'echelle des ages.* Paris: Le Seuil.

Philibert, M. 1974. The Phenomenological Approach to Images of Aging. *Soundings,* 57, 3–24.

Philibert, M. 1979. Philosophical Approach to Aging. In J. Hendricks and C. D. Hendricks (eds.), *Dimensions of Aging,* pp. 379–395. Cambridge, MA: Winthrop Publishing.

Piven, F. F., and Cloward, R. A. 1971. *Regulating the Poor.* New York: Vintage Books.

Plotnick, R., and Skidmore, F. 1973. *Progress against Poverty.* New York: Academic Press.

Pole, J. R. 1978. *The Pursuit of Equality in American History.* Berkeley: University of California Press.

Polenberg, R. 1972. *War and Society: The United States, 1941–1945.* Philadelphia: J. B. Lippincott Co.

Porter, G. 1973. *The Rise of Big Business, 1860–1910.* New York: Thomas Y. Crowell.

Potter, D. M. 1954. *People of Plenty.* Chicago: The University of Chicago Press.

Poulantzas, N. 1973. The Problem of the Capitalist State. In R. Blackburn (ed.), *Ideology in Social Science,* pp. 238–253. New York: Vintage Books.

Powell, L. P. 1937. *The Second Seventy.* Philadelphia: Macrae Smith Co.

Pratt, H. J. 1976. *The Gray Lobby.* Chicago: The University of Chicago Press.

Pryor, F. L. 1968. *Public Expenditures in Communist and Capitalist Nations.* Homewood, IL: R. Irwin.

Putnam, J. K. 1970. *Old-Age Politics in California.* Stanford: Stanford University Press.

Radosh, R. 1972. The Myth of the New Deal. In R. Radosh and N. Rothbard (eds.), *A New History of Leviathan: Essays on the Rise of the Corporate State,* pp. 146–187. New York: E. P. Dutton.

Recent Social Trends. 1933. A Report of the President's Committee on Recent Social Trends. New York: McGraw-Hill Book Co.

Reich, C. A. 1970. *The Greening of America.* New York: Random House.

Rein, M. 1976. *Social Science & Public Policy.* New York: Penguin Books.

Rescher, N. 1972. *Welfare.* Pittsburgh: University of Pittsburgh Press.

Riesman, D. January 1954. Some Clinical and Cultural Aspects of Aging. *Am. J. of Soc.,* **59,** 379–383.

Riesman, D., Glazer, N., and Denney, R. 1950. *The Lonely Crowd.* New Haven: Yale University Press.

Riley, M. W., et al. 1968–1972. *Aging and Society,* 3 vols. New York: Russell Sage Foundation.

Robertson, A. H. 1978. *Social Security: Prospect for Change.* New York: William M. Mercer.

Rodgers, D. 1978. *The Work Ethic in Industrial America.* Chicago: The University of Chicago Press.

Roebuck, J. 1978. When Does Old Age Begin? The Evolution of the English Definition. *J. Soc. Hist.,* **12,** 416–428.

Rokeach, M. 1960. *Open and Closed Mind.* New York: Basic Books.

Rokeach, M. 1976. *Beliefs, Attitudes, and Values.* San Francisco: Jossey-Bass.

Romasco, A. U. 1965. *The Poverty of Abundance.* New York: Oxford University Press.

Roosevelt, F. D. 1934. Review of Legislative Accomplishments of the Administration and Congress. In U.S. Congress, House, 73d Cong., 2d Sess., H. Document 397.

Rossi, P. 1969. Practice, Method and Theory in Evaluating Social-Action Programs. In J. L. Sundquist (ed.), *On Fighting Poverty.* New York: Basic Books.

Rothbard, M. 1962. *America's Great Depression.* Los Angeles: Nash Publishing.

Samuelson, R. J. February 18, 1978. Busting the Budget: The Graying of America. *National Journal,* 256–260.

Schlitz, M. E. 1970. *Public Attitudes toward Social Security, 1935–1965.* Social Security Administration Research Report No. 3. Washington, DC: U.S. Government Printing Office.

Schlesinger, A. M., Jr. 1957. *The Crisis of the Old Order.* Boston: Houghton Mifflin Co.

Schlesinger, A. M., Jr. 1958. *The Coming of the New Deal.* Boston: Houghton Mifflin Co.

Schlesinger, A. M., Jr. 1965. *A Thousand Days.* New York: Fawcett Books.

Schlesinger, A. M., Jr. 1978. *Robert F. Kennedy and His Times.* Boston: Houghton Mifflin Co.

Schorr, A. 1968. *Explorations in Social Policy.* New York: Basic Books.

Schorr, A. 1980. *". . . Thy Father & Thy Mother": A Second Look at Filial Responsibility & Family Policy.* Washington, DC: Social Security Administration.

Schulz, J. 1980. *The Economics of Aging,* 2nd ed. Belmont, CA: Wadsworth Publishing Co.

Science News Letter. June 1, 1963. **83**, 339.

Seltzer, M., and Atchley, R. C. 1971. The Concept of Old. *The Gerontologist,* 11, 226–230.

Shanas, E. 1962. *The Health of Older People.* Cambridge, MA: Harvard University Press.

Shanas, E., Townsend, P., Wedderburn, D., Friis, H., Milhøj, P., and Stehouver, J. 1968. *Old People in Three Industrial Societies.* New York: Atherton Press.

Shanas, E., and Maddox, G. L. 1976. Aging, Health, and the Organization of Health Resources. In R. H. Binstock and E. Shanas (eds.), *Handbook of Aging and the Social Sciences,* pp. 592–618. New York: Van Nostrand Reinhold.

Sheppard, H. L. 1976. Work and Retirement. In R. H. Binstock and E. Shanas (eds.), *Handbook of Aging and the Social Sciences,* pp. 286–309. New York: Van Nostrand Reinhold.

Shock, N. 1957. *Trends in Gerontology,* 2nd ed. Stanford: Stanford University Press.

Simon, H. A. 1955. A Behavioral Model of Rational Choice. *Quarterly J. of Economics,* **69**, 99–118.

Simmons, L. 1945. *The Role of the Aged in Primitive Societies.* New Haven: Yale University Press.

Skidmore, F., ed. 1981. *Social Security Financing.* Cambridge, MA: MIT Press.

Sklar, R. 1970. *The Plastic Age, 1917–1930.* New York: George Braziller.

Skocpol, T. 1980. Political Responses to Capitalist Crises: Neo-Marxist Theories of the State and the Case of the New Deal. *Politics and Society,* **10**, 155–201.

Smith, D. S. 1978. Old Age and the "Great Transformation." In S. F. Spicker, K. M. Woodward, and D. D. Van Tassel (eds.), *Aging and the Elderly,* pp. 285–302. Atlantic Highlands, NJ: Humanities Press.

Smith, S. R. 1978. Death, Dying, and the Elderly in Seventeenth-Century England. In S. F. Spicker, K. M. Woodward, and D. D. Van Tassel (eds.), *Aging and the Elderly,* pp. 201–219. Atlantic Highlands, NJ: Humanities Press.

Smith, T. W. Summer 1981. Social Indicators: A Review Essay. *J. Soc. Hist.,* 14, 739–747.

Social Security Bulletin. See U.S. Department of Health, Education and Welfare.

Somers, H. M., and Somers, A. R. 1967. *Medicare and the Hospitals.* Washington, DC: Brookings Institution.

Spicker, S. F., Woodward, K. M., and Van Tassel, D. D. *Aging and the Elderly: Humanistic Perspectives in Gerontology.* Atlantic Highlands, NJ: Humanities Press.

Stearns, P. N. 1975. *European Society in Upheaval.* New York: Macmillan Co.

Stearns, P. N. 1977. *Old Age in European Society.* New York: Holmes and Meier.

Stearns, P. N. 1978. Toward Historical Gerontology. *J. Interdisc. Hist.,* 8, 737–746.

Stearns, P. N. 1980a. Modernization and Social History. *J. Soc. Hist.,* 14, 189–209.

Stearns, P. N. 1980b. Toward a Wider Vision: Trends in Social History. In M. Kammen (ed.), *The Past Before Us,* pp. 205–230. Ithaca: Cornell University Press.

Stearns, P. N. 1980c. Old Women: Some Historical Perspectives. *J. Family Hist.,* 4, 44–57.

Stearns, P. N. 1981. The Modernization of Old Age in France: Approaches through History. *Int'l J. Aging and Human Dev.,* 13, 297–315.

Stecker, M. L. May 1955. Why Do Beneficiaries Retire? Who among Them Return to Work? *Social Security Bull.,* **18**, 3–12, 35–36.

Steel, R. 1980. *Walter Lippmann and the American Century.* Boston: Little, Brown.

Steiner, G. Y. 1974. Reform Follows Reality. In E. Ginzberg and R. M. Solow (eds.), *The Great Society,* pp. 47–65. New York: Basic Books.

Steiner, G. Y. 1981. *The Futility of Family Policy.* Washington, DC: Brookings Institution.

Steiner, P. O., and Dorfman, R. 1957. *The Economic Status of the Aged.* Berkeley: University of California Press.

Stone, L. May 12, 1977a. Walking Over Grandma. *N.Y. Rev.,* **24,** 26–29.

Stone, L. September 15, 1977b. Growing Old: An Exchange. *N.Y. Rev.,* **24,** 48–49.

Stouffer, S. A. 1955. *Communism, Conformity, and Civil Liberties.* New York: Doubleday & Co.

Streib, G. F., and Thompson, W. E. 1960. The Older Person in a Family Context. In C. Tibbitts (ed.), *Handbook of Social Gerontology,* pp. 447–488. Chicago: The University of Chicago Press.

Sundquist, J. L., ed. 1969. *On Fighting Poverty.* New York: Basic Books.

Thernstrom, S. A. 1973. *The Other Bostonians.* Cambridge, MA: Harvard University Press.

Thomas, W. R. 1981. The Expectation Gap and the Stereotype of a Stereotype. *The Gerontologist,* **21,** 402–407.

Thurow, L. C. 1980. *The Zero-Sum Society.* Baltimore: Penguin Books.

Tibbitts, C. 1952. Social Contributions of the Aged. *Annals Am. Acad. of Pol. and Soc. Sci.,* **279,** 1–10.

Tibbitts, C. 1954. Retirement Problems in American Society. *Am. J. of Soc.,* **59,** 301–308.

Tibbitts, C., ed. 1960. *Handbook of Social Gerontology.* Chicago: The University of Chicago Press.

Tibbitts, C. 1979. Can We Invalidate Negative Stereotypes of Aging? *The Gerontologist,* **19,** 10–20.

Tibbles, L. 1978. Legal and Medical Aspects of Competence in Old Age. In S. F. Spicker, K. M. Woodward, and D. D. Van Tassel (eds.), *Aging and the Elderly.* Atlantic Heights, NJ: Humanities Press.

Tice, T. 1978. Thinking about Values. Unpublished working paper for the "American Values and the Elderly" project. Ann Arbor: Institute of Gerontology.

Tilly, L. A., and Cohen, M. Spring 1982. Does the Family Have a History? *Soc. Sci. Hist.,* **6,** 131–179.

Tilly, L. A., and Scott, J. W. 1978. *Women, Work and Family.* New York: Holt, Rinehart, Winston.

Tipps, D. C. June 1973. Modernization Theory and the Comparative Study of Societies. *Comparative Studies in Society and History,* **15,** 199–222.

Tobin, J. December 3, 1981. Reaganomics and Economics. *New York Review,* **28,** 11–14.

Toffler, A. 1980. *The Third Wave.* New York: Bantam Books.

Towers, Perrin, Forster and Crosby. 1981. *Pensioner Cost-of-Living Increases: Who Needs Them?* New York: TPF&C Special Report.

Townsend, P. 1957. *The Family Life of Old People.* Glencoe, IL: The Free Press.

Trattner, W. I. 1979. *From Poor Law to Welfare State,* 2nd ed. New York: Free Press.

Tropman, J. E. 1976. Societal Values and Social Policy. In J. E. Tropman et al. (eds.), *Strategic Perspectives on Social Policy.* Elmsford: Pergamon Press.

Tropman, J. E. Winter 1978. The Constant Crisis: Social Welfare and the American Cultural Structure. *California Sociologist,* **1,** 1–19.

Truman, D. B. 1951. *The Governmental Process.* New York: A. A. Knopf.

Tufte, E. R. 1978. *Political Control of the Economy.* Princeton: Princeton University Press.

United Auto Workers (Retired and Older Workers Department). 1980. *Planning for Successful Living: A UAW Pre-Retirement Program.* Detroit: United Automobile, Aerospace and Agricultural Implement Workers of America International Union.

U.S. Bureau of the Census. 1976. *Historical Statistics of the United States, Colonial Times to 1970,* 2 vols. Washington, DC: U.S. Government Printing Office.

U.S. Congress, House. 1935. *The Economic Security Act: Hearings on H.R. 4120.* Washington, DC: U.S. Government Printing Office.

U.S. Department of Health, Education and Welfare. *Social Security Bulletin* series.

U.S. News and World Report. September 13, 1958. Should You Be Forced to Retire? **43,** 94.

U.S. Public Law 89–73. "The Older Americans Act of 1965."

U.S. Senate, Special Committee on Aging. 1979. *Developments in Aging 1978,* 2 parts. Washington, DC: U.S. Government Printing Office.

U.S. Senate, Special Committee on Aging. 1981. *Developments in Aging 1980,* 2 parts. Washington, DC: U.S. Government Printing Office.

Valentine, C. A. 1968. *Culture and Poverty: Critique and Counter-Proposals.* Chicago: The University of Chicago Press.

Van Tassel, D. D., ed. 1979. *Aging, Death, and the Completion of Being.* Philadelphia: University of Pennsylvania Press.

Vickers, G. 1968. *Value Systems and Social Process.* New York: Basic Books.

Vickers, G. 1973. Values, Norms and Policies. *Policy Sciences,* **4,** 73–86.

Vickery, C. Winter 1978. The Changing Household: Implications for Devising an Income Support System. *Public Policy,* **26,** 121–151.

Vinovskis, M. A. 1978. Recent Trends in American Historical Demography: Some Methodological and Conceptual Considerations. *Ann. Rev. of Soc.,* **4,** 603–627.

Warner, S. B. 1972. *The Urban Wilderness.* New York: Harper & Row.

Weaver, R. C. July 1935. The New Deal and the Negro. *Opportunity,* **13,** 200–203.

Weinstein, J. 1968. *The Corporate Ideal in the Liberal State: 1900–1918.* Boston: Beacon Press.

Welford, A. T. 1951. *Skill and Age: An Experimental Approach.* London: Oxford University Press.

Wetle, T. 1980. Health-Care Programs in America. Unpublished paper prepared for the Hastings Center.

White, L. D. 1948. *The Federalists.* New York: Free Press.

White, L. D. 1958. *The Republican Era.* New York: Free Press.

Whyte, W. H., Jr. 1956. *The Organization Man.* Garden City, NY: Doubleday.

Wiebe, R. 1967. *The Search for Order, 1877–1920.* New York: Hill & Wang.

Wiebe, R. 1981. Modernizing the Republic. In B. Bailyn et al., *The Great Republic,* 2nd ed., pp. 760–932. Boston: D. C. Heath.

Wildavsky, A. 1979. *Speaking Truth to Power.* Boston: Little, Brown.

Wilensky, H. L. 1975. *The Welfare State and Equality.* Berkeley: University of California Press.

Wilensky, H. L., and Lebeaux, R. 1958. *Industrial Society and Social Welfare.* New York: Free Press.

Williams, R. 1968. *American Society,* rev ed. New York: Knopf.

Williams, R. 1969. Individual and Group Values. In B. Gross (ed.), *Social Intelligence for America's Future.* Boston: Allyn and Bacon.

Wills, G. 1969. *Nixon Agonistes.* Boston: Houghton Mifflin Company.

Wilson, J. H. March 1979. One Historian's Orthodoxy Is Another's Revisionism. *Reviews in American History,* 7, 112–121.

Wilson, J. Q. Fall 1975. The Rise of the Bureaucratic State. *Public Interest,* 41, 77–103.

Wilson, W. J. 1978. *The Declining Significance of Race.* Chicago: The University of Chicago Press.

Wingard, J. 1981. Measures of Attitudes toward the Elderly. *Exper. Aging Res.,* 6, 229–313.

Wishy, B. 1968. *The Child and the Republic.* Philadelphia: University of Pennsylvania Press.

Work in America Institute. 1980. *The Future of Older Workers in America.* Policy Study. Scarsdale, NY: Work in America Institute, Inc.

Wyatt-Brown, B. 1982. *Southern Honor: Ethics and Behavior in the Premodern South.* New York: Oxford University Press.

Yans-McLaughlin, V. 1977. *Family and Community: Italian Immigrants in Buffalo, 1880–1930.* Ithaca: Cornell University Press.

Yarmolinsky, A. 1969. The Beginnings of OEO. In J. L. Sundquist (ed.), *On Fighting Poverty.* New York: Basic Books.

Index